ES OF AMERICA

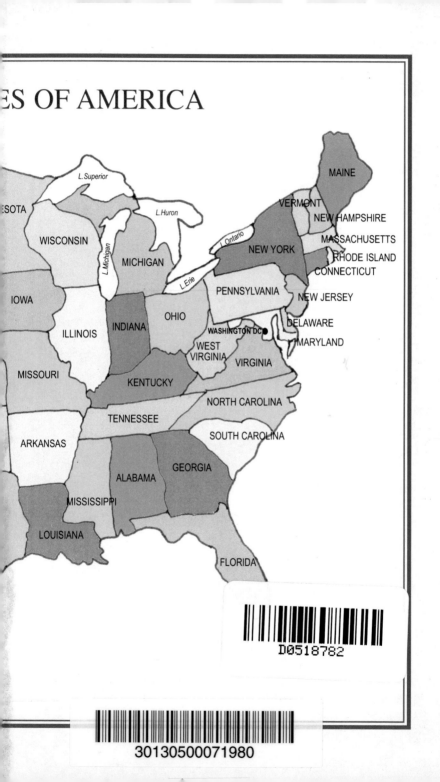

BEYOND THE BYPASS

Also by Mavis Gore:

Where There's a Will – A Year in Canada

BEYOND
the
BYPASS

...to every state in America

Mavis Gore

UNITED WRITERS
Cornwall

UNITED WRITERS PUBLICATIONS LTD
Ailsa, Castle Gate, Penzance, Cornwall.

British Library Cataloguing in Publication Data:
A catalogue record for this book is
available from the British Library.

ISBN 9781852001377

Printed in Great Britain by
United Writers Publications Ltd
Cornwall.

For our children and grandchildren with love
and
in memory of our brother-in-law, who cared
for our home, while we travelled.

Index Showing Routes Taken

Chapter One

'There's nowhere on earth where you can purchase a hula *skurd*. Each *gurl* has to make her own,' explained the buxom, dark-skinned, Hawaiian woman to anyone interested enough to listen, as the lithe dancers shimmied off the open stage at Waikiki Beach. 'Each *skurd* takes about a hun'red leaves. For me: I'd need the whole patch,' she laughed, good-naturedly. Indicating the billowing cloud of vivid yellow silk, in which she was swathed to the ground, she went on, 'This style of dress is called a muumuu.' A lull between dances gave the muumuu-clad commentator the opportunity to enthuse about her native art form, as the sun, an orange orb, gave a dazzling performance before slipping away. It was 6.45pm. By 7.00pm it was fully dark.

Earlier in the day, after our long air journey, we had a traditional lei welcome of creamy-white plumeria flowers, at Honolulu airport. Jeff brusquely removing his blurted, 'For heaven's sake I'm not wearing *that*,' and plonked it over my head, bedecking me with two.

Tall swaying palms; shrubs, hedges, trees smothered in blossom; hibiscus flowers the size of dinner plates; fragrant air; gentle breezes: Hawaii was as anticipated. Eleven hours behind British Summer Time, we were spending the hours gained a second time, revelling in our first tropical sunset, while learning about hula.

The Hawaiian Islands became the 50th state of the United States in 1959. It was our 50th state too; the only one that we'd visited directly from England, not from Canada while holidaying there, as we'd done previously. Despite our jet lag (we had been on the go for almost thirty hours) we were elated by our achievement. Well, more overwhelmed by *amazement* really that, during several visits, we had journeyed through each one of the 50 states. All 50! Although we always relished *any* opportunity to explore new places – anywhere! – finding the unknown intriguing: curious to see what was around every corner, or over the next hill, there had never been a master plan to tour the United States. Ever! What's more we'd done it since Jeff's life-saving, quadruple heart bypass operation, in what he terms with gusto, 'My Bonus Time.' For sure, facing death up close aids enthusiasm for each day of life.

'A blood clot the size of a pin head could kill you at anytime,' the surgeon had stated bluntly, before the operation, as Jeff's arteries, apart from one, were blocked up to ninety per cent.

The Hawaiian Chain of Islands floats in the mid-Pacific Ocean, more than 2,000 miles off the west coast of America. Our journey had come full circle. It was on the Pacific Coast, a few summers previously, that our travels in the United States began, when we drove off the car ferry, from Victoria, British Columbia, at Port Angeles, Washington State, in a hired motorhome.

Thrilled by our *4,000-mile* journey, from east to west through Canada, we'd driven again the route trekked in the early years of marriage; then, on great stretches of *dirt* road through uninhabited bush, prairie and mountains. Jeff had been the sole driver of our nine-year-old Dodge coupé, and I was seven months pregnant! Retirees now, we eagerly looked forward to travelling the northern states of America, back to our son's home (the 'pregnancy' of the earlier trip) near Toronto, Ontario.

On arrival in Vancouver, after our *first* crossing of Canada, we lived there happily for some time, later returning to England. There was a lapse of twenty years with the hurly-burly of raising a family, before we saw Canada again; however, it was only early retirement, because of Jeff's health, that gave us the time and cash to realise our long-held ambition to traverse the continent once more, from Toronto to Vancouver. The medics had cleared Jeff for air travel. But, on the other side of the Atlantic, were we brave, or crazy, to undertake such a long journey by road? Ever the optimist, Jeff always sees the silver lining no matter how dark the cloud cover.

'For more than *thirty* years, between ourselves, we've talked about that adventure and longed to do it again, never really believing that we would. It seemed an impossible dream. Now's our chance. Let's grab it! Let's go!' he urged.

So we did! And it had all been marvellous. That was Canada.

The United States was new territory. . .

A straggle of houses and businesses strung along the highway out of Port Angeles, a commercial fishing port, then we were into heavily wooded country on Highway 101, the road, edged with masses of purple loosestrife, skirting the scenic wonders of Olympic National Park, a diverse area with species of plants and animals found nowhere else outside the park, temperate rain forest with some of the biggest trees in the world, and almost sixty active glaciers. Seattle, where we hoped to rendezvous with a cousin of mine – last seen as a blonde teenager, painting a garden gate in a thatched-cottage-village in Devon, many years ago – was no distance away as the crow flies, but an expanse of island-strewn water means that the road has to make a giant U-turn to get there.

At intervals signs warned: '5 Vehicle Delay – Illegal. Must Use Pullout'.

'5 Vehicle Delay – Illegal. Must use Pullout,' I repeated aloud. 'What does that mean? Anyway, what's a pullout?'

'How should *I* know?' Jeff shrugged.

There wasn't much traffic, but we guessed that the frequent lay-bys – pull-out? – were for slow moving vehicles to pull over to prevent holdups. Not to do so was illegal, apparently. Other frequent signs reminded: 'Buckle Up It's The Law'. Another Washington State law we'd encountered written on large bins, on the ferry from Canada: 'No Apples May Be Brought Into Washington – Deposit Fruit Here'. Washington is the apple state of America and no risk is taken of introducing fruit blight, even if a little sticker on each apple read: 'Produce of Washington'. Ah! But they had been 'foreign' since those stickers were applied! How Americans love The Law! There are federal laws; also, each state thinks up its individual way of shaking a fist: 'It's the Law. . .'

Motorhomes, more usually called RVs (Recreational Vehicles) come in all sizes from van size to coach length; others are huge trailers (often called a 5th wheel) pulled by trucks. In America and Canada, on retirement, many people exchange their permanent dwellings for motorhomes, fully equipped including a computer. *Snowbirds* these folk are called, who follow the sun and warmth as the seasons change. The people on the move around the continent describe themselves more colourfully, often displaying slogans prominently on their vehicles such as: 'We're enjoying spending our Children's Inheritance' or 'There'll be nothing left for The Kids' or 'Grandpa's and Grandma's Playhouse'. In Australia, these travellers of a certain age are referred to as 'Grey Nomads'. Nobody in America admits to anything 'grey' or 'old'; after all they introduced the term 'Senior Citizens' in place of 'Old Age Pensioners'. Jeff and I were in full agreement with their reference to 'wanderers' as being engaged in 'an active post-career lifestyle'. Well said! A much more positive outlook. Truly American!

We called our 24-foot RV, hired privately in Ontario, Canada: Harvi. With two fuel tanks, he guzzled a gallon of petrol every ten miles, could sleep six, had a bathroom: as well as a shower there was a small bath, full-sized fridge-freezer, propane gas cooker, a delightful, comfortable home from home. The only snag was, with only two of us and our equipment, there were many empty cupboards plus four vacant seats, this lack of ballast resulting in the vehicle being light on the road, at times making for a bouncy, rattling ride. Cell (mobile) phones were not then commonplace. Instead, we had CB (citizen's band) radio for emergency use.

As we travelled highway 101, what we could see of the famed Olympic Peninsula, through the rain spattered windows, was attractive with many signs for campgrounds. Despite the weather, they would be fully booked for the following July 4th weekend; however, we weren't looking for a holiday site, wishing to get nearer to Seattle, and didn't expect town sites to be busy then.

At Olympia, the state capital and seat of government, we changed to an interstate: I-5 North.

'Read out the directions to the campground,' Jeff asked.

I did. We came off the interstate as directed, to drive around (tempers getting more frayed with each circuit of the area) stopping several times in the persistent drizzle to enquire of pedestrians – and there weren't many of *them* about in the soggy conditions – while pointing to the advertisement in our book for the campground. All we got in return were blank stares and 'Dunno Guys' or 'No idea!'

Maybe it never existed? Why was it there as a paid-for advertisement in the directory? There were no other campgrounds listed for the vicinity. We drove on to try elsewhere. Eventually – when divorce proceedings looked imminent – I saw, propped against a pillar of a large gateway, a board with a single word on it: 'Overnighters'. Hopping down, from my high RV seat, I opened the double gates. It was a mobile home park, surrounded by lovely, landscaped grounds.

'You're in luck,' the middle-aged, bosomy woman seated at a desk in the office beamed, as if granting us an enormous favour. 'We're permitted to take only two tourers and there's one in already.' She indicated the *exact* place where we were to park Harvi.

On our return, after a fruitless search for anything resembling what we call bread, in nearby shops with Korean names selling nothing but Korean food, the occupants of the other RV came across to talk to us.

'Hello! I'm Jutta. This is Andrew.' They were both tall, athletic-looking, a bit younger than we were. 'You've Canadian registration plates.'

'Yes.'

'You're Canadian?'

'No!'

'English then?'

'Not really.'

'Oooh?'

We explained, as we did on countless occasions, our Irish/English/Canadian connections. 'And you?'

'We live in New Zealand – North Island. I'm a Berliner by birth.'

'My family came from Scotland long ago,' Andrew said, shaking hands.

In Seattle on business, they'd taken time out, hired a motorhome and made a trip to Alaska.

'We've had a marvellous time. It's incredibly beautiful. Saw lots of wildlife, even grizzlies,' they enthused. 'We have to return the RV tomorrow. Any damage has to be paid for. Luckily we haven't any, but we're giving it a good clean-out now. Got to

13

return it empty. Seems such a shame to throw things away. Will you take our leftovers?'

As their RV became tidier ours became less so, as, in between my toing and froing to the laundry room, Jutta would stride across with: a tin of salmon, a little bit of flour, a half lettuce. . . By the end of the afternoon, in disjointed conversation, we had exchanged life histories. Their motorhome was sparkling. Our laundry was done. We acquired, as well as unopened tins and packages, four tomatoes, a few teabags, five scouring pads (when will I use *five* scouring pads? I thought), two large onions, and some much-needed bread. We exchanged addresses and have kept in touch down the years. It was an interesting stopover.

In the morning we drove further north, booked for three nights on a large site near Bellevue, with good facilities and a huge indoor swimming pool.

During the American Independence Day weekend, talking ourselves hoarse exchanging the news of a lifetime, my cousin and family entertained us in their island home with great views, or took us on tours. The celebratory atmosphere was palpable, buildings draped with red, white and blue banners, everywhere a-flutter with flags, a memorable introduction to the United States. (It was all very different from July 4th the previous year! Then, while travelling by caravan in Italy, Jeff collapsed, one lunchtime, in a restaurant. An ambulance ride followed, and a stay in hospital. Subsequently, it had taken him months to regain his health. No reference was made to any of this, because he warned, 'Don't say anything about it to them.') We didn't see anything of the two famous Seattle B's: Bill Gates and Boeing, but Seattle truly is a most lovely city with easy access to fabulous scenery of sea and mountains. On the way to Mount St. Helens, my cousin, a catch in her voice, reminisced, 'Our once-beautiful mountain, now so disfigured, had a conical, snow-covered summit; all went in the volcanic eruption of 1980.'

'Can you believe, six and a half *billion* tons of mountain was blown away? That's a ton for every person on earth,' her husband took up the story. 'A ton. A *ton*,' he went on, slowly emphasising each word. 'Imagine?'

We couldn't.

'It was *500* times more powerful than the Hiroshima bomb. It caused the largest landslide *ever* recorded, depositing ash halfway around the world.'

'Yes, I know,' I agreed, remembering. 'We'd dust from it in our garden – that's 6,000 miles away!'

'Mercifully, only 57 died, because advance warnings were given to evacuate the surrounding area. Those who died had, for various reasons, decided to remain on the mountain,' a woman at a visitors' centre (about forty miles from the volcano), explained. 'My husband is a logger,' she continued. 'His work was in the danger zone. The eruption happened on a Sunday. Had it been Monday,' her face showed remembered anguish, 'who knows. . ?'

On a much lighter note, a liquid note – there's coffee! In 1971, three young men started Starbucks, the city's main coffee company. Seattle is now regarded as the coffee capital of the US. And we all know about Starbucks. . .

The only disappointment that weekend was that there were showers. Lots!

'This is typical summer weather in the Pacific northwest. Couldn't have our precious temperate rain forest without plenty of the wet stuff!' they said, proudly, as we said goodbye.

It was cloudy, but not raining – yet! – when we joined the interstate I-90 out of Seattle, soon after 8am. Major roads, like the one we had driven around the Olympic Peninsula, are called US highways, others are state roads. Interstates, as the name indicates, are the arteries, which connect across several states: even numbers crossing the continent east/west, uneven numbers north/south. At frequent intervals, signs on poles informed us that we were on I-90, the 90 on the blue interstate sign superimposed on the profile of George Washington. In the state named after him, how they love that guy! His famous head pops up in the most unexpected places.

'Has the irony of George Washington's head atop tall poles escaped everyone except me?' I mused, as we journeyed along. He became the first president of The Union in 1789, when at that time in France, in guillotine executions, even kings were losing their heads, which, after decapitation, were displayed – on top of poles.

The road rose and fell, rose and fell, through a wonderful wilderness area of mountains, lakes, forests, an abundance of wild flowers, blossoming bushes, and turkey vultures hovering. At one mountain pass, at an elevation of more than 3,000 feet, we looked across a beautiful valley to a small town, from where a highway on stilts marched off north-westwards into the far distance. And, at regular intervals, George Washington's head reminded us of our road number, in case we forgot.

Milestones along the way gave the mileage from the starting point of the interstate. Seattle was mile zero. Quite suddenly, about mile 100, with an amazing change of landscape, we found ourselves in open, rolling country of fertile land, herds of cattle, and people and machines busy in the fields. The ragged clouds scurried away when the sun broke through.

'I'm hungry,' Jeff said. 'Breakfast was hours ago.'

Gravel shoulders run alongside interstates, but only emergency parking is permitted there, even in areas like this with sparse traffic and limitless miles of nothing all around.

'We only need to park for a short while to make a snack, but it's not worth taking a chance of stopping here,' he groused.

'You're right,' I agreed. 'State troopers would appear in no time: "Doncha know it's 'gainst the law?" '

It's necessary to leave the highway for everything: gas, food, lodgings, campgrounds, even telephones. Roadside signs indicate what's available in the vicinity of each exit. All this we were learning as we travelled, because it hadn't been like this on the TransCanada Highway, where we pulled to the side of the road and used our onboard facilities, whenever we wished.

At last, before Jeff expired from hunger, a big, blue sign promised: 'Rest Area – 1 Mile'. We reached the turn-off, reducing speed to '25mph now' as instructed.

On a rise, the rest area had no amenities. Making coffee, we stood outside Harvi revelling in the rare sunshine. In the distance, great field-length sprayers watered vines, a startling green in the surrounding sweep of pale brown earth, broken here and there by sage, with occasional splashes of vivid yellow.

'Look! There's an eagle!' Jeff said, pointing to a nearby stand of trees. Regardless of having seen hundreds, especially on Vancouver Island, as always, it was a thrilling sight to see one up close. Making wide circles its six-foot wing span caught the sunlight when it swooped low over our heads.

'It's a *golden* eagle!' we blurted, simultaneously.

'Isn't it just gorgeous!' I murmured, mesmerised, mentally recalling a story, heard as a child (a lifetime ago!) of two excited kids transported to a mystical land on the back of a golden eagle.

I don't remember any other details, but that image, buried for so long, flashed before me as I watched this wonderful bird.

'We could've pulled off the interstate at one of the exits indicating food,' Jeff teased. 'Then we could have had coffee in *McDonald's* or *Burger King*!'

Arriving in mid-afternoon at *Big Sun Resort*, near Moses Lake, we booked for two nights. To have any sun, big or otherwise, would be welcome, as the weather bulletins warned of more rain for the already massively flooded disaster area in the midwestern states, where we were heading later in the week.

An enormous outfit pulled onto a sward nearby. Lazing on a lounger, shaded by a lacy-leaved tree (Jeff was snoozing indoors, as he prefers) I watched them setting up home, which was no speedy matter. The woman jumped down. Mid-fiftyish, slim, wearing shorts, T-shirt, flip-flops and sun visor, she called out directions, as the male driver reversed, rather too hastily.

'No! No Vern! Stop! *Stop!* Vern *stop!*' she screeched, her voice rising ever higher.

Her alarm was fully justified. The campground had terraces and we were on the lowest one, beyond which was a steep slope to a large lake.

'Pull forward again, Vern. That's right! Now straighten up!'

Flustered, red-faced, he obeyed.

'Take it back. . . s l o w l y now. . . s l o w l y Vern. . . s l o w l y,' she called moving to the other end of the trailer. 'OK! Right there, Vern! OK! That'll do! That'll do!' she yelled.

He braked. Hairy, bow-legged Vern descended and strutted to the back. 'Jeez! Wota drop to th' lake, Blanche,' he said, agitatedly removing and replacing his bright blue baseball cap a couple of times. 'This goddarn spot's so small!' he complained loudly.

'Not for us it isn't,' I thought. Our 24-footer looked like a toy beside his. This huge 5th wheel had *Prairie Schooner* emblazoned in purple along its startlingly white flank. The horse-drawn wagons, which carried the first non-Indian settlers to the land west of the Mississippi, were called prairie schooners.

'It's an affront to the courage and endurance of the old-timers to give these monstrous machines the same name,' I fumed.

Before unhitching, at the *Prairie Schooner*'s front end two sturdy, steel legs were dropped as anchors. Tow-truck parked, Vern and Blanche then went inside the trailer. From my prone position I watched one then another extension along the side slowly unwind, until each was a six-foot by four-foot protrusion, followed by sunshades popping open over some of the windows. All this was achieved from within, but paunchy Vern had to do the usual connections to power, water and sewer outdoors, like the rest of us.

When next, after a blissful doze, I looked over, they were seated chatting, while playing cards, at a table under a sun umbrella. Perched on the back of a third chair looking on was a colourful cockatoo. Scraps of conversation drifted across from time to time, from Vern and Blanche that is, not the parrot. One had me restraining myself from sitting up in surprise.

'Wot did the Dow Jones say, today, Honey?'

Without looking up, Blanche told him as she plucked a card from the fan in her hand, placing it on the table. Polly remained speechless, eyes closed, calculating, no doubt, that the quantity of its seed depended on the state of the market.

It was cold in the night, the outdoor temperature dipping to 40°F. Warming up to 80°F by afternoon, we watched water sports, then took a ramble in the nearby state park. Big sun aptly described our grandstand view of a stunning sunset slanting across the lake, with the apricot afterglow only fading with dusk.

There's nothing Jeff likes better than planning journeys. At home, early each year, he pours over the map-covered dining-room table planning our camping route in Europe, where we have toured extensively. Because in an earlier life I was a teacher, our holidays always had to be in July/August, with the distance travelled each year governed by the length of Jeff's leave, between three and five weeks. Thanks to our heavenly state of retirement, this year we had *ten* weeks!

Our North American trip started off in Toronto, thirty-six years *to the day*, since we had previously made the then arduous journey through Canada from Toronto to Vancouver. Where possible, we followed our original route.

'It's been a fantastic six weeks through Canada,' I raved. 'Gee, it's so *enormous*, so *empty of people*! The towns and cities have spread out and out – and upwards! Some places have lots of tourists – like Lake Louise. Remember on our visit there, years ago, there were only two cars parked and one of *them* was ours? But little else has changed much. What a marvellous country it is! So huge!'

18

'After all these years. . . the reminiscing. . . the wishing. . . we've actually done it! Done what we set out to do,' Jeff crowed with satisfaction.

'It's *all* been terrific!' I agreed. 'Lovely meeting friends in Vancouver after such a long time.'

'Now there's the long trek back,' Jeff said flatly, after a pause, his voice lacking his usual eagerness for travel.

'Are *you* not looking forward to it? *I* am.'

'Not really,' he replied with a shrug. 'We'll have to take it easy. No long-day driving. *No* side trips,' he warned, as if I, alone, decided on those.

'There're many more campgrounds in the US than in Canada, with much more choice for overnight stops. You won't need to plan ahead,' I suggested, hoping I didn't betray the concern I felt at his obvious rapidly diminishing enjoyment of our adventure. Nearly *3,000 miles* stretched ahead. . .

Maybe the anniversary of last year's hospital sojourn was bothering him after all? He hates to be reminded of previous episodes of illness, of which there have been too many for my peace of mind. He behaves as if they never occurred. I have to stifle my apprehension whenever he seems unwell, as he gets mad with me if I refer to his health. It's as if he regards sickness as a slur on his character!

'Good! I only want us to do 200 miles, even less, a day,' he answered. 'That way we can pull off the road early, and spend afternoons relaxing.'

'You seem fed-up with the whole undertaking?' I ventured, cautiously.

'No, it's just the return journey's hardly likely to give us the same sense of achievement as the Canadian part did.'

'It'll all be *new* for us,' I replied, hoping that his lassitude was owing to nothing more than lack of interest, of challenge.

'That's true,' he nodded.

'Apart from sorties into New York state from Toronto, or here, Washington, from Vancouver, all those years ago, we've not been *anywhere* in the US,' I said, determined to ignite some enthusiasm – for the 3,000 miles ahead!

'Quite amazing, really,' he answered, brightening a little, 'that it's taken us so long. Yes, it *will* all be new.'

Chapter Two

Back on the chilly interstate before 8am, with lots of drifting cloud and only an occasional cluster of farm buildings among trees, etched on the horizon, the gently rolling countryside went on and on, a harmonious blending of colour: gold, brown, dark brown, rust, green, but no telegraph poles. Interstates bypass towns. Unlike in Canada, where telegraph poles often flank the highways, because many settlements are near the road. The TransCanada Highway – *5,000* miles in length, *the longest paved road in the world!* – was constructed over twelve years, mainly in the 1960s, linking together already existing roads in towns and cities, as well as new road, through enormous areas of muskeg, prairies and mountains. The great stretches of road and tunnel through the Rockies cost a *million* Canadian dollars per *mile*.

'Watch out, a bend in the highway!' Jeff said. 'Look! I'm turning the steering wheel. In thirty-five miles it's the first time I've done that.'

For two hours we carried on across flat, treeless country, until a sign informed 'Leaving Range Area'.

'Thank goodness for that!' we agreed.

We stopped in Spokane (pronounced Spo*can*) at *Safeways*, for gas and groceries, the RV needing a double parking space. As we drove out of town, two signs in a store window said: 'Area Rugs' and 'Window Treatments' – carpets and curtains, in less fancy language.

Shortly afterwards, we crossed the state line into Idaho,

milestones beginning again at zero. No more President Washington's head, signboards had a map of Idaho on a dark green background and what a plethora of signs there were. One with an arrow indicated 'North to Canada'. 'Rumble Strips on Shoulders' advised another. A huge billboard had the dire warning: 'Sin When It Is Finished Bringeth Forth Death'.

'There must be rumble strips on the road, too,' I grouched, as we bounced along the corrugated surface.

'This road'll finish us off, before sin gets a chance,' Jeff grunted, struggling to keep lightweight Harvi steady.

The road went over a high bridge spanning a lake and on into trees and hills and torrents of rain. Travelling through the famed Coeur d'Alene recreational area of lush forests and scenic lakes, noted especially for its great number of osprey and bald eagles, we ploughed through many lake-size pot holes and water spilling from swollen creeks, but saw little else through the downpour. Due north in Canada, is Banff National Park with some of the world's most spectacular scenery, and warm sunshine, when we toured there a few weeks before. 'But nowhere on earth could look beautiful in this weather,' I thought.

We drove across the Idaho Panhandle; then at an elevation of 4,680 feet, crossing into Montana, we not only began at mile zero again, but lost a precious hour of life by putting our watches forward to Mountain Time. Through a curtain of drizzle our overnight campground seemed attractive enough, though the solar-panel-heated swimming pool was deserted, not having any 'solar' for yonks. We slept with rain lashing the windows and damp articles of clothing festooned around Harvi, thanks to the laundry's inefficient dryers.

Next morning we splashed and slithered back along the winding, rutted road to rejoin the interstate, on and on through Montana's 145,000 square miles of near-emptiness. Montana, one of the five Old West States, is sparse on population, with few towns of any size. Helena, the state capital, was, then, home to less than 30,000 people. We drove and drove 200 miles non-stop to Butte; sometimes through pine woods, sometimes paralleling a river, sometimes a railway track, where a mile-long goods-train thumptied, thumptied, thumptied; then past masses of pink-tipped, tall grasses fluttering along the edges of rolling, stock country strewn with wild flowers: red, purple, mauve, white

21

ox-eyed daisies and vivid orange black-eyed Susans all the way to the wooded mountains on the horizon, their snowy peaks shrouded in cloud.

Finding space on a car park in Butte, we went for a wander. It was good to be in a town of character with individual stores instead of giant shopping malls. At the end of the 1800s, thanks to a mining boom, Helena, known then as 'Queen of the Rockies', boasted fifty millionaires; Butte was where the hard-working miners lived, a rich ethnic mix of, among others, Irish, Welsh and Cornish. The influence of the latter was evident in Joe's pasty shop on Grand Avenue. A sign in the window encouraged: 'If you have not yet tasted The Pasty (Pronounced Passtee) Step Inside and Try Some'. We didn't. We'd had lunch. I don't even like the real thing produced in Cornwall.

On Main Street, in a gift shop, we asked about the giant white statue – you couldn't *not* see it! – atop a high mountain.

'The statue?'

'Yes, can you tell us about it, please?' I thought, but I didn't say, 'It's amazing to see something so huge, so white, so incongruous, *on top of a mountain*, in this empty wilderness, overlooking a small, unimportant place like this.'

'That's Our Lady of the Rockies,' the young woman answered, in a tone of voice suggesting that *everyone* knew about *the* statue.

'Big isn't it?'

'Yes, Our Lady of the Rockies is 90 feet tall. She stands 3,500 feet above the town,' she smiled, delighted to tell strangers. . . 'the statue rests on the East Ridge, part of the Continental Divide, you know, that means it's 8,510 feet above sea level,' she explained, proudly. The project begun in December 1979, apparently involving people from all walks of life and religious persuasion, took six years to complete.

'Must have cost a lot,' I remarked, still amazed that a statue like this was in a place like this.

'Oh yes! It took years and years to get the money together. Many years. Memorials were a large part of our support,' she went on, 'and they still are today.'

Thanking her, we declined the offer of a seat in a vehicle to take us aloft.

From giant statues to the daredevil, Evil Knievel, who was born in Butte. In one of numerous stunts, he hurtled on a motorbike over thirteen buses in Kings Mills, Ohio. His son, Robbie, was, then, making a name for himself in the same line of action. Outside a Thrift Store (Charity Shop) there was a pair of brand new ski boots for $5. A bargain! But no takers. Now, if they'd been rubber boots. . .

A steep climb out of Butte, high in wooded hills, gave us an eagle's view of a buffalo herd below on the plain, then there was a gradual descent from 6,393 feet at the Continental Divide to 4,800 feet at the campground that we pulled into in late afternoon. It was dry everywhere! It hadn't rained here all day! There was cloudy sun making it almost hot.

The July weather was berated when we congregated, delighted to be outdoors, on a grassy area between the rustic administration buildings and the swimming pool. With the horrendous flooding in the Mississippi valley, we felt sheepish to be complaining about the rain and low temperatures that *we* had, but we complained anyway.

A couple arriving from Yellowstone groused, 'We've had snow, sleet and temperatures of 30°F during the week. Wish we'd stayed home in California!'

'Hope it gets better. We're going to Yellowstone tomorrow,' Dutch people said. (They were true Dutch from the Netherlands, not American-Dutch.)

'We've had awful weather, too, in Vancouver,' other voices wailed.

Jeff and I have camped all over Europe from early days with kids and tents to more recent time with just ourselves in a well-equipped caravan. As the conversation, punctuated by laughter, ebbed and flowed with nothing mentally-taxing being discussed, I recalled to mind a campground in Belgium. On arrival, we were given a double sheet of stiff paper headed: *Camping Regulations*. Stern and unwelcoming, a long, long catalogue had the definite tone of: 'Thou shalt not. . .' like Moses with his tablets of stone, only this list, much longer than his, had towards the end, an admonishment in bold type: 'Discussions between Persons on Religion or Politics are Strictly Prohibited. Anyone engaging in such discussions will be asked to Leave the Campsite Immediately.' At least it said: 'asked to leave'; the mental picture was of offenders being frog-marched off-site by armed police.

The mountains all round loomed big in the darkness, the navy dome overhead studded with stars, as we sat in the large hot tub, while others larked about in the heated swimming pool. The familiar 'Where ye' from?' wasn't long in coming.

We explained.

Debbie, on vacation, from Edmonton, miles away in Canada, piped up, 'I have a friend in England. . .'

Oh no! Not again! I cringed. Usually, the 'friend in England' lives 'somewhere in London' and we live hundreds of miles from there. 'Let's think now. . . what's the address?' they say. Then the *name* of a *road* in London is given! However, this time it was different. Her friend in England was a nurse in the hospital a mile from our home, 6,000 miles away. A strange conversation to take place sitting in a hot tub under the stars, in the middle of the Montana prairies, on the only dry evening there had been for ages, don't you agree?

Montana is called 'Big Sky Country' or 'Land of Shining Mountains'. So far all we'd had were low, leaden skies and anything shiny was wet with rain, but next morning brought improvement. Sunlight striking snowy peaks contrasted sharply with the black mountain ranges. Big sky and shining mountains; wide rolling grasslands; herds of brown and white cattle; little calves; many horses; hay bales galore; wild flowers, but with no viewpoints or rest areas, there was nowhere that we could take a break to admire this ravishing countryside. The only signs indicated meandering roads to named individual ranches up to twenty miles away, with, hanging underneath: 'No Services'. Thanks a bunch!

We crossed the Jefferson, then the Madison and Gallatin Rivers, which join to form the Missouri Headwaters, an abundance of water, just north of us. When we planned this trip, our families in Canada and England were concerned that we would be traversing the endless plains in the full heat of summer. 'They'll be arid and baking,' they warned. We should be so lucky!

The towns had pleasant names: Three Forks for the three rivers, Bozeman from where a road went south to Yellowstone National Park, Big Timber, Prairie Dog Town, Reedpoint. A board suggested 'Take your Horse on Holiday', and indeed we did see an RV towing a large horse box. Even in the vastness of empty Montana, there was no escaping The Law; a sign threatened 'Speed Checked By Aircraft.'

We kept coming upon the names Lewis and Clarke: Lewis and Clarke Caverns; Lewis and Clarke Trail, which paralleled the I-90 for a while; Lewis and Clarke National Forest; and the Missouri Headwaters, where Lewis and Clarke came upon the confluence of the three rivers that form the mighty Missouri. The signs were always the same: a square with two figures in profile, one pointing with his left arm, both looking intently into the distance. Setting out from St. Louis in 1804, their mission from the 3rd President, President Jefferson, was, 'to find the most direct and practicable water communication across this continent for the purpose of commerce'. For the purpose of commerce! Nothing changes? Intrepid explorers, in an expedition lasting twenty-eight months, recording their findings as they travelled, they discovered the land west of the Mississippi through to the Pacific Ocean. Though, at that time, the present borders didn't exist, about a quarter of the miles they trekked lie within the boundaries of Montana.

Shortly after 1pm, pulling off the I-90 at Exit 450, we drove to a KOA site just outside Billings, with a population, then, of 82,000, Montana's largest town. This was our first time to stay on a KOA (Kampground of America).

'Billings is the headquarters of the KOA,' the young, red-jacketed girl clerk chirped when we registered. 'This site was the very first one. Now, ya' know, we're a nationwide organisation.' A first for them and a first for us!

Jeff had been out-of-sorts all week. By the time we'd set up, on a secluded area with the Yellowstone River, on the other side of steep rimrocks, behind us and a small stretch of lake in front, he was downright crotchety. Everything was wrong!

'Why don't you have a snooze?' I suggested, after lunch.

A giant grass-mower throbbed nearby. 'With *that* racket?'

His crankiness was an ominous sign. Past experiences have taught me that spells of lethargy often preceded his episodes of ill-health. I was worried, but tried not to show it, as *that* always made his irritability worse. As usual, any inquiry: 'Are you OK?' or 'What's the matter?' provoked the sharp retort: 'There's nothing wrong with me.' I fretted, quietly.

The previous year we'd taken our caravan to Europe for six weeks – our first trip abroad since Jeff's bypass heart operation, eighteen months before – as a trial run for the long Canadian-US

25

journey we were now doing. Very soon I wished that we had stayed at home! It was evident from the outset that he was unwell, as whenever I ventured to ask how he was feeling, at best he was curt, at other times downright cantankerous. We did less sightseeing than usual, staying several days at each stopover, even two weeks in a gorgeous spot at the water's edge of Lake Trasimeno, Italy. Leaving there, we set out for what should have been a leisurely return to England. A few days later, on a visit to the walled city of Lucca, he collapsed, head down beside his lunchtime pizza, a silent figure amid a gesticulating crowd, everyone – except me! – gibbering in Italian. The ambulance bumped along cobbled alleyways, through the city gates, out to a hospital in the Tuscan countryside. However, it wasn't a heart problem that time, not directly, but the 'Aspirini! Aspirini!', taken on doctor's orders since his bypass, which had caused stomach ulcers to haemorrhage; ulcers that he didn't know he had until then. After a week he recovered a little. Our family, contacted by telephone, together with the hospital doctors, were insistent that we should return to England by air. As I expected, Jeff had other ideas. 'Abandon the car and caravan?' Never! The fact that *he* might abandon this life was briskly brushed aside.

'If *I* don't drive can we travel by road?' he pestered the doctors.

'Your blood count is zilch,' or something like that!

'But we've got a caravan. . .' It was parked on a site twenty miles away. We'd been on a *day* visit to Lucca with just the car when he was taken ill.

'Travelling by. . . what you say. . . caravan?' queried the white-coated Professor, a mirror image of the British actor the late Alistair Sim, though I never saw him playing a white-coated doctor. The Professor seated on a swivel, antique chair, a great bookcase lined with tomes behind him, pivoted agitatedly from left to right and back again several times. 'Caravan? Caravan?' he barked.

'Roulotte,' I explained.

'Roulotte! Roulotte!' he echoed, his chair coming to a stop, as he looked at us disbelievingly across yards of polished mahogany desk, before he fell speechless.

'Every night you stop in different place?' the young house doctor, Dr Neri, stammered, equally as concerned as his senior

26

colleague, the Professor of Medicine.

Some days previously, in faltering English, the younger doctor explained that he could read English better than he could speak it. 'I can read quite well.' There was no arguing with that – among other texts, he knew James Joyce's better than most English graduates.

'Well 'er yes,' Jeff admitted, unfazed by the absurdity of our situation.

'What if you collapse again. . ? when you're in traffic. . ? During the night, somewhere. . ? You're very weak. . . It's such a long way. . .'

Eventually, they ceased trying to reason with Jeff. Giving me a long, sympathetic look the Professor wished us well – probably mentally washing his hands of any consequences – and departed, leaving Dr Neri to see to the signing of papers.

I'm sure that not many folk would consider my choice of books to be light holiday reading: I just happened to have a paperback of classical short stories in English in the caravan, and the author of one story was James Joyce. When bidding Dr Neri goodbye, I handed him this book, duly inscribed with our thanks. He was quite overcome with emotion, genuinely appreciative.

'You'd think you'd presented him with an award,' Jeff said afterwards.

I did most of the driving, towing a folding caravan, on the 1,400-mile return journey, through five countries (each with border controls and a different currency), then got it in the neck from my kids for travelling by road. That might have been because they know I detest driving on the *wrong* side of the road!

Here we were exactly one year later and Jeff not in good mood. Unwell?

The grass cutting finished. While Jeff slept, I had a swim in the pool. With a blizzard of cotton blowing from the many cottonwood trees around the campground it was like swimming in snow, but the water was soothingly warm. Later I basked beside the RV in the sun to dry off. After days travelling in the wide reaches of Montana's grasslands, it was cosy to have such a sheltered spot, heat emanating from the rimrocks behind us, yet adjacent to an extensive wild area for an evening ramble.

During the lazy afternoon, the sound of the Yellowstone River ever present, there was plenty of feathered activity on the lake:

various breeds of duck, some pure white, but no loons, Canada geese, the darting blue streak of a kingfisher, a grey heron standing for ever one-legged, motionless, as if sculpted in stone. Then two geese of a different species crashed down sending up sprays of water, swam to the edge, waddled out, belligerently chasing away anything in their path, making a bee-line for me, necks outstretched, squawking angrily. Deciding that discretion was the better part of valour, or something, I leapt up, knocking over my chair in my haste, retreating inside, banging the door shut behind me.

'What's all that about?' Jeff grunted, waking from sleep.

'I want to get away from. . .'

'What? A bear?' he mocked. (Actually, Montana has the greatest number of grizzlies in the lower 48 states.)

'Two geese,' I burbled.

'Geese!' he chortled, getting to his feet. 'Geese!' He opened the door. They darted necks horizontal, but remained at the bottom of the steps. 'Probably would like some bread.' They weren't easily satisfied. Threateningly, hung around for ages.

For supper we ate meals purchased on the site – roast chicken thighs, potato salad, beans, corn-on-the-cob and ice-cold, homemade lemonade. The raging rain with thunder didn't keep us awake in the night, nor did the mosquito bites that we'd been gathering over several days.

The morning was cool and heavily overcast, the geese, disgruntled, demanding breakfast. I had the easy option each time getting Harvi ready to leave, just making sure everything was stowed away securely, all doors and drawers firmly shut, but Jeff does the outdoor chores, made more laborious and messy if it is raining, or the pitch is muddy. That morning things went smoothly. Driving off the campground, the dashboard clock read 08.06, which was exactly the time to the minute, that it had been the previous morning I recalled, yet one of the joys of our kind of travel is *not* being ruled by time, not having a set routine. Strange?

Billings is in Bighorn County. A few miles southeast of the city is Little Bighorn Battlefield National Monument, also sometimes called The Custer Battlefield National Monument, where in 1876 General George Armstrong Custer engaged in bloody battle with the Cheyenne and Sioux, and lost – hence, Custer's Last Stand.

Six miles beyond Billings we changed to I-94, the start of a new interstate: mile zero again; felt like a game of snakes and ladders, always going back to the beginning, despite having already driven, since leaving Seattle, more than the distance from John O'Groats to Land's End. An extensive area around here is the Crow Indian Reservation, the tribe numbering approximately 11,000, of which only about one per cent practise their ancient traditions. They were once considered to be the greatest horsemen of the plains, living in the coolness of the High Country in the summer, returning to the Lowlands in winter, yet the horse was only introduced to the Crow Tribe in the 1700s, while for generations before that, they moved on foot using dogs to transport their teepees. Like American Indians everywhere they voice grievances. The Crows claim that, as late as the 1960s, their buffalo herds, an Indian life source, were systematically slaughtered, because of the fear of disease being passed to ranchers' cattle. Not true, they say. 'There was no disease. *They* just wanted our grasslands. Put their cattle on our land.'

We stopped briefly in spotting rain to have a look at Pompey's Pillar, a Registered National Historic Monument, where, on July 25, 1806, Captain William Clarke carved his name and date on the 200-foot-high massive sandstone block.

Cordoned off with steel wire, one lane of the highway was being resurfaced. Driving in drizzle, I was keeping to the posted speed limit, for twenty miles or so, when we came to a section without a cordon. Two cars behind pulled out to overtake, their wheels throwing up the loose gravel chippings like a shower of hail, which pockmarked our windscreen, as they speedily disappeared in a cloud of dust. It cost us $250 for a replacement windscreen, not covered by our insurance. So much for speed limits and no overtaking signs. The Law, this time, conspicuous by its absence.

All morning we drove through Wild West film country, though it's never raining in Wild West films; then stopped at a gas station in Miles City to fill both petrol tanks. Judging by the apparel worn by men, cowboy life thrives in Miles City. A signboard gave the population of the place as 8,000. Bet that increases dramatically during their famous Miles City Bucking Horse Sale every May, with its three days of horse trading, rodeo and street dancing entertainment.

'Hope they'd better weather than this!' Jeff remarked, when we parked, to buy groceries and have a coffee, on the outskirts of the sodden town and picked our way gingerly around great pools of water. There had been no rest areas, only roads for 'Ranch Access' or 'Valley Access', with 'No Services'.

Arriving in early afternoon, we booked into a campground in Glendive, a town of less than 5,000. A big sign informed proudly that the Yellowstone River, which joins the Missouri just north of here, is the longest undammed river in the lower 48 states. 'It remains wet, wild and dam-free' over its 650 miles thanks to the people of Montana, who took action in the 1970s to safeguard the river's future. Later, after Jeff had his now customary afternoon sleep, we explored a tiny corner of Makoshika State Park. Makoshika is Sioux for bad earth or bad lands. Wind and water erosion constantly changes this landscape, carving the sandstone rock formations into weird shaped knobs and caprocks with quirky protuberances here and there, while others are so smooth and regular they could have been produced by precision tools. Evergreens, sage brush, cacti, yucca, wild flowers, grasses grew in different areas of the park contrasting with the red scoria rock of the hillsides. Fossils of ten different species of dinosaur have been found in Makoshika. Just two years before, a triceratops skull and skeleton had been excavated. No doubt our young grandson in Ontario, who could rattle off the names of dinosaurs, the way other kids lilt nursery rhymes, would know all about it.

The river and stream beds north of Glendive are an excellent place to search for stones of the famous Montana, or Yellowstone, moss agate, we'd been told by a couple of rockhounds, when we were registering and they were setting out hunting. 'Don't need much in the way of equipment,' they grinned, 'just rock hammers for digging, ye'know and a bucket for carrying stones. Oh, and strong shoes!' On our return from Makoshika they were back, too. It was hard to believe that the grey potato-shaped bits of rock in their buckets were indeed gem stones in the raw.

By the time we finished our home-cooked steak dinner, followed by some fruit and quality ice cream from our freezer, it was fully dark.

'It's not yet 9pm,' I commented. 'On other evenings we've had daylight much later than this.'

'Must be nearing the edge of a time zone,' Jeff said.

Chapter Three

'Hello! We're back!' We were greeted outside church on Sunday by the Dutch couple with whom we'd chatted on a campground miles away, several days before, who were heading to Yellowstone National Park. On hearing of their proposed visit to Yellowstone, I asked Jeff, tentatively, if we could detour there too, and it was his tetchy refusal to go that alerted me to the fact that he wasn't well, because normally he would have readily agreed to such a jaunt.

The Dutch were as excited as kids who'd been to Disney World. Yellowstone was very different from The Netherlands!

'Did you see any bears?' I asked

'Lots of other wild life, but no bears,' they admitted, regretfully.

Jeff shot me a look as if to say, *see*? We had several sightings of bears in the Canadian Rockies, a few weeks before. I shouldn't have been miffed that he hadn't detoured. His health was really my prime concern, but I was peeved nevertheless. Yellowstone was the world's *first* national park and we had passed *so* close. Now I would never see it! As the Dutch were staying around Glendive for the day, we said cheerio and headed for Wibaux, the last settlement on our route in Montana.

Pierre Wibaux was a Badlands cowboy, who bestowed cash and his name to St. Peter's church, built in 1885. The church, its exterior clad in lava rock, was not open; the few other buildings on the verge of collapse, the surroundings overgrown, were deserted, apart from a stag with great branching antlers, who surveyed us with a contemptuous gaze for some moments before ambling off.

Shortly afterwards a roadside sign on the edge of miles of waving grassland welcomed us to North Dakota. Even more welcome was the sun shining in the wide blue dome of sky now that, after all that driving, we had left Big Sky Country for another state! 'Think North Dakota. Think The Great Plains. Think Badlands,' I trilled. 'The I-94 crosses the Badlands; so we'll see plenty.'

Home on the Range, Buffalo Gap, Painted Canyon were intriguing names of places in this prairie wilderness. At Theodore Roosevelt National Park South Unit, we stopped at the Visitors' Center and Painted Canyon Overlook to eat a late lunch at one of the picnic tables, from where there was a grandstand view over a great sweep of colourful badlands, with their weather-ravaged pinnacles, spires and buttes. Pushing on to Bismarck, arriving at a campground later than usual because, now on Central Time, we had 'lost' another hour, we booked for two nights.

'American feet are not made for walking,' Jeff observed, when we took an evening ramble, all alone in the huge, still world outside the campground. Americans will get in a car to drive to the house next door – honestly! They'll move the car several times on a parking lot if visiting different stores. They'll drive to the gym or sports centre. Use a motorised buggy on the golf course. They just don't like *walking*. Oh yes, they *do* use their legs: to run marathons, or jog, or power walk, with faces set in grim lines of concentration. A few will hoist enormous backpacks on to their shoulders and depart with a compass into the wilderness for weeks on end, enduring all manner of deprivations, even encounters with dangerous wild animals. But nobody takes our kind of gentle-paced, three-or-four-mile walk. Nobody! Not only were we the only campers walking, but we were the only ones enthralled by the first sunset for days, a stupendous spectacle, a great ball of fire throwing searchlight beams of crimson across the hushed, immense prairie, before slipping slowly towards the far distant horizon to vanish in an instant. Wiped away by an unseen hand. Gone! Its going cannot be delayed, not even by a split second, sobering, this utter powerlessness in the face of nature. I have always felt a pang of loss at the sun's disappearance – even more now that old age is staring me close up, another day down the slippery slope. That evening I was quite overcome by the awesomeness of this daily event. Native Americans, the first inhabitants of this vast land, are so in tune with the world that they treat all of creation with great deference. Good on them!

In the morning it was raining – heavily. Not the weather to spend the anticipated lazy day on site. And not a pleasant one for Jeff's outdoor chores, before we could leave in Harvi. At times like this, shopping malls have their uses; Bismarck had several. Spacious, self-service stores are great to whizz around 'til reaching the check-out, as we found in *K-Mart*. Our plump, girl checker, new to the job, (that's why there was no queue for her) slowly scrutinised each item, then, while mouthing its name, a stubby finger searched a flyer by the till in case it was on special offer, laboriously registering the bar code, at last, each price flashed triumphantly. On and on, item by item. Eventually, we made our escape. 'By now,' Jeff hissed, 'those from the other queues are home eating a cooked lunch!'

Bismarck's attractive 19-storey Art Deco limestone and marble state Capitol building on the east bank of the Missouri River is visible across the prairies from miles away. In between heavy rain showers we stopped in town to have a closer view. There were many well-preserved Victorian buildings, too. In contrast a starkly modern one was The Dakota Cyclery with a notice offering bicycles for rent and the suggestion: 'Why not follow the Lewis and Clarke Bike Tour, the 246-mile route along the Missouri River?' As a 200-mile stretch of the Missouri had caused devastating flooding requiring federal emergency relief, rafts might have been more appropriate.

'Some farmers are not going to get any kind of crop this year. Here, in North Dakota they're set to lose $21 million,' Craig said, while manoeuvring great fistfuls of popcorn around his beard into his mouth, alternating with swigs from his bucket-sized coffee. At an eating area on a Bismarck mall, Jeff and I were having a snack, when this dark-haired, well-built 6-footer in jeans, leather jacket and giant boots, pushing a laden trolley, sat down at the next table, the small chair disappearing from view beneath his girth.

'Hi folks, how are you today?' he greeted us like old friends. 'I'm Craig. Where you guys from? England! What brings you to flooded North Dakota?'

Throwing back his head, he laughed uproariously when we explained that we hadn't expected rain like this in the Midwest.

'We've had eight dry summers in a row, now this. . . I've not gotten my hay in yet – too wet. Weather girl this mornin' said of the past forty days there's been rain at some time on thirty-seven of them.'

'Thought it would be hotter than this,' Jeff went on.

'Yeap, sometimes up to a hundred Fahrenheit in July. Today it's fifty-two degrees!'

In town on business from his buffalo ranch, 130 miles away, his wife, shopping in the department stores, was already one and three quarter hours late. Watching him waiting patiently, munching contentedly, I wondered if buffalo chewed the cud like cows – like this rancher.

'Properly called they're bison, but Native Americans call them buffalo, and that's good enough for me,' Craig answered my question about the beast's correct name. 'French traders called the great humped cow: boeuf. English couldn't pronounce boeuf, so used buffalo and the name stuck, but *water* buffalo, now they're totally different from bison.'

His wife hadn't yet turned up when we left him consuming ever more popcorn and coffee. 'Have a great day,' he boomed after us. 'Nice talkin' to ye'.

There was plenty more rain, 1.7 inches overnight, with an electric storm, which lit up the campground for hours.

A messy time for Jeff disconnecting the hoses at the start of a second soggy day. Driving in rain, on cruise control, 220 miles across North Dakota past vast fields of uncut, black, rotting hay, not a tree in sight, the I-94 as straight as a tightrope, Harvi could have made it driverless. Jeff was always happier when driving required concentration and skill; rolling along at a steady pace for hours on end he found boring. It was boring!

It was a relief to leave the endless American highway for a couple of hours, at Exit 258 to Jamestown, to visit the re-constructed Frontier Village with trading post, one-room school house (surprisingly, the first building to be moved to the site), dentist, sheriff, church, post office, jail, saloon, all with fittings and fixtures from a bygone age, testifying to the tough life the Pioneers had worked and lived, but it was all much too spick and span to feel authentic. Something aeons older, on display in the small museum, was a Bison Crassiconis skull dating from about 3,000BC, which had been found in the vicinity. A sea of squelchy mud surrounding the buildings prevented us from exploring outdoors. A buffalo herd was out there somewhere in the mist.

In the late afternoon we stopped in Fargo, parking on West Acres Mall. This time the conversation about the weather was not with a rancher, but with ageing cowboys – 'cowmen' might be more appropriate. We'd grown used to seeing many wearing Stetsons and boldly checked shirts driving 4x4 trucks or flashy cars, but this pair dressed in full kit including neckerchief and spurs could have stepped off a film set; I wondered where they had tied up their horses.

'In Sioux Falls (in South Dakota, directly south from Fargo) things are *r e a l b a d* ye' know,' number one cowboy drawled; 's o b a d they're turnin' to *pra-yur*,' he said bemusedly.

'Tried ever'thin' else,' his mate twanged, from under the too-big, brimmed hat which dwarfed him, 'so can't do no harm.'

Waterlogged Midwesterners were holding church services to pray for favourable weather and the relief of those affected by the flood, 'as sandbags, levees and dams had all failed to keep out floodwaters'. Considering this, we and Harvi weren't doing too badly. Not badly at all!

The twin towns of Fargo/Moorhead sit right on the state line, Fargo in North Dakota, Moorhead in Minnesota, or, so we thought, but confusingly the address of our campground that night was: Moorhead, North Dakota. Next morning, crossing the Red River of the North, which forms much of the boundary between the two states, we were very definitely in Moorhead, Minnesota.

Then, it was all change! The road, the weather, the scenery. . . Only that we were still travelling in Harvi, it was as if overnight we had been transported to a totally different country. Driving in sunshine (though the unfortunate flooded areas to the west of us could expect more rain) on a state highway instead of the interstate, we left the enormity of ranching country for more conventional farming, with man-sized not buffalo-sized fields. It was more like European countryside than any we had seen in our extensive travels in Canada, or, so far, in the US. We felt quite at home. In fact, the Red River Valley, with some of the world's most fertile land, was settled by Scandinavian and other northern

Europeans in the late 19th century. The regular, angular fields of yellows, greens, browns, stretching for miles, had the neatness of a coloured drawing, and more trees scattered about than there had been for ages. Clumps of pink-tipped grasses waved us on our way as they had done right across the continent; the abundant black-eyed Susans, cheery as always, were now jostled for space by great splashes of another equally colour-strident plant: orange hawkweed. Its common name, the Devil's Paintbrush aptly describes its riotous behaviour.

From time to time the tops of silos shining silver in the sunlight were a give-away that farm buildings were hidden behind a screen of trees, when there was no other sign of habitation on the teeming acres of agricultural land. The highway ran through towns and villages with attractive houses each with its pretty lawned, treed garden, or front yard, as Americans say. At the outskirts, the population was given on roadside signs with punctilious precision: '4,242', '421', '12,500' (by far the greatest) '2,073', '144', '533', '132'. . . We wondered if the signs were changed yearly or more frequently taking into account every birth, every death. The small shops were interesting, too, offering everything from 'Helicopter Rides' or 'Antiques & Used Music' to 'Hunting & Fishing Supplies' or 'Harness & Saddle Shop'. No doubt these last two would also stock guns of various kinds, but they weren't blatant about it as in Billings, Bismarck, Fargo. . . where the Gun Shop had windows crammed with an arsenal of destruction, and outside: weapons hanging stiffly like a fringe of shining steel.

As always in America, Jeff and I were amazed at the number of churches: Presbyterian, Methodist, Seventh Day Adventist, Catholic, Assembly of God, United Evangelical. . . but here in Minnesota, the frequence of Lutheran ones (subdivided: Salem Lutheran, Evangelical Lutheran) was a reminder of the influence of northern Europeans. Even the smallest of villages, in every state, had several churches, often outnumbering the stores, and all well-maintained. With sparse populations, who funds them?

'Hi. How ye doin'?' a cowboy, dressed in black Stetson and a blue boldly-checked shirt, asked as he filled up his hefty 4x4 at the next pump, when we stopped for gas. Guzzling a gallon of petrol every ten miles, Harvi was a thirsty vehicle; Jeff topped up the two tanks frequently. Luckily gas was cheaper in the US than anywhere else we've driven. This 18-gallon top-up costing just $21.

'Have a good day,' the cowboy called as he drove off. I wondered if cowboys had their hats glued to their heads, because I've never seen one remove his headgear. Soon, we stopped again – surprised! – because an unadorned, white sign said simply: 'THE MISSISSIPPI'. Somehow we hadn't expected to see it this far north. Here, the wide, placid, brown river gave no indication of its destructive force, which had devastated several states. On its long journey from source to the sea at New Orleans, the Mississippi gathers water from 31 states and two Canadian provinces – that's a lot of water – which now had overflowed swamping, in places, farmland under 20 feet of water. Unlike a tornado or hurricane that hits and runs, this disaster had crept up over six weeks owing to abnormal rainfall.

Much as I felt sympathy for all the folk who had lost their homes and livelihoods, I was thrilled to see this river. At last! We both have several ancestors who travelled far and wide – in an age when travel was not customary. One of Jeff's grandfathers, when he was a boy of twelve years, walked with his family – *walked!* – across Europe from Russia to escape a pogrom. I have nobody that I know of who can equal that feat, but my maternal grandfather, a Yorkshireman, *did* spend some time working the boats on the Mississippi in the mid-1880s, around the time that Mark Twain (my grandfather always gave him his real name, Samuel Clemens) wrote *The Adventures of Huckleberry Finn*, though, of course, the book refers to the time *before* the American Civil War (1861-1865). I have an early edition of *Tom Sawyer* given to me by my grandfather, who duly inscribed the flyleaf; (a sister got *Huckleberry Finn*). By the way, in his early working life Samuel Clemens was a journeyman printer; so, too, at the very same time, was my grandfather's father, in Yorkshire.

We carried on through places with fascinating names: Ottertail County, Eagle Bend, Deerwood, Crow Wing River, to our overnight campground in a state park, where we had a meander in marvellous surroundings teeming with wildlife all quite unperturbed by the constant roar of the turbulent St. Louis River, a seething mass of white topped water, adjacent to the park.

The sun was striking down through the maples from a clear sky when we got under way next morning, having tussled with the temptation to stay longer in our idyllic surroundings. As family from England would be joining our Canadian family, we wished to return there soon, although there was plenty of time before returning Harvi to his owners.

'Any spare days we can spend near one of the lakes,' Jeff suggested, in better humour than he had been for ages, now that 'home' was not far away.

On and on we drove through trees; a big-eyed fawn stood transfixed for a few minutes at the roadside, before scampering into the safety of the forest. Most days we'd seen squashed animals pasted to the tarmac, on one occasion, two spotted deer together in a ditch. 'Deer! Deer! – bet they did lots of damage to whatever collided with them,' Jeff commented. 'Poor creatures.'

On a high bridge over the St. Louis River estuary near Duluth, one of the largest ports on the Great Lakes, we crossed into Wisconsin and stopped in attractive Ashland on Lake Superior, where the spired church of Our Lady of the Lake, with its nearby school, were preserved historic buildings.

The Great Lakes: enormous inland seas, Lake Superior is the size of the island of Ireland – can you believe? Previously, we'd travelled along its Canadian side; the Wisconsin section includes the offshore Apostle Islands, named by French missionaries. In fact, there are 22 islands in the group, spread over 600 square miles of Lake Superior. The missionaries travelling by *canoe* could be forgiven their miscalculation. Anyway, when the islands were recounted nobody renamed them. Diverting for a while from our intended route, we followed the scenic shoreline of Superior for some distance, before stopping to cook lunch on board Harvi. Afterwards, clambering up the steel ladder at the back, I stood on the roof, nine feet above ground – my arthritis only in the early stages! – revelling, in silent wonder.

'Take some film from your vantage point,' Jeff suggested, handing up the video camera: a huge, ugly, rest-it-on-your-shoulder-job, which he had bought in a secondhand-cum-pawn shop in Church Street, Toronto, because he hadn't brought his own nifty, lightweight one from England. When I was ready to hand it back, so that I could come down from the roof, there was no sign of him, but I could hear chuntering, then a yell, followed by another, 'Come quick.'

'Lord, what can have happened?' I thought, struggling with the cumbersome camera, transferring it to my left hand, while gingerly feeling backwards with my right foot for the top rung of the narrow ladder – nine feet above ground, remember – my right hand grasping the rail, breaking out in a sweat, wanting to hurry, but needing to take care as I descended slowly, the same foot leading each time feeling for the rung beneath.

'Where are you?' I called, placing the camera on the ground.

'Here!'

'Where?'

'Here!'

My God! Where? What's happened? I panicked. Why? would have been a better question, when I spied him partway underneath the RV, his backside in the air.

'There's a wet patch on the ground; something must be leaking,' he gabbled, in a muffled voice.

'Is it oil?' I asked, dropping to the ground beside him.

'No.'

'Petrol?'

'Don't think so.' He dabbled his fingers in the liquid. 'No, it's not. Did you spill water, when you washed up after lunch?'

'Of course not!'

'Then it must be one of the holding tanks leaking,' he wailed, even more worried. 'We'll have to find out which one,' he announced, getting to his feet, wiping droplets of sweat from his face with the back of a hand, leaving behind black streaks. 'Can't park up on a campground like this.' He peered underneath again. 'There's *more* dripping now!' His voice rose. The puddle grew bigger.

We both went inside Harvi to read the gauges for the various tanks, not that they would tell us anything, but it gave us something to do in our confusion. 'Can't hear any dripping above the racket of that damned thing,' I said, in annoyance, indicating the air-conditioning unit in the ceiling, which was going full blast.

The front of his dark hair was clinging in damp curls to his knotted forehead. 'Ah! – *that's* probably the cause,' Jeff said, relief ironing out the tension in his face. 'It's condensation from the air-conditioning,' he laughed, with a complete change of mood. 'Can't be anything else.'

'We haven't needed to switch it on for ages. When we *did* use it a week or more ago, we must've been on more absorbent ground than this firm, dry surface, so we wouldn't have noticed the moisture,' I agreed, as I retrieved the camera from where I had abandoned it in the grass.

'Been here a couple of hours,' Jeff replied, looking at his watch as he swung up into the driver's seat. 'Time we got moving.'

Skirting the edge of Bad River Indian Reservation with signs offering 'Cigarettes for Sale' – no taxes are levied on cigarettes sold on Reservations – we carried on for a few miles, then crossed the state line into Michigan thereby 'losing' another hour.

'We're on Eastern Time again, the same as the kids in Toronto,' I said, adjusting my watch.

'Bear Crossing For Six Miles' made a change from the more usual leaping deer signs, but we hadn't expected to be in bear country here. At the next service area we filled up with gas: twenty-six and a half gallons into the right tank, five and a half gallons into the left, $31.50 in total – less than one dollar a gallon. After weeks travelling in Harvi, each time we got fuel we were delighted anew at the low cost. Great! And, we weren't accosted by bears.

'I've got a map of the scenic route.' Jeff waved it, as we drove off the forecourt. The road wriggled along the state line between Wisconsin and Michigan, so we were never quite sure which state we were in; not that it mattered, it was all truly gorgeous. Sparsely populated, the sign for any settlement read 'Township Village of' – and then the name of the place; the number of residents was not given, obviously being few, instead, the *names* of the families, who lived along each byroad were displayed. Harvi almost filling the narrow road, through forest – still no sign of bears! – our 60-mile detour around the area billed as 'Wisconsin's Last Wilderness' was certainly lovely; there was a lake, waterfall and the famed Township Village of Presque Isle with its couple of wooden fronted shops, a post office, and, surprisingly, we only saw one church: St. Rita's.

'All very scenic,' Jeff agreed, 'but we'd better press on.'

Our overnight campground had, as well as the usual swimming pool, its own lake, fed by underground springs, with birches and pines edging the slick of sandy beach. In the evening, the light of many camp fires dotting the dusk, we weren't bothered by drifting smoke, as on other occasions, but the ubiquitous aroma of barbecuing steak filling the air could have reached 'bear country' a hundred miles away. However, the bloodcurdling shrieks, which shattered the silence of the sleeping campground at 2am were not those of someone being attacked by a marauding grizzly but only loons having an argument. The two black ducks with distinctive white markings, I had seen when I swam in the lake in the afternoon; consequently, we didn't join those rushing outdoors to investigate the racket, as we knew, from past experience in Canada, what an incredible sound loons can make.

There was no sign of them on the lake, glinting golden in the slanting sun, when we departed. For hours we carried on through attractive countryside, the road dodging in and out of Wisconsin, before settling in Michigan, and on to Escanaba on Little Bay de Noc, giving us our first view of Lake Michigan, the only Great Lake we'd never seen, because, unlike the other four, it has no shoreline in Canada. We took a long rest stop in pretty Escanaba, then drove to Manistique and our overnight campground adjoining a hotel, overlooking the lake. The French names everywhere a reminder that European missionaries were among the first white people there.

Chapter Four

'Come an' join us,' a man's voice called from a lively group near an enormous blazing, log fire as we returned to the camping area from the hotel after dinner.

Fully dark, by the firelight we recognised the brood of assorted children and four adults, encountered earlier on Manistique Beach. For most of the afternoon we'd had the great curving sweep of golden sand to ourselves, the pine-studded dunes behind strewn with bell-like flowers as vivid blue as the lake; then, a straggle of kids whooped down to the beach, followed by two couples, mid-thirtyish, who instantly introduced themselves. Some of the children were theirs; others not; all were 'goin' to have a campin' vacation to remember' – or something. Leaving them enjoying the beach, we made use of the hotel's indoor pool and spa, and later, restaurant.

'There's space here,' Chuck invited. 'Tracy, Jamie, would you like to sit at the table?'

Tracy and Jamie, aged about four years, obligingly vacating their camp-stools tried, without success, to squeeze on to the already full benches of the wooden picnic table, liberally strewn with paper plates, bottles of pop, great bags of chips (crisps) tubs of popcorn. . .

'There's no space, Dad,' pretty, blonde Tracy whispered shyly. Hefty, broad shouldered Chuck scooped her gently onto his knee.

'I'll sit here,' Jamie declared, skipping away from the group to swing on a low bough of a tree.

'Careful Jamie,' his mother, Lisa, warned.

The possibility of danger was an immediate attraction for two bigger boys, who darted to join him. In no time, all three were pushing and elbowing each other off the perch to roll around on the ground like playful puppies.

A call: 'Time for marshmallows,' put a halt to boisterous behaviour. Getting to their feet, brushing pine needles from chubby hands on their already mucky sweaters and leggings, they returned to the fireside. Blazing log fires and toasting marshmallows are a must for holiday camping with kids. The squidgy squares skewered on long sticks are held over the flames for a few seconds before being dipped in melted chocolate and scoffed – nauseating! – but we gamely joined in for a while. However, mustering mosquitoes were having a scrumptious feed, too; Jeff and I, not expecting to be outdoors for long, hadn't doused ourselves with repellent.

"The mosquitoes botherin' you?' Jean exclaimed, surprised, when I murmured that we'd have to retreat from the festivities.

'That's 'cos you're newcomers, don't bother us,' dark-haired Lisa added. It's true, the bugs don't like everyone equally. Too bad they loved Jeff and me – lots!

'D' ye know it's only female mosquitoes that bite?' Jean went on, in her high-pitched voice. 'They need blood to lay their eggs.'

'We've supplied plenty, more than our share. There'll be squillions of eggs!' we laughed, slapping and scratching, as we said good night.

Despite getting through the RV door speedily, several mozzies buzzed in too. 'I'll give them a blast of spray,' I said, grabbing the canister of repellent, which was to hand since being invaded by a swarm of the pests a few weeks before in British Columbia, when they discovered a minute tear in a window mesh.

'Glad we're not in a tent,' Jeff said. 'D'you remember that night near Ottawa?'

'How could I forget?' Some years before, on our first visit to Canada in more than twenty years, with our teenage daughters, we camped in two tiny tents, all very basic, but hugely enjoyable, until one night we came close to being devoured by marauding mosquitoes. Vicious vampires!

Jeff made porridge for breakfast. 'Why porridge?' I queried.

'Might cancel out those blasted marshmallows. . .'

Recommended for lowering cholesterol levels, Jeff ate porridge regularly, but not often while we'd been travelling. I swam in the hotel pool before taking to the road later than usual, because nearing the end of our trip, with time to spare, we could go at a more leisurely pace.

Our journey followed the shoreline of Lake Michigan around to St. Ignace, where just after noon, booking into a campground for the weekend, we left a 'Pitch Taken' sign in our spot, before heading into town a couple of miles away.

Several sweeps of the small town – which actually is classed a city – proved that all parking was full. Soon irritability soared. Tempers frayed. Harvi seemed to grow more ugly and cumbersome and the roads narrower, as we bumbled around. And around. And around. Still trading comments loudly, Jeff, yanking the steering wheel, drove past the 'Private Parking' sign on to the empty parking ground of St. Ignatius' church.

We fell silent, owing more to shortness of breath rather than the inappropriateness of our behaviour. An oblong, wooden sign placed prominently over the presbytery garage threatened: 'Thou Shalt Not Park Here'. Jeff, in no mood for levity, driving to the other side of the lot, pulling up with a jolting application of the brakes, stated, 'Well, I'm not moving from here, except to go back to the campground. Are we staying or going?'

I approached a gangly youth who was hoeing a patch of garden.

'There's a service at 5.30,' he told me. 'Need all this parking then.'

'We'll be returning for Mass,' I assured him.

'Oh! Oh! OK, then,' he answered slowly, while eyeing Harvi's licence plate. 'You from Canada? Live in Ontario?' he asked.

'Yes,' I replied briefly, not wishing to spend time on explanation.

'Better make yourselves *small* as possible,' he advised, when I thanked him.

I relayed this to Jeff.

'Huh, what's he want us to do, rub down Harvi with vanishing cream?' He re-parked alongside a perimeter fence, where we wouldn't cause any obstruction. Sideways on, Harvi looked bigger than ever, decidedly scruffy, much in need of a wash and polish.

At the north end of the lakeshore boardwalk in St. Ignace we spent a fascinating afternoon at Marquette Mission Park and Museum of Ojibwa Culture. Archaeologists consider this site to be one of the most important in the Midwest. Digs have uncovered thousands of artefacts dating back 300 years, many of which were displayed in the small museum, a converted 19th century church. There were tools of stone, bone, copper and pottery with explanation of their uses, from three periods of the Ojibwa people's history, some original, some clearly marked as reproductions.

Michigan comes from a Native word meaning 'large water'. Michigan state, consisting of two peninsulas, is surrounded by the waters of four of the Great Lakes; Lake Ontario alone has no shoreline in Michigan. (Canada, on the other hand, has a shoreline on all the Great Lakes except Lake Michigan.)

On Sunday afternoon, bundled up in rain gear against heavy showers, we walked through lovely countryside to the bridge. Pronounced Mackinaw, the Mackinac Bridge, a 5-mile feat of engineering, joins the Upper and Lower Peninsulas. During a dry spell, we had a superb view of the bridge, but annoyingly had brought neither camera nor binoculars. On our return, we stopped off at a Native craft store. It housed a marvellous array of beautiful objects from full-sized bark canoes, to carved wood, to exquisite beadwork, to intricately designed jewellery, a veritable Aladdin's cave. Only it wasn't a *cave*. The *building* that housed all these treasures was itself a work of art. The high roof of the wooden structure was supported throughout on the boles of birch trees and the entire inside of the building was 'wallpapered' in birch bark, everywhere shimmering silver. It was delightful! There was much to look at and admire. Two of the many things we bought are among our all-time favourite purchases, both made from agate. One is a piece of polished brown agate, half an inch thick, measuring roughly three and a half inches by two inches, on top of which a tiny Indian paddles his canoe, the miniature wrought in silver with great precision; the other is a thin slice of agate with a bear and pine trees silhouetted against a sunset, cleverly using the colour of the stone.

'We'd better leave before we buy up the whole store,' I suggested, reluctantly turning away from the displays.

That evening Jeff lit an enormous fire in our fire-ring in an attempt to warm us, hoping also to dispel the gloom of the near-deserted campground, as all the weekenders had gone home. 'We'll stop before reaching the bridge in the morning to get some snaps,' Jeff said, sending up a shower of sparks, when he threw another log on the fire.

But we didn't. The toll-bridge was shrouded in dense fog. This 5-mile span of steel crossing the Straits of Mackinac has the water of a different Great Lake on each side: Lake Michigan to the west and Lake Huron to the east. And we didn't see any of it! Nothing except the tail lights of the creeping car ahead of us.

The fog cleared slowly, but it remained heavily overcast. Continuing south on Highway 75, down the centre of the Lower Peninsula, we took exit 310 and followed signs to The Cross in the Woods Shrine in Indian River. 'As you're goin' that way, you *must* stop by,' we'd been encouraged by folk on the campground.

Built in the form of an Indian Long House, the church sits in beautiful grounds surrounded by tall trees, all very tranquil. 'The Last Supper in Beads', on loan from a museum, was on view in the adjoining gift store. Measuring eleven and a half feet by five and a half feet, this amazing bead tapestry, a copy of Leonardo da Vinci's fresco in Milan, had been created in the late 1960s by a Native woman.

Information boards gave details: 'My name is Mary DeGuvara, a Chippewa and Ottawa Indian. When I was a little girl my mother taught me to do Indian beadwork.' Her story continued, 'One day, many years later, I decided to make something special. The Last Supper of Our Lord came into being created.'

Drawing the pattern took her *ten* months. Then on a 6-foot wooden loom made from salvaged wood by her husband, Sylvester, she 'began the actual beading'. With help from her son, it took *seventeen* months to complete. The tapestry 'weighs 43 pounds 5 ounces'.

Using 121 different shades of seed beads, Mary DeGuvara recorded the total number of beads she used down to the last one: a staggering '1,788,761' – nearly *two million* tiny beads! The halo surrounding Christ's head was done in 14 carat gold beads, purchased with money which had been donated from all over the continent. *Each* bead was 'reinforced by going through it four times with nylon thread', thereby using more than 'ten and a half miles of thread' and more than '200 beading needles'. The result of all this dedicated work is a stunning masterpiece in vibrant colour. With no pictures of it on sale, we took photographs.

A section of the adjacent museum was devoted to dolls – a permanent display, not on loan from a museum, as the tapestry was, but researched and created painstakingly many years before. This, too, in its own way, was unique. There were 525 dolls of similar size arranged side by side on shelves in glass cases. Each doll was dressed differently. No vibrant colours here. No fancy bows or frills. No pretty clothes. There were bonnets, yes, or more accurately, veils: these dolls were nuns!

Every one of the 525 orders of Religious Sisters in the US was represented here, attired in the cumbersome, floor-length habits that, at one time, were customary, but have long since been modernised. However, like manuscripts or ancient cathedrals, these dolls dressed as in a bygone time, also were church history. Cards gave details about each order of nuns and the dates of arrival in the US.

The first Missionaries in this part of the continent were French, usually coming from what is now Canada, being active from the1500s. In later times religious from European countries came. As I was reading, I remembered that the school I attended had sent religious sisters to – of all places! – Los Angeles. Would I find here a doll dressed like my head teacher of long ago? What a sobering thought!

The French Sisters of St. Louis (named for King Louis of France) suppressed in their homeland during the wars of religion, had been re-established a long time after that in Ireland, in 1842. Much later, they had convents in England, then parts of Africa, then Los Angeles. I was about to give up, cross-eyed from my scrutiny of the glass cases and their hundreds of miniature nuns, when there she was on a bottom shelf: my head teacher, dressed identically to my teachers of English literature, history, art, all of whom had influenced my continuing interest in these subjects. (When I became a teacher, knowing the long-term effect for good or ill that I could have on my students was, at times, disconcerting, to say the least!) How strange, here in rural Michigan, to be transported back to school days in Dublin. Then I could hear the music teacher, Sister Clotilde, berating the school choir – it was definitely time to move on!

Fast forward. Where was Jeff? Obviously not delighting in

nostalgia about nuns! In conversation with a couple fascinated by our mode of travel, cups of coffee in hand, they were viewing Harvi's engine, having marvelled at the compactness of the interior of the RV.

As we continued south a roadside marker declared: 'You are now crossing the 45 Parallel – half way between the Equator and the North Pole'. Well, we were glad not to be in either of those places, but still in lovely Michigan with the temperature in the low 70°F; farms with silos; wild flowers edging fields; an occasional eagle or group of turkey vultures circling effortlessly; a lone cowboy astride his horse riding into town; on an enormous, sloping field a herd of buffalo grazing; a forest of Hardwick Pines with a sign saying: 'One of Michigan's largest stands of virgin white pines, the remains of forest that used to cover much of the north of the Lower Peninsula'; the startling green of a well-watered golf course. . . Then a reminder that the real world has grim features too, a board warned: 'Prison Area, do not pick up hitchhikers'. We'd seen similar signs in other states, but in more isolated places.

Delayed by extensive road construction plus a detour, when eventually we found our intended (not pre-booked) RV park for a two-night stay, we got the very last vacant space, much to my relief as I was feeling guilty because Jeff had driven all the 201 miles that day. Truly, I hate driving. I felt happier – or less unhappy! – in the driver's seat on an interstate, in sparse traffic, where I could stay on cruise control with no fluctuations in speed, no obstructions, no worries except not to fall asleep through boredom. Manoeuvring Harvi along narrow or single lane roads I left to Jeff and he kindly did not complain.

Both tired, I headachy, Jeff's ankle, hurt weeks before, in Vancouver, was aching again. Once set up, we raided the fridge for an easy meal: turkey burgers with Spanish rice; scraped the ice cream container empty, followed that with a handful of grapes, all washed down with cold drinks.

The sun broke through, the first we'd seen for a couple of days, creating a beautiful sunset; slender, upright trees darkly etched against the turquoise and apricot sky, just like my slice of agate bought in the Upper Peninsula, though no bear!

Before going to bed we turned off the noisy air-conditioning, opening the roof and several windows instead; despite the coolness I didn't sleep well. There was a starry sky, but no moon visible, when I peaked out about 2am. Then, for spite on a rest day, we both were wide awake early. I was feeling quite rotten, but Jeff's foot, thankfully, was less painful. Parked right at the river's edge, I opened the curtains on a sunlit picture-perfect view, with the nearby ornamental bridge and the fringe of trees reflected in minute detail in the mirror-like surface of the placid water.

Deciding to spend time on a bay on Lake Huron, we set off in Harvi. One of the great joys of the RV was having our home with its on-board facilities, thereby enabling visits to quiet, out-of-the-way places. We parked on a level piece of ground, away from the boat launch. The few vehicles had empty trailers. Even viewed through binoculars, the boats, no doubt with occupants happily fishing, were mere dots in the distance. For the entire day we had the place to ourselves to wander the beach; admire wild rock flowers; have a swim; take a walk to a lighthouse; gather wild raspberries; watch busy sandpipers on their stick-like legs making their funny little runs in and out of the water; snooze; read. Restored, nine hours after leaving, we arrived back at the campground.

After dinner I tidied, and cleaned the oven and hob thoroughly. We spent hours sorting accumulated notes, papers, brochures – what a lot there were! – checked that we had gifts for grandkids, family and friends, organised to return to base.

A gloriously sunny morning for our last full day in the US, yet other places were not so blessed, the weather forecast on the radio warned, 'One inch of rain is expected in St. Louis and Kansas City today.' Rising waters of the Mississippi had already broken a levee in St. Louis and now another inch of rain. 'Three billion dollars in emergency aid' had been granted to help those in the flooded areas. While some parts of the US were experiencing record high temperatures, even drought, in other states the rain continued to pour down. Little wonder that there is a need for a TV station in the US reporting nothing but The Weather.

There were acres of cultivated fields; in some, potatoes were being harvested, in others, corn. As always, eagles, once to my delight a golden one, or vultures, glided overhead. Near some cabins oozing smoke, there was a makeshift sign saying: 'Jerky and Smoked Fish for Sale'. Jerky is dried buffalo meat. Not being adventurous enough to try *fresh* buffalo meat the dried stuff had no appeal whatsoever. Then, incongruously, in this vast agricultural area an enormous sign gave directions to 'The World's Largest Christmas Store – Open Every Day Including Sundays'. And it was only July! And Christmas is not the main public winter holiday for everyone in the US, but Thanksgiving is, at the end of November. The notion that Thanksgiving dates from the time of the Pilgrim Fathers is doubtful. It only became an official celebration in 1863. At least Christmas has been around for a while. Anyway, we didn't detour for the Christmas shop, but we did, near Flint, for a Farmers' Market.

Once we had turned off the main highway, there were no further signs for the market, so we stopped to ask directions from two black men, who were cutting the grass verges along the road. One was about to help with, 'Go straight down, 'til you reach. . .' when the other butted in, 'We'll take you there,' and with a sweep of a muscular arm, 'Com'on.' Abandoning their work and implements, they jumped into an old jalopy parked nearby and, without waiting for us to get moving, took off like a bat out of hell, their car making ominous rattling noises. We followed as best we could. Shortly, we could see further along the road a great iron gateway with 'Farmers' Market' emblazoned overhead. Arriving there, the gates were firmly locked. Our two friends, standing beside their jalopy, scratching their heads in disbelief, blurted in unison, 'Gee folks, it's closed!'

'Yes,' we agreed, pointing to a big board beside the gates, which said, 'Open Tuesdays, Thursdays, Saturdays.'

Our friends continued to look puzzled. 'Today is Wednesday,' Jeff grinned.

'Oh Jeez! Wot d'you know.'

'Thanks for trying,' I called, as we climbed back in the RV.

They were still standing outside the locked gates, slapping one another on the back, laughing uproariously, while Jeff manoeuvred Harvi in the narrow road to return the way we had come.

'Hope they find their way back to their grass cutting,' I said.

'And that their tools are still there,' Jeff laughed.

Early in the afternoon, we pulled onto a campground near Port Huron for our last set-up. Jeff couldn't get through the bushes with our cable to the electric point, which was annoying because it had taken some time to park on blocks to be level for the fridge. I had to go back to the office to sort out another site, while Jeff extricated Harvi. We moved elsewhere.

Reminiscing endlessly that evening on our ten-week adventure, we admitted that, all down the years – *thirty-six years* to be exact – when we used to say wistfully, 'Someday we *will* do that trip again through Canada,' we never really believed that we would, not even when our Vancouver-born baby grew up and returned with his wife to live in Ontario. In more recent times, Jeff's heart trouble scuppered any thought of extensive travel. We always acknowledged that living in Canada, overcoming the difficulties we had encountered there as hard-up newly-weds, had taught us to cope with whatever life threw at us. Now, not only had we repeated the trip from Toronto to Vancouver, despite Jeff's quadruple heart bypass operation, but we had returned through seven American states, *travelling by motorhome*, and we'd not seen the inside of one, let alone driven one, until we hired the RV. It would be a wrench to say goodbye to Harvi, but apart from that we were mighty pleased with ourselves!

In readiness for returning the RV on our last morning we filled up with fresh water and dumped the grey and black water. A few miles down the road we topped up with gas – cheaper in the US than Canada. The RV had to be returned in the same condition that it was on collection. (We had to pay extra for a new windscreen, pockmarked by those speeding drivers. . !) We carried on to the Duty Free for some goodies including 24 Labatt and 24 Molson (not for us, Jeff doesn't like beer; I don't drink alcohol), we said a regretful farewell in the direction of the US as we took the Blue Water Bridge.

Driving off the other end in Sarnia – we were back in Canada!

'We'll head for Port Stanley,' Jeff said.

'Why?' I queried. 'That's in the opposite direction to home, isn't it?'

'Well,' he replied, with a grin. 'The other day you mentioned that we'd been on four of the Great Lakes this holiday, but not on Lake Erie. Well, Port Stanley has a beach on Lake Erie. We'll detour there. It'll only take a couple of hours. Then we will have seen all five Great Lakes on the same trip.'

What a lovely surprise! Not one of the biggest of the Great Lakes – but still resembling an ocean – it was our first time on

Erie. Blue, blue water and a gorgeous sandy beach, I had a swim, took some snaps, then back to the highway. Three hours from Port Stanley and more than *7,000* miles since we had waved cheerio to the family at the start of our trip, we pulled up at 1066 – truly, that historical date is the number of their house!

'Oh! Hi!' our seven-year-old grandson, clutching a basketball, called out matter-of-factly before taking aim at the net, as if we were only returning from driving around the block. A pretty big block, but in reality that's what we had done!

Chapter Five

During the next two summers we caravanned in Spain and Portugal, poking about in obscure corners of the peninsula, each with its own treasure of beauty or interest. After our Big Trip in Canada and the US, which we'd talked about endlessly for months, it was good to be exploring new places on Europe's familiar continent.

Following a fly-drive vacation at the Grand Canyon, our daughter-in-law suggested that we should also go. 'Put it top of your list of places to visit. Soon!'

There was no list! Nor, after our 'once-in-a-lifetime' trip in North America, had we any plans to tour there again – soon, or ever! But constant dripping wears away a stone. Eventually we succumbed to her continuing entreaties and gave a trip to the Grand Canyon some thought. Well, actually, lots of thought. . .

'What about doing a trip to celebrate our Ruby Wedding?' Jeff suggested.

'But I don't want just to go to the Grand Canyon; there are other places, too, that I want to see.'

'Like where?'

'Yellowstone National Park for one,' I answered, peevishly, our not diverting there on our Big Trip still rankled. 'If we *do* travel in the US again, aren't there places *you* want to see?'

'Um, I suppose so. I'd love to tour California.'

Yellowstone, California and the Grand Canyon are hundreds of miles apart. From Toronto to Yellowstone, travelling through six states, is *twice* the distance of that from Paris to Moscow, and that was just the beginning. Fly-driving wouldn't do. Our very own motorhome was needed!

In early April, travelling sixty miles north of Toronto, through white, ice-stiff countryside with occasional pines, or stark leafless trees, we purchased *secondhand* a small motorhome, more easily manoeuvrable in towns than the hired one. Given sufficient headroom it could be parked in a standard parking space.

The RV, which we again called Harvi, was a Dodge. A good omen for doing our trip in celebration of forty years of marriage, as the nine-year-old car in which we crossed Canada, as newly-weds, was a Dodge coupé. Jeff, who knows *all* there is to know about such things, declared that our purchase was in great shape mechanically and I, who know *nothing* about the inside workings of a motor-car (and little about the outside, only ever noting size and colour, not the model, so that I've disappointed many by failing to be impressed with their limousines) was very taken by the deep pile, rose pink carpet and matching upholstery; woodgrain panelling and solid oak drawer fronts and cupboard doors; everything in immaculate condition. This was definitely going to be Gran's and Granddad's Playhouse!

Though congratulating herself on her persuasive powers, our daughter-in-law thought that we were crazy. 'I never intended you to *drive* to the Grand Canyon!'

There had never been anything haphazard about our camping trips. Heavens no! Jeff is an organiser par excellence; it's not in his nature to be unorganised. While waiting to return to Canada, he spent much time pouring over maps, calculating distances and deciding a route to take in the various points of interest that we wished to see. Later, he enlisted the help of the Canadian Automobile Association. Their suggestion of allowing two and a half hours travelling time for each 100 miles travelled, taking in meal and rest stops, meant that at least nine weeks were needed. The CAA produced an individually tailored routing on strip maps: bulky, but in use the Triptix, despite its size, was easy to hold. 'Even *you* should be able to follow it,' Jeff teased.

A send-off party of five lined up on the driveway of 1066, bemused at the reversal of roles. 'You oldies should be staying at home and waving *us* good luck!' they laughed.

Refreshingly cool in the USA customs-immigration office, our passports and car documents were checked fairly speedily. Then back to the steamy 90°F on I-94, for several more hours. On a campground near Ypsilanti, Michigan, we decided against paying the extra charge to use our air-conditioning. Boy did we pay for our ignorance! The clammy heat didn't abate until the early hours; only then could we snatch some sleep.

Bleary-eyed in tune with a heavily overcast sky, shortly after 8am we rejoined I-94, where, apart from avoiding bad sections of road liberally strewn in places with remnants of burst tyres, or being buffeted by overtaking trucks thundering past with total disregard for any speed limit, the only diversion was the numerous roadside signs: 'Free Wine Tasting', 'Antiques', museums for this and that, birthplaces of famous people, 'Off Track Wagering Facility' – a betting office, the exit for 22 And 1/2 Mile Road. . .

'22 and 1/2 miles to where?' Jeff queried. 'Or, for that matter from where?'

'Yes there really is a Kalamazoo', read the sign at the interstate exit for the university town. The I-94, following the shore of Lake Michigan, crossed into Indiana, becoming I-80; then we crawled through road works into Illinois, the dashboard air-conditioning making it tolerable in the RV.

'Small van: small site seems to be the policy on this campground,' Jeff observed, as he backed Harvi into our designated place in a corner of the campground, when, mid-afternoon, we escaped from the traffic.

'Yet the charge is the same for each pitch regardless of size. Doesn't seem fair,' I whined.

'One of the consequences of not booking ahead, but I didn't know if we'd get this far today. Just look at the size of that outfit!' On a swathe of grass *The Snow Bird*, a gigantic white trailer pulled by an equally big white truck, with a TV satellite dish alongside and a car on an A-frame for towing, was parked across from us.

Determined that we were not going to suffer again without air-conditioning, as soon as Jeff plugged into the electric mains, I switched the air on – great value for a $2 fee for the following eight hours that we needed it. Airy indoors, liquid heat outside, even the water in the swimming pool was too warm to be refreshing. After being cooped up in Harvi all day, once we'd eaten, despite the stifling conditions, we set off for a walk, taking a well-trodden path surrounded by extensive, gently rolling cultivated and livestock countryside.

'The corn is as high as an elephant's eye, as in *Oklahoma*,' Jeff warbled off-key. Very true! Closely bordered on one side by woodland, on the other by acres of tall, golden grain the path became a rough farm track. Tiny corn flies swarmed, getting in our eyes, up our noses and sticking to every inch of exposed, sweaty skin.

Slapping and flicking away the gnats, a hubbub of noise ahead grew louder as we strolled. The cornfields gave way to open land with farm buildings. A lawn, splashed with two beds of multi-coloured petunias fronted a neat bungalow sitting behind a fenced enclosure: a quiet oasis amid a scene of feverish activity. Beyond the bungalow, the ground sloped upwards before levelling out to a big farmyard; so that, seen through the metal bars of the locked farm gate, the action taking place there was like watching a drama on a stage, against the backdrop of a magnificent coral sky, streaked with narrow bands of cloud. Two braziers of glowing coals stood on one side. Nearby, under some shady trees, the weighing and branding of cattle was progressing noisily. Cowhands, male and female, only the colour and pattern of checks on the shirts varied, otherwise each wearing like a uniform, jeans, boots, checked shirt and Stetsons worked as a well organised, vocal team.

Judging by the amount of cow dung everywhere, slippery or dried, the job had been going on for some time, but now only about a dozen or so cows stood waiting. With a flick of its head and shoulders setting it in motion, the front animal did an about turn, 'Not today, thanks all the same. I'd rather not, if you don't mind.'

Before any of its mates in the restless group showed agreement with those sentiments, a whack on the cow's rump and a hefty shove changed its direction straight into the weighing enclosure, with many mooing protests, the gate clanking shut behind it. Cowhands exchanged shouted statistics to the accompaniment of further belligerent bellows. Another gate opened, the cow bounded out to slither into a second enclosure, a hot branding iron applied, a gate at the far end opened and the cow with, 'Stuff you, I'm off,' loped away to join the herd in a distant field. One by one the process continued. As the sun slipped away and the light dimmed, all the figures became black silhouettes against the sky.

The stench of scorched hide mingled with the acrid smell of cows and, with dusk falling, mosquitoes on the rampage, we were glad to leave the buzzing, shouting, lowing, slithering to return to our clean, cool, compact motorhome.

After a long night's rest, we hit the road early hoping to cover a good distance before the heat of the day. A big, green roadside board said 'Great River National Park', but the bridge over the Mississippi being under repair, as well as roadworks, meant the adjacent rest area was closed – no stopping to have a look around. Shortly, we were in a new state: Iowa; an information sign said: 'DesMoines – 174 Miles'. At least it gave the distance to the state's capital city, unlike many roadside signs everywhere throughout the United States that point in the direction of a named place, but give no indication whether that place is two miles or 200 miles away. In Harvi, perched high above our surroundings, which were flat, flat, flat, I swear the 174 miles to Des Moines was one great cornfield with the I-80 cutting through like an infinite airport runway, on and on. This was our fourth time to drive across the Great Plains of North America.

'God it's boring!' Jeff complained.

'Yes, it's all the same, but I don't think the prairies are as completely level in the United States as they are in Canada,' I replied, as I took over the driving. 'The road does go up and down occasionally. We're roughly south of Winnipeg here.'

'Yeah, you're probably right, but it's damned awful boring anyway in both countries. Here, we must be in the very centre of the continent, *about 2,000 miles from any ocean*. Imagine! Well, imagine, if you can, sea breezes,' Jeff said.

'I'm not that good at imagining! It's golden corn not golden sand. The dashboard air will have to do. The contrast with the deep blue of the sky is gorgeous; you'll have to kid yourself it's sea and sand.'

Passing Des Moines the corn-belt continued way, way beyond, fields of grain stretching from sky to sky. Dodging into Nebraska for a while, the farmland there was no different. We stopped off at a Nebraskan mall or two to break the monotony (and to look, without success, for postage stamps), but depressing in their uniformity they were like every other strip mall in the entire continent. So, we got back on to I-29 North, paralleling the Missouri River. Our overnight campground was near the Lewis and Clarke State Park. Being back in their territory again cheered us.

Continuing north we detoured a couple of times into towns; one had a Minnehaha Street, also signs for 'Emergency Snow Route', a reminder that the Central Plains really have only two seasons. However, a post office proved to be as elusive as a parking space, where we could have stopped to ask directions. Crossing the state line into South Dakota, joining the I-90 West, the sideways draught of overtaking double-wagons, hell-bent on being first, rocked us as they careered past.

'Mitchell must be a good-sized town. We'll try for parking there and have a decent break,' Jeff said, when we came upon a succession of advertisements giving details regarding the 890-acre Lake Mitchell Recreation Area; The World's Only Corn Palace; several museums and galleries; even a Prehistoric Indian Village.

'Attractions! – just try finding a post office to buy stamps!' I muttered in exasperation.

'A post office? Dunno,' a smartly-dressed young man answered, before hurrying away.

'I'm not from these parts. . . I don't know,' an older woman apologised, smiling. 'I'm so sorry.'

'Oh there is one somewhere,' a young woman told me. Of course there's a post office in a town this size you pretty, blonde dope, I thought unkindly, but I didn't say anything, not wishing to disturb her concentration.

'I come into town from time to time and I *know* I've *seen* one. Can't remember now where it is,' she giggled. 'Gee! Ain't that funny?' ('No!' I thought.) 'Guess you'll have to ask someone else,' she giggled, again.

'You wanna post office?' queried a plump woman in a too-tight T-shirt and matching shocking pink shorts.

'Yes, please.'

'You from outa town?'

'Yes, I am.'

'An' you wanna post-office?'

'Yes, to buy stamps.'

'Just stamps you're wannin'?'

'Yes, for postcards for overseas.'

'Overseas!' she exclaimed, her voice rising in alarm.

My turn to be a dope, with neither youth nor good-looks to compensate for stupidity! 'Overseas' is hardly an expression in common usage in the *middle* of this vast continent. Most probably she'd never seen a large lake let alone a sea.

'If it's only stamps you're wannin', you'll get 'em at the big supermarket. Go down to the end here,' she continued, helpfully, 'Make a right. Go to the end. Make a left. . .'

Ten minutes later, after righting and lefting and reaching the supermarket I still had no stamps for the cards that I'd been carrying around for days, because the only stamps available were for use within the United States. 'Ye'needs to go to a post office.' No she didn't know where it was.

'We might as well have a look at the world's *only* corn palace before we leave Mitchell,' Jeff suggested. Dating from 1892, the Corn Palace was built to encourage settlement by proving the richness of the soil in the eastern part of South Dakota. A fanciful Moorish-style building, the exterior more funfair than regal residence, decorated inside and out with designs and murals constructed from local corn, grain and grasses – between '2,000 and 3,000 bushels' go into the creation, which is renewed annually – it proved to be an interesting museum, though hardly a haven for hay fever sufferers. Near the exit we asked an attendant about a post office. 'Sure. No problem. . .'

And it was no problem to drive there quickly, park, deposit the cards, and buy plenty of stamps for future use. After Mitchell, there was very little heavy stuff on the road, but there were many cars towing motorbikes on trailers, also an ever increasing number of two-wheelers tearing along noisily.

Crossing the Missouri River was like entering a different world. The flat 'breadbasket' behind us, rangelands rolling from horizon to horizon lay ahead. The West unfolded before us. 'Can't fathom out why hundreds of bikers are heading this way. Cowboys on horses would be more appropriate,' Jeff muttered.

'Yes, this is cowboy country, real and celluloid,' I agreed. 'Many famous films have been shot in this area. Motorbikes seem incongruous.'

At a rest area adjoining a Scenic Overlook, an information board informed us that the altitude was 1,300 feet. A great panorama, with the Missouri snaking through, spread out below us, bathed in afternoon sun. Quite lovely! And scores of motorbikes parked. A couple of bikers at a picnic-table under a tree, black-haired, swarthy, kitted out in leathers – in this heat! – sat with their backs to the table section, legs spread out in front, cups in hand: 'We're on our way to Sturgis,' the woman volunteered. Quickly realising that didn't mean anything to us, she went on, 'Every August, Bikers come from all over to meet in Sturgis.'

'Sometimes as many as 200,000 the man bragged.'

'200,000!' we echoed in surprise. 'Is Sturgis a big place?'

'Nope. We camp. Meet up with folk each year and getta know som'others.'

'Donna drink. Donna party, yet we hava swell time,' the woman assured us.

130,000 was a more accurate number, we later learned. Still impressive! Sturgis, with a resident population of less than 6,000, annually hosts the Black Hills Motor Classic. Enthusiasts come there from around the world.

We booked ahead for two nights at a KOA campground on the Badlands National Park, still 150 miles away. Changing from Central Time to Mountain Time we gained an hour, but thunderstorm warnings, followed by a tornado alert for the area we were driving through, were worrying. Motorbikes shattered the peace of the open, wide-skied countryside as the road carried on and on through vast livestock ranches. At a gas station, dwarfing Harvi to Lilliputian dimensions, an intimidating monster wagon, with forty-four wheels, was the size of a row of houses in England.

The sun of the early afternoon had long vanished by the time we reached the Badlands National Park. With menacing cloud cover, the grassland bordering the approach road to the campground was blown almost horizontal by the wind.

We set up speedily on our reserved spot. The water in the nearby swimming pool, which had a big 'Closed' sign on its padlocked gate, began to slosh around over the edges. Some campers were already indoors; others were hastily taking down awnings, or rounding up children and toys before retreating to safety. While telephoning the family in Toronto, now 1,400 miles away, lightning zigzagged across the sky, as simultaneously a tremendous roll of thunder crashed overhead and a great gust of wind, sweeping all manner of clattering objects before it, swooshed across the campground sending the swaying trees into a frenzy. Thunder, lightning and torrential rain continued through the hours of darkness, the wind rocking the RV alarmingly throughout the sleepless night.

People were about earlier than usual surveying damage. Harvi had stood up well to the onslaught apart from being liberally splattered with mud, bits of tree branches and debris. We'd been on the edge of a tornado, which, though destructive where it ripped through, mercifully had not claimed any victims. On the campground, apart from the mess wrought by the storm, everyone was safe.

Setting out in Harvi soon after 7.30am we had a long day to explore the bizarre wonderland of the Badlands. French Canadian trappers in search of beaver were the first men to record their impression of this desolate region, calling it 'les mauvaises terres a traverser' – bad lands to travel across. The Native Americans referred to it as 'mako sica' – badlands. No good for anything. Useless. Except that now it has become a picturesque national treasure: an attraction.

The ravaging forces of nature, in particular wind and water (like last night for instance), over aeons, ruthlessly carved the colourful pinnacles and spires, massive buttes and deep gorges, which make up the 160 square miles of the Badlands National Park. With nine scenic overlooks along the 32-mile loop road, each one giving a different panorama, all weirdly beautiful, with only one or two cars at some stopping places, none at all at others, we had the park to ourselves. Against the deep blue of a cloudless sky, the morning sun enriched the colours in this place of sharp ridges, pyramids and knobs, some shading from grey to dusky pink; others from gold to rust; others were banded with rock of a different colour with such precision they looked as if the bands had been carefully painted. We ambled along nature trails, disturbing a coyote, who growled at us before running off disgruntled, while the occasional deer we encountered seemed unperturbed by our presence. In the distance on a green mesa, which accented the rugged outcrops, a herd of antelope grazed. Far away in the roadless wilderness, black dots to the naked eye, grew to a herd of bison, when viewed through binoculars.

Always, turkey vultures or eagles floated effortlessly on the updraughts above this mysterious land.

The narrow, dirt road, the Old Northeast Road, between the overlooks was edged with low weedy greenery and yellow black-eyed Susans and beyond that, waving golden grasslands. Though all morning we encountered little traffic, at one point three hay wagons in convoy, with enormously wide loads, filled the entire width of the track ahead; Jeff had to drive Harvi on to a small piece of firm, level ground to enable them to lumber past.

'Thanks! Hava-great-day!' each cheery driver waved from his high perch.

South of the Park, on the Pine Ridge Indian Reservation, is the Wounded Knee Massacre Monument, where more than 300 Sioux, mostly women and children, were slaughtered in 1890, when soldiers opened fire during a skirmish.

Some of the world's greatest fossil beds of prehistoric animals are preserved within the park. Excellent exhibits of these bygone beasts were on display in The Ben Reifel Visitor Center, operated by the Oglala Sioux Tribe under contract with the United States National Park Service, along with detailed explanations of the history and geography of the region. 'Fossil mammals from the Eocene and Oligocene Epochs, 37-26 million years ago', stated one information card. Awesome! I can't even begin to understand *millions* of years ago, about 5,000 and that only sketchily, is my limit, but our geologist son, in England, would have been fascinated.

It had been energising to trade tarmac roads, traffic, and advertisement boards for such a wonderful experience. However, during previous days there was one board that had been repeated again and again since we crossed the state line into South Dakota, now 300 miles away: it was for Wall Drug. 'Wall Drug – Famous Drugstore – 270 Miles'; 'Wall Drug – Window to the West – 220 Miles'; 'Visit Wall Drug Wild West Wax Museum – 160 Miles'; 'Wall Drug – Internationally Known'. Repeated again and again, always giving the mileage, until, with diminishing distance, there was the invitation to: 'Stop In For a 5 Cent Cup of Badlands Coffee' and while there, 'Why not Visit The National Grasslands Visitor Center, Downtown Wall?' Another giant billboard promised, alongside 'Free Water' and 'Admission', a 'Travellers' Chapel'.

What an intriguing place? Anyway, a country road lead from where we were in The Badlands National Park back to I-90 and a short distance away was Wall. So we went! Thousands of bikers were there before us. Maybe not all 130,000 from Sturgis, it just seemed like that, way too many for a place whose resident population was less than 900. Enormous car parks and a restaurant with seating for 500 indicated that Wall *expects* crowds and the pervading atmosphere was testimony that today's thousands were having a great time. Not only does Wall claim to be: 'The World's Largest Drug Store' but also boasts 'an internationally known emporium of galleries': twenty-six shops, selling all manner of goods from hand-crafted treasures to mass-produced trash.

There were other buildings: a pharmacy, a museum, the chapel patterned on a church in Iowa, built by Trappist monks in 1850, with beautiful stained glass from a reordered church elsewhere; even – look out all those bigger South Dakota towns! – a post office, brightly painted dark blue and red with red benches outside, where I was glad to sit in breezy shade as a respite from the humid heat to listen to a group of Native Americans, with flutes, strings and percussions, compete with the cacophony of noise and the ever-present vrrum vrrum of bikes revving up. Signposts gave the mileage from Wall to places all around the globe. There was no mention whether those far-flung cities had signposts giving the mileage to Wall!

Dating back to the 1800s, there were countless photographs featuring South Dakota and The West, together with more recent photographs taken of people visiting Wall: Presidents of the United States, Foreign Heads of State, Hollywood stars, celebrities of this and that – a veritable roll call of the famous – covering every perpendicular surface.

Situated on the edge of The Badlands in the Black Hills, how did this place become so well-known? In the early 1930s Ted Hustead and his wife, Dorothy, came to Wall to open a one-room drugstore. Ted is quoted as saying that he 'Thought the folk passing by in summer would be pretty thirsty', so he travelled back along the road *100 miles* or more to put up signs advertising 'Free Ice Water' and a successful business grew from that. Grew from giving away *free* ice water? – selling all manner of things for *cash*, surely! Interestingly, it's claimed that three college textbooks have used Wall Drug Store as a case study.

Dorothy Hustead had died some years before, but Ted, then in his 90s, smartly dressed, wearing a tie, exuding bonhomie, whizzed around in his wheelchair, notebook in hand. During the summer months more than 200 are employed here and he seemed to know each of them by name. Periodically the wheelchair would stop when Ted got into animated conversation with someone.

'Hello. Wotcha name?

'Where ye' from, Jeff?'

'From England, now Ain't that neat. You're the first from England for quite a time. Folk come from all over,' he added, proudly. 'Here, sign your name. Give your address,' he commanded, handing Jeff his notebook and pen. That done, 'Goodbye. Nice talkin' to ye'. Hava good day,' he called over his shoulder, already propelling the wheelchair on its journey through his kingdom.

Early the next morning we drove for a couple of hours through beautiful countryside deeper into the Black Hills, so called because of the dark pines which cover them, to view one of the most treasured monuments in the United States: Mount Rushmore National Memorial. Driving almost deserted roads, under a great dome of sky, we passed a flock of turkey vultures, about twenty, squatting heavily on the flimsy branches of small trees. Further along an eagle rose up startled from the ditch, a mass of ruffled feathers, its breakfast hanging from its great, curved beak, its wings filling the width of the windscreen, as it scooped swiftly upwards and away.

'Gee what a wingspan!' I exclaimed, amazed.

'About five feet,' Jeff said. 'Lucky we didn't collide. Would've made an awful mess.'

Two and a half million people visit the Mount Rushmore Memorial every year. There was only a handful of cars and one coach on the terraced parking. High on the granite wall of Mount Rushmore, one of the largest pieces of sculpture ever carved, the colossal faces of Presidents George Washington, Thomas Jefferson, Abraham Lincoln and Theodore Roosevelt gazed down, stunning in the morning light against the deep blue of the cloudless sky. Art on a monumental scale.

The coach passengers, a mixture of ages, trouped towards the entrance. 'Oh my God, how marvellous!' squealed a young woman in red T-shirt and shorts, her hand to her mouth in excitement, while her young child tripped over his feet in attempting to keep pace with her.

'Wow! Taka look at that!' a gruff man's voice could be heard above the babble of admiration.

Sculptor, Gutzon Borglum toiled for *fourteen* years carving these faces of such amazing expressive likeness; each head is *60-feet-high* and the group is 5,500 feet above sea level. Sadly, he died before they were finished; the memorial was completed by his son, Lionel, in 1941. An interpretative programme, that outlined the purpose and national significance of the carvings, was displayed in a pavilion, one huge wall of which was entirely glass. We could look out and up at the faces, while digesting all the available information about their construction. Yet, in the early days, during The Depression, there had been an outcry not only about the expense but that carving a national monument from a mountainside in the Black Hills 'would be as incongruous and ridiculous as keeping a cow in the rotunda of the Capitol'. Now the Mount Rushmore National Memorial ranks in importance, for patriotic Americans, with The Stars and Stripes and The Statue of Liberty.

An hour later when leaving, the car parks were filling up with vehicles displaying licence plates from all around the continent. 'Thank goodness for people of foresight like Gutzon Borglum – and Ted Hustead, with his free ice water – who ignore cruel ridicule to create something of enduring worth,' I said, sancti-moniously.

The road quickly carried us from the world of Presidents of the United States to that of Cowboys and Indians, as we passed places called Custer State Park, Crazy Horse Mountain, Spring Creek Road, The Fort Trading Station, The Black Hills National Forest. . .

'I'm starving,' Jeff complained.

'So am I. It's ages since breakfast.'

'I could do with a proper cooked meal.'

'In an air-conditioned, decent restaurant would be lovely.'

'Fat chance of that!'

There wasn't even another car in view, and with few settlements along our route where food might be available, though hardly with desirable ambiance, Jeff parked at the side of the narrow road. Our onboard propane cooker could be used in transit, but not wanting to add to the considerable heat, I made some sandwiches. The fridge-freezer working off a battery while travelling, there was ample cold food, but not the appetising meal we both craved. Then a swarm of wasps buzzing around Harvi meant we had to keep the doors shut. 'Not quite the Ritz, is it?' I laughed.

It wasn't the London Ritz, but Moscow which came to mind when, some time later, curiosity getting the better of us, we stopped to investigate a sturdy structure standing all alone in acres of deserted countryside. Whew! we didn't need to go far to know that it was a 'long drop': a pit lavatory! It was the miasma that awakened memories of visiting Zagorsk (not far from Moscow) the seat of the Patriarch of All Russia, with a small group of Quakers, a couple of years before. Across from the fabulous, golden-domed churches glinting in the sun, black-robed clerics rushing between buildings – it was the Russian Orthodox Good Friday – hidden from sight behind bushes was a long, low building, the only 'restrooms' amid all this splendour. There was no scent of attar of roses, I can tell you. No way would anyone wish to 'rest' there. Men to one side, women to the other, *doorless* cubicles, a stupefying stench, two pitiful, head-scarved women attired in black dispensed single pieces of toilet paper with such frugality they could have been handing out sheets of gold-leaf. The pit toilet in this remote place, in South Dakota, had it been required, was luxury in comparison.

I took over the driving. Jeff promptly fell asleep. He often did this while I was at the wheel and assured me that he could relax because he had such confidence in my driving. True? No! I knew that it was because he is incapable of sitting still for more than two minutes – no, that's an exaggeration: thirty seconds is nearer the mark – before boredom sets in; therefore, he would rather switch off completely and sleep. Hundreds, yes hundreds, of clacking grasshoppers formed a cloud around the RV, smashing themselves into the windscreen, the washer and wipers working overtime struggling to keep a view hole clear. Watching this slaughter was horrible. What could I do? Jeff was still in the land of oblivion. Afterwards he had the nasty job of cleaning up!

We crossed into the wide, rolling, yellow grasslands of

Wyoming at an elevation of 4,000 feet. The road carried on for ever, just an occasional hamlet or small town with shops named 'Outlaw Motors' and 'Corral Rest' selling all manner of cowboy gear; then paralleled a railroad for many miles, where there was more activity than on the road – only two persons per square kilometre in Wyoming. An ambling train of assorted wagons pulled by five locomotives, one named Santa Fe, took an age to pass; shortly, one with steel carriages, like a great, grey snake, swept along travelling the opposite way. By the time the four engines of the next train came into view Jeff was awake, and counting loudly one by one all 92 wagons gave him something to do.

A huge hoarding standing alone, incongruously, in acres of scrubland dotted yellow and grey like a pointillist painting, said: 'Powder River for Native Furs and Skulls'. Skulls? Skulls of what? It didn't say. With the temperature now a murky 96°F furs didn't seem much of an attraction either. The nearby Crazy Woman Creek was aptly named – this heat was definitely sapping my sanity.

We drove through Buffalo, once the scene of many battles between the Sioux and Cheyenne Indians, passing several churches, Johnson County Library, a lovely building, and the Pawn King, and out on US 16, where Jeff took over the wheel to drive through the Bighorn Mountains. As soon as the road becomes tricky I prefer the *passenger* seat. The posted speed limit kept changing, because of this and the acute steepness of the road, Jeff had to use a low automatic gear. Harvi responded well. A sign warned 'Open Range Loose Stock' with, standing forlorn in the road alongside, three stray cows. 'Clever beasts,' Jeff joked, 'they must be able to read!' At the top of the Powder River Pass; the road widened sufficiently to park to admire the vista and read the Information Boards. We had the place to ourselves.

'The elevation here's 9,666 feet,' Jeff exclaimed. 'No wonder the road was steep; we've climbed more than 5,000 feet in the last 30 miles.'

Standing on 'Pre-Cambrian rock 3 billion years old' we read that, 'Only Alpine Tundra grow at this Height'. There were snow-fences at an angle to the road to catch snowdrifts. The mountains are snow-capped all year.

In less than an hour a scenic route dropped us down into Ten

Sleep, so called, we read on a small board in the village, because Indians 'measured distance by the number of sleeps, and it was 10 sleeps from here to each of their main camps'. At the bottom of the board, two upright hands with outstretched fingers and a drawing of a Teepee was Indian writing for 10 Sleeps. There was no sign of any Indians, or anyone else, when we drove on to the camping. A horse was tethered to a post by the open door of what appeared to be the office. There was nobody inside, but from the living-room at the back, loud snores rattled and whistled. A heavily-built man sprawled in a rocking-chair, the large, white Stetson lying on his stomach rising and falling with each breath. Stifling a laugh, Jeff rapped loudly on the office counter. The snores ceased abruptly. The chair pitched forward as the man bounded to his feet simultaneously donning his precious head-gear – we had actually seen a cowboy without his hat! – and on long legs loped towards us. 'Hi, wha'canado for you folks, today?' he drawled, unabashed at being caught sleeping, though possibly disconcerted at being seen without his hat.

Usually on registering we were given a hand-drawn map showing a one-way road system, sites (pitches) individually numbered, the location of the amenities' block and so on. As it was only a small camping, not a campground, we expected to be directed by pointing from the office door. Imagine our amazement when he untethered the horse and mounted it. Picking up the reins, he called, 'Follow me,' as if he were about to charge bareback across Wyoming. Jeff started up the RV. At *walking* pace our cowboy lead the way for all of twenty yards – the office still in full view – stopped, and with an expansive gesture indicated our *small* pitch. 'Here we are folks. It's *all* yours. Hava great evenin'.' He ambled back the twenty yards, dismounted, tied up the nag once more and went indoors. He may even have gone back to sleep.

The laundry-room's *new* equipment I soon put to use. The other really nice thing about sleepy Ten Sleep (population 500) was the drinking water, which came from artesian wells, unlike all the previous water we'd had, which varied from just-about-all-right to downright awful.

The next morning at 6.30am we set out to drive the 270 miles to Yellowstone, America's first National Park, created in 1872. *We'd driven 2,000 miles across seven states for this.* A couple of hours later, stopping on the edge of Cody for gas, we carried on downhill along Stampede Avenue, littered with notices for all manner of tourist attractions; on through scenic Buffalo Bill State Park to join the bumper to bumper queue (fender to fender line-up) for the manned pay booths at the East Entrance to Yellowstone National Park.

In the crawl, because of road construction, a big yoke directly ahead of us belched out black smoke and choking fumes. Jeff, eventually, managed to overtake it. There were viewpoints from where vistas of mountains and Yellowstone Lake and River and the wildlife which frequented these areas, could be seen, but had we stopped we might never have got back again into the line of vehicles. Anyway, we were hoping to get on to a camping – if we ever reached one.

Winter snow means that most of the roads through Yellowstone are closed for several months, yet more than *three million* people visit every year. Were they *all* here today? Yellowstone Park covers roughly the area of Devon and Dorset combined. The campgrounds, which don't take reservations and have only pit lavatories, were full. We were hugely disappointed.

It was a nightmarish drive for Jeff with cars edging out of side roads or attempting to leave viewing areas. As we drove we saw little of the glorious surroundings, just keeping our eyes riveted on the stop lights of the car ahead, as Harvi inched along the lower loop road making for the park's main visitors' centre.

We found a space on the enormous car park; like Mount Rushmore it had vehicles with licence plates from all around the United States; and followed the signs for Old Faithful, Yellowstone's most famous feature. The Park with *thousands* of thermal phenomena, created as scalding water escapes from the earth, has more geysers than any other spot on earth, but Old Faithful remains *the* most popular tourist attraction. The geyser (Americans say guy-sor) spews hot water hundreds of feet into the air. 'It doesn't shoot the water as high as it once did,' a man standing beside us volunteered, 'but it does it more frequently now; used to have to wait round for more than an hour between eruptions.'

In the company of a large motley crowd, squealing with appreciation, we watched several upsurges of varying heights and duration, before carrying on to view further delights. Wooden walkways lead among other spurting geysers, bubbling mud pots, steaming mineral pools and colourful springs, yet none of these had many spectators. The names throughout the park were enchanting: West Thumb, Fishing Bridge, Paintpots, Fountain Paintpots, Beehive Geyser, Firehole River. . . One pool, a glorious deep blue in the centre edged by vivid yellow, was aptly called 'Morning Glory'. The ground around geysers was white as were the plumes of water. Seen against a background of green trees and deep blue sky, each made a lovely picture. Reluctantly, after a couple of hours, we got back on to a roadway, which though busy was not horrendously jammed so that we were able to avail of viewpoints along our route to view wildlife, mainly bison and moose. There were no bears around that day – they had more sense! Yellowstone is renowned as a successful wildlife sanctuary.

The West Gate of the park and the town of West Yellowstone are in Montana. We were many miles further south than we had been on our previous travels through the state. Beautifully situated, ringed by mountains, our campground was jolly cold during the night, because of the elevation. Jeff declared that he badly needed a couple of days' rest with 'little or no driving'; he also declared quite emphatically that no way was he staying 'this close' to Yellowstone! In case I cajoled him to return? – he knew how much I would have liked that. Though hugely disappointed, I understood his feelings, because *I* very definitely didn't want to be the *driver* in Yellowstone.

Our visit to the World's First National Park had been fascinating and frustrating in equal measure.

Chapter Six

After driving for a couple of hours, the next morning we got to a campsite in Idaho Falls. We had two golden days to swim, loll in a hot tub, take strolls along the bank of the Snake River, admire the half-mile-wide Idaho Falls with a white, wedding-cake-style Mormon Temple on the other side of the river, which looked magical when lit up after dark. A reminder that Idaho experiences extremes of weather was the notice *painted* on the heavy door of the Public Washrooms in town: 'Please Close Door To Avoid Freezing' – the August temperature at 6pm was 98°F. The glorious weather continued, matched by glorious scenery through Idaho into Utah.

'I've had enough traffic. I'm keeping off the interstate,' Jeff announced, taking the Scenic Route. In Idaho, we saw a large roadside plaque dedicated to the FORTY-NINERS, many of whom had perished along this way during the Californian Gold Rush, in 1849. Apart from knowing that Salt Lake City is the capital, and that 'almost everyone in Utah is a Mormon', we knew nothing else about the state. On a deserted road, flanked by farmland, we came upon a big, colourful board headed: BRITISH SETTLERS with written underneath, to our amazement, 'Most Early Bear Lake Settlers Came From Britain'. Of these, one was the *first* woman convert to the LDS (Latter Day Saints: Mormon) Church in *Europe*. Born in England in 1806, she had lived in Illinois, before *driving* an 'Oxteam to Utah in 1849'. Fortunate to survive, countless men, women and children died travelling the

71

route west, she lived in Utah, until dying there in 1890.

Leaving a fertile valley, the serpentine road rose sharply, giving us marvellous views of incredibly blue Bear Lake, twenty miles by eight, in a landscape of greens and gold, limestone particles suspended in the water accounting for the lake's turquoise colour, to 7,800 feet at the summit. Harvi did us proud taking the gradient and numerous bends without complaint. Then the road descended quickly for twenty-five miles through winding Logan Canyon to another fertile valley, renowned for its fruit, especially raspberries, followed by a 60-mile stretch of interstate into Salt Lake City, where we booked on to a campground for three nights, and got a schedule for the bus, which departed for town from the entrance.

'No need to move Harvi for *three days*,' Jeff declared with delight, while we were setting up home.

I hoped he regained his pleasure in driving soon – we had a long way to go!

A plain, ringed on three sides by the snow-capped Wasatch Mountains on the edge of a vast salt lake and hundreds of miles of desert, doesn't appear to be the ideal spot for a settlement at the end of a gruelling *thousand*-mile trek, during which many died, but Brigham Young, then leader of the Mormon sect, on arrival in this hostile environment on July 24, 1847 asserted, '*This* is the right place.' The self-styled Chosen People had arrived in the Promised Land.

Since the church's establishment by Joseph Smith in Fayette, New York, twenty years before, the Mormons had been banished from one city after another, because of their practice of polygamy, and also their interference in politics. In this place, then outside the area of the United States (Utah, named for the Ute Tribe of Indians, wasn't incorporated into the Union, as the 45th state, until 1896), they felt safe from persecution to settle permanently. Within a few days of arrival the pioneers were tilling the soil and planting crops. A city was planned. Blocks in 10-acre squares were arranged on a grid pattern, separated by streets 132 feet wide to enable 'a team of four-oxen and a covered wagon to turn around' with ease.

Our campground was not a haven of rest, but noisy all night with road, rail and air traffic. To crown it all, the engine of a bus, sited nearby, starting up roused us at 5am. The throbbing

Mavis and Jeff with Harvi.

Reconstructed native longhouse at St.Ignace, Michigan.

Last Supper in Beads, Indian River, Michigan.

Nearly all campgrounds have individual fire-rings.

Badlands, South Dakota.

Mount Rushmore, South Dakota.

At 9,666ft: Powder River Pass, Wyoming.

100 miles of Salt Flats, Utah.

Overlooking Bear Lake, Utah.

Golden West train crossing in the centre of Reno, Nevada.

Cacti at Spanish Bay, 17 Mile Drive, California.

Las Vegas – where else? Nevada.

Reconstructed stores at Seligman, Route 66, Arizona.

Entrance/exit East Gate, Grand Canyon National Park, Arizona.
(There are only two in this vast park.)

Walking down Bright Angel Trail towards Plateau Point,
Grand Canyon.

vibrations and fumes continued for twenty minutes, or more, as the chattering passengers (pilgrims?) stowed numerous small tents and copious camping paraphernalia before boarding. By the time they departed, we were too wide awake for any further sleep, though we were both headachy with scratchy throats, sore eyes and frequent bouts of sneezing.

During the morning Jeff traipsed around on foot in search of a connection for the RV's water filter, which had been troublesome for several days. When he finally succeeded in getting one, having worn his legs down to the knees, he had a sweaty time fitting it. He well deserves his family nickname of Mr Fix It. If Jeff can't diagnose the problem, or better still, *mend* it, whatever IT is, (anything from a motor car to a delicate wrist watch) it truly is irredeemable! Apart from all his repairs and restorations back home, our Canadian family has a special box in their basement, where during the year broken items and toys are relegated, 'Till Grandad gets here'.

I busied myself with routine household chores that could only be done when parked on site, hence Jeff walking everywhere. Living in such confined space, it was necessary to return everything after use to its allotted place. Most items were stored inside something else, with often something else inside that, and so on – a bit like a Russian doll – requiring a good memory, invariably failing miserably when called upon in an emergency, with the frantic search for the crucial item resulting in such disarray, as if a turbulent tornado had torn through. Tidiness was vital. Everything stowed carefully in transit.

We sited Harvi with the awning on the shaded side, despite that, the temperature there, while we ate lunch al fresco, was in the high 90s. Out in the full glare of the sun it was hotter still, but for the first time on this trip there was no humidity, just dry, baking heat.

The number 50 bus from the campground set us down near the centre: the 10-acre Temple Square, containing the six-turreted Mormon temple; the Tabernacle with its famous pipe organ; Assembly Hall; and Visitor Center. Our first impressions were how ordered the city was with an absence of hoardings and advertisements, so evident elsewhere in the United States, and the width of those ruler-straight, spacious streets. Only Mormons may enter the Temple and its Enclosure (not that we had the

73

tiniest inclination to do so) but through the encircling railings, we could glimpse small wedding groups posing for photographs on the manicured lawn with several precision-planted flower-beds. The uniformity of hairstyles and attire meant each beaming couple looked a replica of the previous one.

As I had done some family history research using, among other resources, the Mormon Library in Kensington, London, I was eager to visit The Genealogical Society Library, the first (and biggest) of all the Mormon places of records. Jeff, who has done no research at all, nor ever shown the slightest interest in it, astounded me by saying, 'I'll come with you. Maybe it will be possible to learn something about my Russian forebears.'

Despite the attentive assistance of a rosy-cheeked, middle-aged female member of staff, who patiently showed Jeff where to *begin* his search with his paucity of information, once she left him, he quickly became frustrated.

'I've had enough of this,' he growled, eyebrows meeting in a frown. Pushing back his chair, beads of perspiration making little curls of hair on his forehead, he got to his feet; slapped his big ledger shut and hauled it to the main desk, lingering just long enough to arrange to meet me outside the building, a couple of hours later. 'Not inside!' he stressed. Then he swiftly turned tail and was gone.

Deciding against spending time doing any research of my own, I explored all three floors of the enormous building. It was truly awesome. Order and organisation reigned; there was a map for each floor with sections named and clearly signposted; more information here on every nation under the sun than there would have been available in the home country. Hundreds of thousands of volumes of family trees and catalogued rolls of microfilmed documents; millions of family group records; archives; church records. . .

On another sortie into the city we split up for several hours, as Jeff didn't want to visit the places I wished to see (though, if time allowed, I'd love to see his choice of places, too). This is our customary way of sightseeing, or shopping: spending time together, then separating to do our own thing, sometimes to meet up again, other times making our individual way back to base. Prolonged travel, especially in the confines of a caravan, motorised or otherwise, is considered to test a marriage – very true! For some, wedded bliss 'Till death us do part,' has been known to become wedded boredom, or worse: divorce. Our pleasure in travelling, with the freedom that camping allows, has survived a long time: this trip celebrating forty years together. Our interests don't coincide on everything. In the British Isles, or Europe, I am quite happy to explore alone: museums, gardens, art exhibitions, churches, ancient ruins, even going solo to the theatre. Here in the US, uncomplicated by language problems, I found life delightful!

In the Visitor Center there was no wandering about; instead, in the entrance hall, I was shepherded into an enclosure by an earnest young man in black, knife-creased trousers and immaculate, white, well-ironed shirt, 'To make a Tour'. A gentle, spiralling, carpeted slope lead upwards past huge murals in primary colours, each depicting Christ in copious, startlingly white robes, with a verse of scripture written underneath. '140 feet of paintings,' the guide declaimed, proudly. All the while a recording issued admonishments from the old and new testaments – chosen selectively in favour of *their* interpretation of the texts. It didn't actually say, 'This is Christ calling' or 'Here's a message from your Leader,' but that was the drift. At the top an enormous statue of Christ – in *white* plaster, what else? – dominated the vast circular hall painted to look like space, with the earth, moon and stars swirling around in a dark blue sky. Their emphasis on Christ is ironic, as there is much controversy, because of their startling departure from Christian orthodoxy, as to whether Mormons are Christians at all, with some even claiming that it is the first 'new' religion since Islam. Around the perimeter, glum groups of tourists sat on settees waiting for our guide – this time, a fresh-faced, smiling girl with tied-back hair, in an up-to-the-chin, down-to-the-wrists, white blouse and a long black skirt. (All the blinding whites would have made an ideal washing powder commercial.)

The Greatest Work You Will Ever Do Will Be Within The Walls Of Your Own Home was written under the heading: 'Strengthening The Family' on the wall of a big hall (no mention of multiple wives). With hardly a pause for breath, our young guide rattled off her spiel, giving the impression that if anyone as much as coughed she might lose the thread of her memorised talk and be unable to finish. But finish she did, with a triumphant smile. Of course, there was no invitation to ask questions. No well-brought up Mormon queries anything. Brigham Young, of whom we heard quite a bit, had more than twenty children, needing a substantial dwelling, paid for by his followers. How many wives did he have? Not a mention! Yet he did have several. Today, in spite of it being outlawed in 1890, upwards of 30,000 Mormons are believed to practise polygamy clandestinely, making a nonsense of their ban on teenagers holding hands, and their strict code of dress to be observed by believers.

The Salt Lake Tabernacle Auditorium, on Temple Square, has been in use since its completion in 1867. It is claimed that the dome-shaped building is so acoustically sensitive that a pin dropped at one end can be clearly heard 170 feet away at the other. A dark haired, young girl (were they all young and dark haired? Clones?) demonstrated the amazing acoustics of the place by tearing strips from a sheet of paper and lo and behold their claim was true: she could have been standing beside me and not 150 feet away. During this, a recording of the Tabernacle choir and organ was playing quietly. Had there not been the background music, a pin would have dropped with a resounding clang. The Tabernacle Choir's radio programme, one of the longest running in the United States, dates back to 1929.

The red carpeted aisles were roped off half-way along; despite the barrier, there was no missing the famous organ, brightly lit, with its 11,623 pipes. I took some photographs. Then, unexpectedly, all lights were extinguished leaving the handful of visitors to stumble to the exit.

Affluence was evident everywhere. Commerce is as well-organised and regulated by the Church of Jesus Christ and Latter-Day Saints as everything else. The first department store opened in North America was in Salt Lake City, and it developed into one of the *largest* shopping malls in the nation. Utah has anti-alcohol and anti-gambling laws, yet since 1946, when Utah-based loans helped the gangster Bugsy Siegel to open the first gaming house, Mormons have had a presence in Las Vegas and now *own* much of that city. Sort that out!

However, not everyone in this city is a Mormon; there were churches of other denominations on the periphery. Out near the mountains, a Catholic cathedral had stained glass and carved woodwork from Germany. 'Not everyone here *wants* to be a Mormon,' Jeff said, chuckling at the memory. 'Yesterday morning, when I was scouting for the water filter, there were two black-suited young men doing the rounds knocking on doors. They were unceremoniously chased away from several places. One woman, brushing her front steps, shook her broom at them accompanied by a torrent of words, that didn't sound like endearments.' Even in the city of their headquarters they still tout for business. Extraordinary!

It was too windy on the campground to sit outdoors, or for me to have a swim. 'This doesn't auger well for tomorrow's journey across the Nevada Desert,' I said. This was the part of our extensive trip that our kids were most worried about.

'It'll be sweltering. There'll be few places to stop for help if you've any problems,' they warned. And now it was windy, too, and all that sand. . .

Luck was with us; by morning the wind had died. We set off before sun-up. In fact, the sun didn't show itself, and then only hazily, until late afternoon. Being fully overcast for most of the day, it wasn't unbearably hot thanks to the dashboard's efficient air-conditioning, though nudging 100°F outdoors.

Without a shadow of a doubt, it was the most tedious, the most boring day of this trip. Or any trip. The all encompassing murky, grey sky merged on one side with the enormous expanse of grey Great Salt Lake, then Salt Flats, and on the other with flat scrubland stretching for miles to a continuous chain of mountains, a fuzzy frieze in the distance.

Part way across the 120 miles of Salt Flats, like driving in dirty snow, we crossed into Nevada. The never-changing scenery compounded by the fact that, at the state line, we changed from Mountain Time to Pacific Time, putting our watches back one hour, made us feel as if we were on a treadmill. For all our driving we weren't getting anywhere!

Three and a half hours after leaving the campground in Salt Lake City, we stopped in Elco, a pleasant, small town in the desert, to get gas and to shop for groceries, before having lunch of sourdough bread, cold beef and gallons of tea on board Harvi.

'When we park up, we'll phone Canada to let them know we're safely across the desert,' I croaked, as I still had a raw throat.

'We're *not* safely across yet. Not by a long chalk!'

Without the air conditioning it quickly became too warm for comfort; we got moving again. Soon the road took us into high country, the Sierra Nevada Mountains, like crumpled fawn velvet all around. Just out of Elco, at Adobe Summit, a sign read: '6,548 feet above sea level'; in this arid landscape it was difficult to imagine a cooling expanse of sea. The road continued up and down, a sign giving the height at each summit – with no billboards, that was the extent of our entertainment on this journey.

Winnemucca. Yes, it's a real place! You've heard the name before? Butch Cassidy and the Sundance Kid robbed a bank here, then obligingly sent a painting of themselves to the manager. After our tiring, monotonous drive of more than 360 miles, arriving in Winnemucca, we booked on to a campground, situated in the mountains (which meant it was cold at night) with a spa, good-sized pool and masses of colourful wild flowers, and for those wishing to avail of Nevada's gambling, they ran a free shuttle bus to the casinos in town, as well as having lots of slot machines in the camp shop and games-room.

In the morning we drove to Reno, through dun-coloured, mountainous country, the lower hills resembling the mounds of earth deposited after excavations. Reno used to be the place where Hollywood stars went for a quickie divorce. Casinos and pawn shops were everywhere. The former necessitating the latter.

Because of Harvi's height, we parked in the open on a casino parking lot, not in the nine-storey (an entire block!) town parking. At 11am the casino was busy when we walked through to have our parking ticket validated. The place was cool and dim, though a bright 80°F outdoors, with a thousand pinpoints of winking lights; the steady hum of machines disrupted occasionally by the clatter of coins cascading for a hit. I would like to have lingered, maybe even tried my luck. Jeff wouldn't have any of it.

'I only went in to have the ticket stamped,' he blurted, squinting in the sun. 'All those staring morons sitting mesmerised, feeding coins into machines. . . throwing away money as fast as they can. . . It's pathetic!'

The pawn shops promised 'Money on Almost Everything'. Open from 9am to 8pm seven days, boards declared the items each had for sale, from jewellery to left-hand holsters, sporting goods, antiques, buckles. . . even an automobile.

'Wonder how the guy got home without his car?' I said, bemused.

'Shot himself,' Jeff answered, flatly. 'The car sold to pay his debts.'

We were held up in traffic for ages as a goods-train lumbered through the centre of town. Seen up close, we were amazed at its *height*, with huge wheels in comparison with those in Europe, though we were well used to the extraordinary *length* of American transcontinental trains. Crossing the state line into California, Jeff said, 'We've covered three thousand miles since waving cheerio to the kids in Canada.' We felt mighty proud of ourselves – quite thrilled, really! Not bad for two retirees, eh? In a huge, unfamiliar country. . .

Our month-long sojourn in California began at beautiful Lake Tahoe. One third of the lake lies in Nevada, where gambling is legal, two thirds in California, where it is not. We chose scenery not slots. The busy road crossed in and out and in again to California, affording tantalising views of shimmering lake through the trees, but there were few stopping places. Vehicles jostling for parking, eventually Jeff found a precious spot for a brief stop.

We had pre-booked a site. 'Thought we'd have found the camping by now,' Jeff said, with mounting exasperation, after driving for miles in chaotic, slow-moving traffic. Tempers igniting, a lively exchange of words followed, because, on leaving the parking, we'd headed in the *wrong* direction, driving almost the entire 72-mile shoreline of Lake Tahoe, instead of the short hop required. Several campgrounds that we passed near the lake had 'Vacancy' boards; our pre-booked was five miles inland.

Knowing that the elevation at Lake Tahoe is 6,225 feet, we prepared with extra bedding for the night-time cold (I drew the line at wearing a woolly hat in bed, as I once did when tenting, in summer, near Hadrian's Wall in England). Nearing 8am, the temperature having warmed up a little, dressed in jog-suits, we ate a big breakfast under the aromatic pines, the quantity of egg determined by the number that I salvaged earlier from the slithering mess of broken ones in the fridge.

To reach Lake Tahoe we'd have to drive, in busy conditions, and then park. No thanks! Instead, leaving Harvi to have a well-deserved rest, intending to keep well away from crowds, with food, water and sun screen in our backpacks, we walked uphill through Eldorado National Forest. Ignoring us, a couple of steller jays close by squawked in disagreement – they really have the most beautiful blue plumage, if lacking musical voices. A chipmunk scurried across. From the valley below the yapping of a dog could be heard, otherwise our feet crunching on the rough track and my out-of-condition, laboured breathing were the only sounds. Even here there was no escaping written warnings. A large, wooden information sign said: 'Backcountry Travellers Avalanche Control Area – Unlawful if 36 inches of Snow Lying. Violators are Guilty of a Misdemeanour Punishable by 6 Months Jail'. So there!

At 7,450 feet, we arrived, near the sky, at an expanse of deep blue water: Echo Lake. We looked down, down to our campground and Lake Tahoe, the distance hazy with smoke from three forest fires, raging for days. There were some chalets and a small area for tenting, a shop-cum-coffee bar – where we had coffee, and later, delicious ice cream – and, at a distance from everything else, Pit Lavatories!

The lake was fringed with a profusion of greenery banked by various trees, mostly pines. In the RV I had a book on North American trees and wild flowers, which I perused whenever I could. I was quite puffed-up at being able to identify some of the trees here, and eager to display my newly-acquired knowledge, I pointed:

'That one's named for you.'

'Whachamean?'

'That's a 3-needle pine called a Jeffrey pine.'

'Huh! To me it's just another tree.'

End of self-congratulation!

There were lodgepole pines with their smooth, straight trunks, ponderosa with long, incredibly sharp needles, also an abundance of very tall trees with light-coloured, pendulous cones only on the topmost branches, that were unfamiliar. Later, on checking in my book, I learned that they were sugar pines. Further edifying information explained that, 'The Indians and early settlers chewed the sweet sap as a laxative.' Not even *pit* toilets then!

On our return from the nine-mile round trip I had a swim to cool off; then, while Jeff prepared supper, I did some laundry, putting it in the dryer just as the food was ready.

'I thanked the guy in the office for telling us about Echo Lake,' Jeff said, as we tucked into an appetising meal. 'I'm not sure whether he was impressed, or worried about our mental state. Anyway, he was amazed and blurted, "You *walked* there? Most people *drive*!"'

'Most people our age, particularly with health problems, don't tour in a small RV around America, especially when they're from Europe!'

'We're not like most people. . .'

We *did* spend time at different locations on Lake Tahoe by getting there before 6.30am, when we usually had the place to ourselves. Even viewed through morning mist, it well deserves its reputation for scenic vistas. At the parking area high above Emerald Bay, we were joined by a lone, middle-aged man, wrapped up against the early chill, savouring the view and his big, red mug of coffee.

'Mornin'. Frosty last night – cold in the tent,' he volunteered, his free hand indicating the tent-camping area hidden among trees well back from the road. Eyeing our Ontario licence plates, he remarked, 'You guys have come a long way – must be 'bout 3,000 miles from Ontario.'

'Correct,' we agreed. 'But we've come 6,000 miles. We're only visitors to Ontario.'

'Oh! Where ye'from?' I gave our usual answer. 'Really! My folks come from those parts. My mother was born in Ireland. Her family came out when she was a child. My father's part Dutch part Welsh. Myself, never been out of the States.'

I didn't ask, though I wondered, if by Dutch he meant Deutsch – German. Part of the state of Pennsylvania referred to as Dutch Pennsylvania, was settled by Germans, Deutsch becoming Dutch. I didn't ask, because he mightn't have known the difference! Many Americans are incredibly uninterested, and therefore ignorant, about *anything* outside the United States. For some even Canada the other side of the 49th Parallel is unknown territory!

We were the only humans on the golden, coarse sand beach, backed by snow-capped mountains, at Baldwin Bay. There were numerous birds feeding. A solitary cormorant stood forlornly shaking its outstretched wings. Far away, over the misty water, three hot-air balloons moved so slowly that they seemed stationary.

When planning this year's big trip, we intended to explore widely in California. Tahoe was beautiful, but after a few days it was time to move on.

Chapter Seven

Petaluma (sounds like a flowering shrub?) is an attractive town in Northern California, where we spent a few days. The following year, thousands of miles away: in a line-up for the Empire State building, New York, there was the usual exchange of 'Where ye' from?' A group answered, 'From California,' and on being pressed further, replied, 'Oh a lil' place near Petaluma.' When we, from England, said that we'd stayed there and named restaurants and stores in town, and the garage where Harvi had an oil change, there was much exclaiming: 'Howdya like that?' 'No kiddin'?' 'Isn't that somethin'?'

Northern California is stunningly beautiful. It has everything from marvellous coastal scenery – viewed from twisting, climbing roads with precipitous cliffs, or at sea level with vistas of mile-long breakers fringing deserted beaches strewn with tree-length driftwood – to forests of giant redwoods, to rolling fertile farmlands. In the lower busier area vines grow in the famous Napa Valley, and there are the delightful towns of Santa Rosa and Sonoma.

We hadn't anticipated, though, how cool and gloomy it often was, needing a sleeping bag on top of our usual bedding. In California! In August! To use the RV's propane furnace, the made-up bed could not be left in place and we would have to stow the bedding. Where, in our compact motorhome?

'What we need is an electric fire,' Jeff declared.

'Small, free-standing electric fires are hardly commonplace in this land of universal central heating. 'You'll be lucky!' I answered.

After much rummaging in small shops and thrift stores in one-street towns, Jeff procured, second-hand, exactly what he wanted: a fire with a thermostat control, in good condition, for the princely sum of $10.

A couple with a lively bunch of kids told us, 'We come here most weekends to *escape* the sun and heat of Sacramento. When it's 100 degrees inland, the coast is kept cool by fog or cloud.' Another garrulous guy explained that the luxuriant maritime pines all around us were 'watered' by the moist fog during months of prolonged drought.

With logs available from the office, fires blazed each evening in fire-rings. We didn't toast marshmallows, as others did. On one occasion, Jeff, adopting the spirit of *rough* camping, dried a pair of his colourful shorts (bought for $3 Can. at *Bargain Harold's* in Ontario) on a long forked stick over our fire, instead of using the dryer in the laundry room. Talking of marshmallows, they sure go a bundle on the squidgy, oversweet treat – an ice cream was spoiled for me because bits of marshmallow, which felt slimy in my mouth, lurked unexpectedly in the big chocolatey dome.

A hamlet, population 440, had a Catholic church. The priest, originally from Co. Kerry, Ireland, served three Mass centres, spread over a wide area. With no attempt at artistry, five large sunflowers stood stiffly in an enormous vase. The hymns were accompanied on a tinny piano. However, whatever the lack of sophistication, the liturgy – the same on that day as in every Catholic church across the world – here, in such humble surroundings, seemed, somehow, as it must have been long ago. On the return journey we stopped to buy roma tomatoes and strawberries from three chatty children selling at a table in their front yard, and later, for a grandstand view of seals frolicking off shore.

After a few days, leaving the coast, travelling quiet winding roads through undulating farmland, Harvi's front brakes began to play tricks, not always responding instantly. They also squealed in protest every time they were applied, which in that terrain was often. Disconcerting! 'I think the brake pads are breaking away from the backing plates,' Jeff explained. Relieved at eventually, after an age, reaching a town, he found a garage willing to help. It is a definite advantage that Jeff always can diagnose the problem and *tell* a mechanic what is required, *before* the bemused mechanic has had time to investigate, as was the case here. Fortunately the repair job took only a few hours.

Sequoia sempervirens, the coast redwoods, are the world's *tallest* living things, also they are among the world's *oldest* living things, some are 2000 years old. Armstrong Redwoods State Reserve, does not have the tallest or oldest trees in California, but neither are the adjacent roads choked with traffic, nor the trails throughout the wood full of noisy humans, as happens at other forests elsewhere.

We paid the entrance fee; parked Harvi; picked up a printed information booklet at the visitor centre and took a self-guided stroll through a grove of these ancient redwoods. The trees growing closely together are of such height that leaning right back – had I been young and agile I could have done a back somersault, instead, I almost fell over – I couldn't see the tops. An information board read, 'The Parson Jones Tree is 310 feet high'. Named for the lumberman who, during the 1870s, had the foresight to set aside this area as 'a natural park and botanic garden'. The Colonel Armstrong Tree 'is more than 1400 years old'. Within the forest there are also tan oak, California laurel and big-leaf maple, but it's the towering redwoods in this semi-dark place that create an atmosphere of reverential awe reminiscent of a great medieval cathedral at dusk.

Wandering further, we came to a clearing with more light, filtered sunlight, and long logs placed to be used as seating. In this amphitheatre chipmunks and birds, especially steller jays, were enjoying their playground. A family group arrived, young Mom pushing a baby in a small buggy, Dad with Junior, head lolling in sleep, in a carrier on his back. Introducing themselves, Lynn and Chuck were from Oregon.

'Where're you from?' they queried.

Chuck summed up, laughing, 'You're Irish. . . live in England. . . visit Ontario, Canada each year. . . where some of your kids live. . . now, in a motorhome, you're travelling 'round Northern California. . . before movin' on.'

Swiftly interrupting, 'Know somethin'?' Lynn quipped, 'you've gotten lost!'

We'd have been quite happy to be lost – for ever! – in this part of California.

84

Our next campground ran an all-day minibus trip to San Francisco.

'It's not called the Golden State because of the endless sun, not even because there was a gold rush here once,' Nancy lilted, in her Alabama accent, as she manoeuvred the minibus through the campground gate, heading south.

'Why then?' Bradley's deep voice called from the back.

'It refers to the place like now, nearing the end of summer. . . dried up. . . no green grass anymore.'

Slim, in her thirties, white, Nancy gave us a rundown on her background in her high-pitched voice; then, without taking her eyes off the busy road, she asked each of us, 'Where ye from?' The couple who delayed our departure, because Hans had forgotten his wallet, were from Germany, the rest: American from various states.

The city of San Francisco has retained its name since the Mission of San Francisco de Asis was founded in 1776, by Spanish Franciscan friars. Anyone who has asked me, 'After all your travels, where is your very favourite place?' knows that, Assisi, built in a great cleft in Mount Subasio, in Umbria, Italy, the birthplace of Saint Francis, is way ahead at Number One. Then, any enquirer who asks, 'Why?' has to listen while I extol the virtues of the place, with its pink marble churches and Giotto's fantastic frescoes (dating from after Francis's time and not all of it in keeping with his life of poverty and simplicity), flowers cascading on to cobbled streets, which climb up the wooded hillside towards the Hermitage, near where we had parked our caravan, all alone, the peaceful surroundings only broken by bird song. Breathtaking! It was easy to understand Francis's joyous appreciation of God and His universe as seen in people, plants, trees and animals. Wonder what Francis would think of today's rampant environmental destruction?

Good-humoured Nancy was a mine of information. I marvelled at how she continued with her commentary while negotiating busy streets; even at intersections looking left, right, left, right, like watching an interminable game of tennis, she kept up the flow of chat. Stopping briefly, if traffic allowed, she pointed out things, which would have been missed otherwise, 'In case you come back into town again to look for yourselves.' Sightseeing this way gave a great overview of San Francisco. With its reputed fifty-two hills, we were glad not to be walking! It would have taken several visits by ourselves to see as much.

'The city can be cold, foggy too,' Nancy warned, echoing what my daughter-in-law in Canada had told us. They were both right. Unfortunately! We all trooped towards the Golden Gate. Where was it? Completely obscured by fog, the fog-horn bleating repeatedly.

Away from the bridge area there was no fog. A marble gateway erected in Golden Gate Park (McLaren Park) is from the remains of a house hit by the 1906 earthquake. The park's three miles by half a mile requires a million gallons of water a day to keep it flourishing. Not a high-rise concrete city, there is a great variety of architecture. What looked like a continuous row of houses was, in reality, several detached dwellings, Nancy told us. 'If there's one inch (one inch!) between houses they are regarded as detached,' she giggled. Earthquakes over the years have caused much destruction. 'The guys who paint those,' Nancy said in amusement, pointing out a row of Victorian houses, 'call themselves colour consultants, not decorators or painters.' The houses have featured in several movies. Frequently we had a sense of déjà vu, as much of San Francisco is familiar from films or TV.

We beat the Germans to front seats for the clanging cable-car ride from the top of Van Ness down to Drum in the business sector, with its pyramid TransAmerica building. There was a long lunchtime stop at Fisherman's Wharf with views of Alcatraz. Another lengthy visit in China Town; then we rejoined the minibus. Pausing at each intersection like an elevator on each floor, Nancy drove carefully down the steep hill where *Bullet* had been filmed. Steve McQueen's car, she told us, had to be rebuilt every two blocks – 'The hill is twenty blocks long.' On our return, we stopped again at the Golden Gate Bridge. Despite the sunny weather all day elsewhere in the city, the fog-horn mournfully echoed in the fog-shrouded stillness.

California joined The Union in 1850. Woefully ignorant of the *settlement* of what is now California – we *did* know that it didn't begin with the gold rush of 1849! – Nancy's references to the early mission complexes with their museums, whetted our interest; we decided that where our route took us in the vicinity of a mission we would have a look around.

In San Juan Bautista a diminutive, frail woman swamped by her faded, floppy hat and long voluminous dress, the *owner* of the campground, in answer to my query, replied softly, 'No we've no swimming pool here.' It was evident that there wasn't any shade either. Thanking her, we drove off to look for an alternative. On and on along quiet roads through golden countryside, until the pungent aroma of garlic filling the air spoiled the idyllic pastoral scene a little – well, a lot! Later, we discovered that this area so loved its smelly produce that they actually make a garlic flavoured *ice cream* – something much, much worse than mushy marshmallow.

Giving up on finding a campground, we doubled back to return to the little old lady. With her demeanour and manners of a bygone era, making no reference to our earlier visit, bright eyed, she beamed at us from under her hat, while indicating where the amenities were, before writing our receipt in copperplate script.

There were only four outfits on the large, all hard-standing campground with its few scrappy trees. We rolled out Harvi's sun awning to give us a little protection from the baking heat, but it was still too hot for Jeff, who retreated indoors to have a snooze, with cool air blasting. In the evening, after we'd eaten, he spread out his maps; I perused literature on historic buildings. First we had to calculate how much time we still had for California, before moving on to other states. We began by working backwards from the approximate date of our return to Canada.

'Don't forget, leave plenty of time for the Grand Canyon, the main reason we're doing this trip, remember?' I fretted.

'And when we get *there* it's then nearly 3,000 miles back to Canada,' Jeff retorted, roughing out a schedule for the following couple of weeks in California, planning to leave Harvi in situ for at least one day, preferably two or three, between each driving day.

After it grew dark, we sat under the awning in the delicious, warm stillness marvelling at the enormity of the full moon hanging low in the sky. It was one of numerous such remembered scenes from our long years enjoying camping. It remained luminously bright until daylight took over.

In many instances the name of the Franciscan Mission became the name of the modern town or city, as is the case with San Francisco, Santa Barbara, San Diego, San Luis Obispo. . . The town of San Juan Bautista, dating from the founding of the mission there in 1797, is enchanting in not looking modernised, though it has been reconstructed following earthquakes. The lovely old town with its many red-roofed, adobe buildings and the only remaining Spanish military plaza in California, seems at ease with itself – even The *Faultline* Restaurant on a corner! – quite content to be caught in a time warp away from the bustle elsewhere.

With three aisles, the church, which has been in continuous use since it was completed in 1812, is the widest of all the mission churches. It has an original reredos painted in 1816 and, though not intentionally artistic, some animal prints in floor tiles dating from the following year were made while the tiles were left outside to dry in the sun – not exactly fossils, but 200 years ago is ancient history in modern, western America. Low buildings had once enclosed a quadrangle which, as at all Missions, would have been the centre of activity where the skills of carpentry, tanning, weaving and candle-making were learned. That space was now a lovely, long-established, informal garden with tree-size cacti, flowering shrubs, everywhere strewn with roses.

'The mission is beautiful but it is not perfect. Only God is perfect' read an information board, which gave a warning to take care with low doorways and uneven surfaces. Infinitesimal concerns here, surely, as a mere couple of hundred yards away, under its little wooden awning, a seismograph makes a continuous recording of the interior movement of the earth. The San Andreas Fault runs along the base of the hill near the church, whose three-feet-thick adobe side walls collapsed in the violent earthquake of 1906, and were only restored 70 years later. Way below us, in the extensive fields stretching to the ever-beautiful, crumpled-golden-velvet mountains in the far distance, Mexicans in wide-brimmed hats toiled in the heat. Not much changes! Native Indians working then, Mexicans now. Two hundred years afterwards, the impact of the missions, both positive and negative, on the Indian population of the time, is still debated, but it's worth keeping in mind that Indians in the US – *Native* Americans in the land of the free! – did not have the vote until 1920, one hundred years *after* the last mission was founded.

Everyone in California was going camping to Monterey for the weekend, even those who had never camped in their lives before, or so it seemed judging by the difficulty we had in making an advance booking. After many phone calls we got one. On arrival, some days later, we found it to be a small space on hard-standing at a motel, without a swimming pool and not within walking distance of a beach. We hadn't realised that Labour Day, the first Monday in September, marks the end of summertime and everyone wants to spend a last weekend on the beach, regardless of the weather. As it turned out it was cool, overcast and windy. Great if you like sand in your food; our camping spot miles from a beach suited us well. After that weekend we had no difficulty getting on a campground, lower rates too!

Arriving too early on Friday morning to occupy our reserved space, having paid for three nights, we set off to drive the privately owned roadways around the Monterey Peninsula through the Del Monte Forest and along the famous 17-Mile Drive. Paying the toll, we were handed a map and a small brochure giving the conditions of entry into this earthly paradise owned by the Pebble Beach Company. A warm day of cloudless skies, with few visitors, we drove short distances in between parking often, to enjoy the surroundings: exotic greenery screening from view the homes of the ultra wealthy; two exclusive golf courses; great vistas of white sand beaches with crashing waves; Spanish Bay; Bird Rock with its countless shoreline birds; Seal Rock and its ungainly creatures; one of California's most familiar landmarks: The Lone Cypress atop a rocky outcrop (commercial photographers need a licence to take pictures of it!). Most amazing of all was to watch the turbulent waters off Point Joe, where ocean currents collide.

Harvi's Ontario licence plates were often a conversation opener. Near one of the beaches, a resident of this exclusive place stopped to chat and ask questions, interrupting his daily, post-heart-surgery walk; tall, slim, tanned, mega rich folk are like the rest of us in that respect. He had recently returned from his first visit to Galicia, northwest Spain, for a big family re-union of countless relatives. 'My folks came from there. Both of my parents came to California from Galicia.'

Hearing that we'd been there a couple of years before, he was eager to talk about it. (Doubtless *he* hadn't been *camping*!)

'We thought the Galicians were quite different in looks from those in the rest of Spain,' I commented.

'Thought they were Irish looking, especially like people in the west of Ireland,' Jeff said. 'Many western Irish are descended from the shipwrecked Spanish Armada of the 16th century, you know,' he continued.

After a long pause, our friend nodded slowly, as if he was only then making that connection, not having thought of it before. 'True! How very true! I've been to Ireland to play golf a couple of times. Now that you draw my attention to the resemblance, I can see it. And the same warm hospitality in both places too,' he laughed. 'Great talkin' to you,' he smiled, before continuing on his way.

In need of hospitality ourselves, we drove to Carmel, which Americans pronounce *Car Mel*. Clint Eastwood was once the mayor of the town. Boy is it a tarted up arty place, too many beautiful trees, shrubs, flowers, all impossibly perfect, opulence oozed everywhere, lots of trendy eating places and boutiques with quaint names. We didn't like it at all! Jeff read from a brochure, 'In 14 Streets in Carmel there are 56 galleries for art or antiques'. We stayed just long enough to eat, then drove south to Mission San Carlos Borromeo. It's an important one, as Fr. Junipero Serra, founder of nine of the twenty-one missions, is buried in the church. Franciscan churches usually have flat ceilings, simplicity being the keynote in decoration, but here is a noted exception. The interior walls curve inwards gradually as they rise and the ceiling follows the sweep of the walls forming a catenary arch, a lovely effect. Restoration is ongoing as at other mission complexes, most of which are dependent on voluntary funds.

We camped, once, beside Lake Maggiore, Northern Italy. For centuries the wealthy Borromeo family were Big, as they say, in that area, but one of them in the sixteenth century, Charles, renouncing privilege lived an ascetic, exemplary life as a priest, later: archbishop of Milan. There is a statue of him, more than 350 years old – its enormity quite intimidating! – called the Colossus of St. Charles Borromeo. Made from copper, his right hand raised in blessing, a great tome under his left arm, standing an incredible 35 metres high, it is probably the largest such statue in the world. Exploring on my own, Jeff was elsewhere, I paid, actually *paid*, to climb this hollow structure. On the inside, wrought iron, spiral stairs went up to a platform from where, through openings, there were sweeping views. The rivets, both small and large, holding the structure together, were visible and the spine of the book held a water chute. To ascend further to get inside the head for a bird's eye survey, it was necessary to scale a fixed perpendicular ladder. There was nobody to ask, 'What's it like up there?' All alone *inside* this metal monster, I should have retreated. Instead, hand over hand I climbed aloft. My bag slung diagonally in front of me taking up precious space in the narrow, airless tube made it difficult to keep clear of the scorching sides. Claustrophobic panic overcame me. My confused state compelled me *upwards* – thinking that all would be well when I reached the top. But there was no platform, or extra elbow room! Overcome by heat (and fright!) anxious not to pass out, or touch the sun-baked metal, I didn't delay to look out of the viewing slits in the statue's eyes, before hastily beginning my descent, the darned bag a greater hindrance now, bumping my stomach each time a fumbling foot felt for the next rung below. (I later discovered that *that* ladder measured *15 metres*!) At last reaching the platform, disregarding my earlier delight at the outside panorama, just relieved to face forward to *see* the stairs, sweating profusely, I clumsily clattered down. Never so glad in my life to stand on terra firma, I almost kissed the ground.

No adventures like that at Carmel. There *was* a statue of Charles Borromeo, in the garden adjoining the church, a perfectly ordinary solid statue, an irreverent, squawking seagull perched on its head.

August gone and summer too! At home I always feel a yearning for bright evenings and heat, and dislike approaching autumn. I want to hang on to every bit of warm sun, blue sky, roses. . . 'Maybe this year in California it'll be different,' I thought. It was a cool and heavily overcast Labour Day, when we left Monterey soon after 7am. Single-lane SR1 wiggling along the coast through drifting fog, driving needed Jeff's full concentration. The area is renowned for its spectacular scenery, but any time the fog cleared sufficiently for me to have a good view, not all my gasps were ones of appreciation. A printed note on the map read, 'The northbound lane hugs the inside of the highway providing a feeling of greater security for a more pleasant trip'. We were travelling *south*. I was in the right-hand seat. The narrow, twisting road edges precipitous cliffs. Yes, I felt alarmingly insecure. Yes, the scenery was *breathtaking* in every respect. We stopped from time to time at turnouts from where, often, there was a better prospect than from viewpoints.

9am on a civic holiday was hardly the time to expect a free concert – at one of the turnouts, a young guy was banging hell out of a full drum set, enveloped in the mist swirling up from the sea, meeting that spilling down the mountains. In these weather conditions the wail of bagpipes would have been more appropriate; after all this was supposed to be sunny California. Nearby, an enterprising pretty young woman was selling cups of coffee from the doorway of her RV. In other places there were motorhomes which had parked overnight. Talking to a fellow returning from Alaska en route to Florida, he said, 'I've been here for three nights.'

'I thought it was illegal to park like this?' Jeff suggested. There were notices saying that it was prohibited.

'Well,' the man drawled, 'it's not exactly *legal*, but the cops don't say nothin' – jus' drop by each day. That guy over there's been here *six* nights.'

Our three nights at Monterey, for little more than a parking space, had cost us over $100!

Conversely, one of the best pitches ever (and over the years we've been on thousands) came our way a few days later. Awash with colourful flowers, high up on a corner of a tiered, hillside campground at Malibu, we had a balcony view, on three sides, of sea and spectacular sunsets. The girl in the office said that they had been booked solid all summer, 'But after Labour Day y'know, there's not so many.'

When registering, we also booked a pricey day-long trip to Los Angeles for later in the week, not run by the campground, I hasten to add. Gee was that a disappointing day! Was it ever! Honestly, I can't even remember the guy's name. Notice I don't call him a guide, mainly because he wasn't one. With seven paying passengers the cramped vehicle was not suitable for the trip. His frequent phone conversations indicated that all was not well with his staff back at headquarters; also – disconcerting for us! – that *he* was not accustomed to conducting tours. He made no reference to any of this, when he managed to squeeze in a bit of commentary here and there between phone calls, or dropping in to businesses to pick up items unconnected with our tour. From time to time he decanted us to see things from a standing position

'For twenty minutes' or 'thirty minutes' and once we got a whole hour. Jeff and I were the only ones from our campsite, and English was not the first language of the others. No introductions were made and for once there was no 'Whereyefrom?' We were not a bunch of chatty companions, no way!

The following day couldn't have been more different. I had a fantastic time for the cost of a cheap bus ticket. The J. Paul Getty Museum was then in Malibu. (The following year a much bigger museum complex opened in west Los Angeles.) Admission was free but 'under the terms of an agreement with local homeowners' on-street parking was not permitted; reservations for the limited space at the museum had to be made two weeks in advance; also there were regulations regarding taxicabs, private automobiles and school coaches. Bus No. 434 passed within half a mile of the museum, but arriving that way had stipulations too, 'You must obtain a Free Admission Pass from the bus driver and present it to the officer at the Front Gate Guardhouse'. Was it worth all that hassle, plus the hike uphill in the heat? Yes it was!

The museum was a re-creation of an ancient Roman country house of the First Century AD at Herculaneum, and in the various gardens surrounding it, tended by eleven full-time gardeners, were trees, flowers, shrubs, herbs and water features similar to those of 2,000 years before, with replica bronze statues and frescoes based on ones found in Pompeii and Herculaneum, unearthed during the eighteenth-century explorations of the ancient cities. (The originals are in the museum in Naples.) It was a fitting building to house Getty's extensive collection of Greek and Roman antiquities – originals not replicas! – on the main level.

'Are you goin' to be cremaded?' a plump, blonde woman asked a plumper one in tight, red trousers, as they were looking at a Roman sarcophagus.

'Cree-maded? Dunno, haven't thought 'bout it,' the plumper one replied. Then after some frowning consideration, indicating the sarcophagus, she asked, 'Wouldn't you finish up in an *urn*, not one of those?'

'Maybe,' the plump one said with a shrug, obviously losing all interest in the subject. 'Let's go eat; they say the food here's good.' And they departed.

There was a vast array of other priceless treasures on the upper level, with stunning views out to the blue Pacific. I had a marvellous time!

Our month-long meander through California was coming to an end. For me, the enduring mental picture of California is of panoramas of gold and deep blue: sand and ocean, or rolling, yellow landscape against a dome of cloudless sky. The state is roughly 850 miles from north to south; we'd seen much of the scenic Pacific coast's warm, soft-sand beaches and cold, thrashing waters; mountains and farmland; many cities and towns; and a number of the historic mission complexes.

Though all the missions had many aspects in common, each also had its own unique features of interest. One, where we spent a half-day exploring, had turned the clock back nearly 200 years – La Purisma Mission, near present day Lompoc, founded in 1787 was later destroyed by earthquakes, then lay in ruins for almost a century until the 1930s, when rebuilding began through a combined effort of state and federal agencies, resulting in the most fully restored mission of all, in its original setting, reproducing California as in the 1820s. Billed as *A Place in Time*, it is one of only three preserved within the State Park System. It was fascinating! Hundreds of thousands of adobe bricks, floor and roof tiles, all hand-made, and hand adzed beams were used; concealed within the adobe walls and hidden in the attics are modern building techniques, which make the structures earthquake safe. The complicated water system, beginning at springs more than a mile away, had been re-created, and the gardens and orchards replanted to reflect the period. There were thirty-seven rooms with authentic furniture; though the church had a forlorn atmosphere precisely because it was a museum showpiece, not a working church evolving with time, as at other missions. Surrounding the buildings there were over 900 acres maintained in their natural state. Livestock included burros, four-horn churro sheep, longhorn cattle and the more usual farm animals, but not in the numbers of previous times – a corral inventory of 1820 recorded 12,600 sheep and 9,500 cattle.

Mission San Antonio de Pala is the only one to survive for its original purpose of service to the Native American Indians. Hearing about it while at another mission, we set off immediately, one Saturday lunchtime, to drive twenty miles, ten of them along a narrow, dusty road, to its remote location in the middle of an

Indian Reservation. The chapel, in the form of an Indian longhouse, with an uneven tiled floor, great rounded roof beams tied into sturdy uprights, the interior decorated with Indian symbols, together with some other parts of the complex, stand as they were when built in 1816. In more recent times other buildings had been replaced using adobe bricks and cedar logs brought from the Palomar Mountains. It is now regarded as the most faithful of all the mission restorations. In the school we met a husband and wife, white American teachers, who were busy doing unpaid out-of-school-time chores – like teachers everywhere! 'We speak to the children in Spanish, or Indian dialect,' they explained, 'but all teaching is done in English to comply with government regulations.'

While making purchases, ably assisted by a middle-aged, Native lady in the small shop, well-stocked with Indian craftware and jewellery, another assistant came in. Detecting her accent, instead of us being asked: 'Where are you from?' I asked her, 'Are you Irish?'

She was. We introduced ourselves and got chatting. Barbara came from the town in Ireland which was Jeff's birthplace!

'Can you believe that?' she said, pink-faced with excitement, turning to the other lady, who then joined in the conversation enthusiastically to tell us that she had visited Ireland with Barbara some years before. When we all recovered from that surprise, there was more to follow. Jeff was born when his family, including his east-European grandparents, English-born parents, aunts and an uncle, lived in a big, rambling house, set back from the road, in southwest Ireland, which they all left three years later to live elsewhere. Barbara, a Franciscan nun, (the Native lady was a nun, also) came from the same road and knew the small estate of houses which had replaced the large dwelling of Jeff's birth. Not only that, but the *origins* of her family had startling similarities to his, extremely unusual for that era in an Irish country town, more so that it was the *same* town.

'Just think,' Barbara exclaimed, 'if you had left with your purchases before I came into the shop, we'd never have met. . . here in the middle of an Indian Reservation. . . more than 6,000 miles from our birthplace!'

The following Christmas we sent a substantial cheque for use with the Native American children and got a thank-you letter from them, beautifully decorated with Indian motifs.

Our last mission (we saw fifteen of the twenty-one) was in San Diego, actually the first one founded from Mexico; we had been visiting from the opposite direction. The city of San Diego, the sixth largest in the US, is lovely. In all our travels in Europe we had never *walked* from one country to another. There is always a first time – in San Diego we took a trolley to the American side of the border and a short walk took us into Tijuana on the Mexican side. Not the most salubrious of places, well not the part we could visit on foot, anyway, but it was interesting to see, if only for the stark contrast with prosperous San Diego, which ironically, along with much of what is now California, was settled by Europeans from Mexico.

Soon, reluctantly, it was goodbye to California. We didn't have a single drop of rain while there, sunshine all the way, except for the occasional fog or mist on the coast. We headed northeast, then east across the Mojave Desert, with its Joshua trees, cacti and scrublands for many miles, over passes through mountains, which looked unreal, more like giant sandcastles of quaint design, into Nevada again, 338 miles from San Diego to Las Vegas with just a couple of stops to eat. At our lunch-time *fast-food* venue the man in front of us – because of all the choices he was given – took *seven* minutes to place his order!

Las Vegas, once a Mormon trading post, now they own many of the casinos, though as already mentioned their religion doesn't permit gambling, has half the population of the entire state of Nevada. What a place! With its *millions* of lights, it's the only city on earth which can be seen easily from space. We'd a mini view of casinoland in Reno, but Las Vegas was huge. . . It was great fun for a couple of days. We didn't gamble, and Bingo from 7am onwards had no appeal, but we enjoyed excellent food, cheap and abundant, with some laughs thrown in – as in one restaurant where a printed notice hanging above bundles of white, plastic cutlery read: Silverware.

We knew that there were just two campgrounds within Grand Canyon Park, both near the only village, with places reserved five or six months ahead; other campgrounds are miles away, outside the park. Maybe it was because I was phoning from Las Vegas that Lady Luck was with us: I booked a space for the RV for four nights. Our daughter-in-law was as thrilled as we were that *the* highlight of our trip – the very reason that we'd bought Harvi and journeyed as far as this – was now less than 300 miles away, in our next state, Arizona.

'Enjoy it!' she said. 'Hope you have a great time! Keep in touch!'

e

Chapter Eight

The first view of the Grand Canyon was one of the great moments of my life. Nearing sunset, we stood gazing in silence for some time, quite overcome by the stupendous spectacle, before Jeff murmured, 'It's unbelievable! Unreal!'

True! No words, no pictures can adequately describe the magnitude, the magnificence, of the multi-coloured stone in the Grand Canyon of the Colorado River; nothing prepares you for that first breathtaking encounter. It surpasses all expectations.

On checking in and paying for a 7-day permit at the South Entrance of Grand Canyon Park, soon after 3pm, we were given *The Guide*, a 12-page newspaper, with a detailed map, packed with information on the Canyon. We drove on to Trailer Park (the only other campground caters mainly for tents, not having any hookups) taking care not to startle the mule deer, with their longish ears and white tails tipped with black, browsing on the mosses along the gravel roadside and between the parked motorhomes. After setting up, while having a snack washed down with gallons of tea, we checked Sunset Times – which are given to the minute, daily – and the best Sunset Places, printed prominently on the front of the newspaper. Taking the free shuttle bus from near the campground to The Village, we had a quick look around, then walked the three-quarters-of-a-mile trail to Yavapai Point, getting there about half an hour before sunset, which was scheduled for 6.32pm.

The scene was ever-changing, as minute by minute the shifting sunrays threw into prominence different areas of varied coloured rock with glowing highlights of pink. . . orange. . . crimson. . . and where sunlight didn't penetrate there were enormous shadows of deep purple shading to black. It grew cooler. We went indoors.

The Observation Station at Yavapai provides a panoramic view of the Canyon through the building's large windows. From there, with other mesmerised onlookers, we watched a giant sun slip to the horizon, then disappear. Away in the distance a lone tree became a solitary silhouette against the vast apricot afterglow. Within half an hour it was fully dark.

Perusing the exhibits on display, before the Station closed, a man's questioning voice beside me made me turn to face him. 'Oh! Oh! I'm sorry, I thought you were my wife,' he spluttered, apologetically.

Staying in a hotel some miles outside the Park, they were making an evening visit before moving on the following morning. From Birmingham (England) their home was in the next road to that where friends of ours live!

Retracing our way to the village, beyond the Rim Trail, the Canyon was in total blackness. We peered into the nothingness: the earlier magical scene – gone!

'Let there be light!' Jeff intoned.

This giant hole measuring more than 200 miles by 17 miles had disappeared with the sunset. Vanished!

'Do you think it's been filled in?'

We walked to the Visitors' Center and on to the Mather Amphitheatre, where a Ranger, in love with his own voice and more appreciative than the rest of us at his attempts to be amusing, related incidents concerning visitor mishaps in the Canyon.

'I'm going back to the RV,' Jeff whispered to me after a while. 'Anyway, I don't want to walk in the Canyon. I'm not going to. You stay if you want.'

Zipping up my jacket, now too shivery for comfort, I listened, with the few remaining, to the Ranger's advice. I was determined to walk in the Canyon, despite his several hair-raising stories. What *would* my daughter-in-law say about making all this effort – even *buying* our own motorhome – and *not* going, even a little way, into the Canyon? Back home, too, all our gang were eagerly awaiting details of our adventures, our brief phone calls and cards whetting their appetites.

Leaving the amphitheatre, not having brought a flash light, I was unprepared for the lack of illumination in the village: the lights stood only about forty inches off the ground, beyond that: darkness. Total darkness! Everywhere had closed. Not a soul about. The few that had remained at the Ranger's talk now cosily in their village accommodation. I berated myself for not going with Jeff, as I hurried in the direction of what I hoped was the bus route. Not knowing the schedule, would there be a bus? Where would it stop? Should I walk on? When I left the village with its low pools of dim light and plunged into the blackness, the Ranger's remarks about coyotes on the prowl added to my anxiety. After only a short distance, I became disoriented. Where was I? I couldn't see a thing. Nothing! Not a sound apart from my thumping heart. Panic set in. Which way should I go? Which way? Which way? Then, after what seemed an age of stumbling about, what was that noise? Mercifully, not the yowl of a coyote, but men's voices. Humans! I stumbled towards the sound. I could make out two shadowy figures. It was the other campground.

'OK, see you tomorrow. Good night.' I heard one call.

Oh! nooo! Flustered, increasing my speed, I was just in time to accost a startled young man as he retreated into his tent.

Pointing into the blackness, he said, 'That way. Make sure you keep to the track.' Easier said than done! Shortly, a near-empty bus – the last one! – a bouncing chariot of blazing light arrived. I was saved!

Back at Trailer Park, apart from the half-moon shining, with no light pollution for miles and miles all around, we stood outdoors – as we were to do for the next few nights – revelling in the dazzling, vast firmament, the quantity and brightness of the stars just a memory from childhood holidays in the Irish countryside.

'Couldn't be a greater contrast to Las Vegas, could it?' I said. 'I know which I prefer.'

'Me, too!'

It was cold in the night, down to minus figures having been in the 70sF during the day.

By next morning, Jeff had changed his mind – not an uncommon thing for him to do, though he never admits to it – about a walk into the Canyon. We set off a couple of hours later than I'd intended if going alone, because, just as it was time to depart for the shuttle bus, Jeff managed to lock us both out of the RV with everything we needed still inside. All he had were his binoculars, not much help in our situation. Anyone hearing the ensuing verbal exchange (only the stone deaf in the next state would not have heard) would have believed that *I* was the culprit. Eventually after a lot of bother – for me! – he managed to break in and we retrieved our kit. By then he was in a foul mood – oh, not with himself.

'No I'm not taking any cameras. We've' – *We've*! – lost so much time. . .'

I couldn't see how taking photographs had anything to do with anything. So that explains why *all* the views taken that day were by me.

From the Trailview Overlook on the western edge of the village there was an unobstructed view away to the south of the San Francisco Peaks, one at 12,670 feet is Arizona's highest mountain. Below us we could see the Bright Angel Trail zigzagging downwards, then, distance diminishing it to a thread, out across a plateau.

'Time for action. Let's get down there,' Jeff said.

The canyon is a mile deep, but the switchbacking trail takes eight miles to reach the bottom; anyone going that far needs a permit to stay overnight, not being possible to do the return trip in one day (not our intention). Bright Angel Trail has a steep descent; 'It should be attempted only by persons in good physical condition,' the Ranger had warned. We were properly shod; wore sunhats; had food and plenty of water in our backpacks; one of us had an as-good-as-new heart, enthusiasm to succeed would have to sustain the other of us. We were about to test our fitness. The elevation at the top of the canyon, where the temperature was 70°F, is 7,000 feet; therefore, apart from the heat of our exertions, it grew warmer as we went down. In places it is very steep. With sheer rock walls on one side, which get taller and taller, the other side falling away, scrubby greenery, bushes and stunted trees sometimes screening the depths, other times just a yawning emptiness, there is nothing to hold on to. The surface of grit and loose small stones made it difficult at times to keep a firm grip with our feet, especially when being passed by young breezy types walking much too fast, so that they kept breaking into sliding runs dislodging the surface of the trail. Contrary to the advice on footwear that was readily available, we saw several walking, or rather sliding, in flip-flops. After only a short time they didn't look too happy. But they were no more glum-faced, nor incongruously clad, than the folk in the photographs we had seen in the museum. The first passenger train arrived at Grand Canyon Village in September 1901. Posing on the tracks by the engine, were women and girls in long voluminous dresses, or ground-length skirts with frilled and bowed white blouses, and picture hats, men in suits and hard hats, large watch chains slung over ample stomachs. Another photograph showed Theodore Roosevelt astride the leading mule descending Bright Angel Trail, attired, like all the other men and women, in formal clothes and a hat.

The mule train goes down at 8am each day. The pungent smell from a heap of droppings reminded us to be back on top well before it returned in late afternoon, because the rule of the 'road' is that the mules and riders pass on the rock side; walkers must stand on the open-to-the-abyss side to enable them to pass on the narrow trail.

We out-walked the flip-floppers. Then there were only the occasional ones or twos, properly equipped, puffing their way back up. Often we had the place to ourselves. Total silence in this land of stone monuments. Black ravens with great fringed wings soared effortlessly on updraughts in the dome of cobalt blue. While eating our sandwiches, we took care not to drop any titbits for the rock squirrels scurrying around. There are strict regulations about not feeding any wildlife: 'They might be carriers of bubonic plague'. Bubonic plague! Every year in Arizona there are a couple of cases of the disease in humans.

I was elated at having walked *in* the canyon, nearly six miles for the return trip. An acquaintance of mine, on hearing that we were planning to visit the Grand Canyon, said, 'I have read about it and seen *so* many pictures, to go there wouldn't interest me in the slightest.' Well, bully for him! It would be impossible to explain the thrill of experiencing it in person. I didn't intend to try.

Jeff was keen to 'do a proper walk' along the unpaved nine-mile Rim Trail. Next morning he set out early. For four summer months each year the road west of the Village, West Rim Drive, is closed to traffic apart from the frequent free shuttle buses. (The original road was built by the Santa Fe Company in 1912 and automobiles were banned then, because they *frightened the horses* drawing the open-topped stages!) On the outward journey the buses stop at each of eight viewpoints. That was my mode of travel, hopping off at each stopping place to enjoy a spectacular panorama at leisure, then either walking the trail between viewpoints or hitching a lift by bus. Many of the rock formations have romantic names: Isis Temple, Tower of Ra, Shiva Temple, Cheops Pyramid, Vishnu Temple, Wotan's Throne, a flat-topped butte; the names of others aptly describe their appearance: The Alligator, The Colonnade and, close up at one viewpoint, The Battleship was spot on regarding its shape, but not its brick-red colour.

Hopi Point is named for the Hopi Indians, who used to live in or near The Canyon, but now are 100 miles east. From the promontory I could see a section of the Colorado River snaking like a long, brown shoelace a *mile* below me, the water muddied at the end of summer. It must be a gorgeous sight to see its more usual turquoise colour. I loved Hopi Point with its extensive views of Mount Trumball, sixty miles away, and below me massive tumbling walls of rust-coloured rock down to the river. Here, as at each viewpoint, good-humoured spectators exchanged banter with strangers about one of the world's great Natural Wonders. 'Can you see the rapids?' a cheery woman asked me. 'Would you believe that thread-like river is actually 350 feet wide? Oh! I'd love to ride the rapids. Take a look through my binoculars,' she enthused.

I could see a portion of Granite Rapids (there are about 170 rapids throughout the canyon). Handing back her binoculars, I laughed, 'I wouldn't do white-water rafting if I were bribed with gold bars!' Many find it thrilling, including some of our kids.

'Ah! that figure's familiar. . .' but Jeff wasn't looking my way as the bus passed close to the trail. I waited for him to catch me up at the next stop, The Abyss, which possibly has the most awesome view of all. The sheer steepness of the rock wall drops 3,000 feet to a plateau, and clearly visible are six layers of differing rock showing the geological past of the canyon. It is said that nowhere else in the world is such a view of time on show, as each stratum of rock marks a period of the Earth's history from two billion to 250 million years ago. How our geologist son in

103

England would understand and appreciate it! Havasupai Point looked close, but we knew it was fourteen miles away. The Havasupai Indians, who used to live in this area, now live further west. Together, walking the two miles to the penultimate stopping place, Jeff then continued on foot, while I took his backpack on the bus.

Hermits Rest is the last viewpoint, the end of the Rim Trail and the end of the paved road, where the buses turn around. There are no roads whatsoever through the wilderness west of there, though the Grand Canyon stretches, unbelievably, 180 miles further on. With no amenities or buildings since leaving the village, nine miles away, the snack-bar, the drinking water tap, and especially the restrooms were busy! I sat on a cold rock in the shade of a pinyon tree, waiting for Jeff. Glowing with delight at his achievement and looking remarkably fit, I took a photograph of him standing underneath the Hermits Rest sign. Five years ago, in the weeks before his by-pass operation, how could I ever have foreseen a triumph like this. He was amazing!

Pouring over maps spread on the bed, Jeff worked out our route back to Canada, while I spent the morning of our last full day tidying and cleaning. Life spent on board Harvi instead of in lodgings had enabled us to maximise our enjoyment of the great outdoors. Jeff put away his detailed notes.

'Do you realise we've to travel through seven states to get back to the international border? Two and a half thousand miles – like driving across Europe and back. And we've ten or eleven days to do it.' Together we brushed down the awning and rolled it away. 'No more long stopovers. . . Travelling north. . . Won't need its shade. . .'

During the afternoon we explored The Village, where many of the buildings open to the public are on the National Register of Historic Places. At Hopi House there was Indian craft galore: jewellery, baskets, pottery, rugs, blankets – we spent more cash than we could really afford, but how can a price be put on the *time* taken to create such beautiful artefacts? For a grand finale, along with a motley throng of vocal, camera-toting onlookers, we shared a stupendous sunset with much lively camaraderie at Hopi Point. All for free!

Dawn is another favourite time for viewing the canyon. We left that until our last morning, but were thwarted: the office didn't open until 7am and sunrise was at 6.15am. Our invoice showed: Trailer Space Rent and Room Tax. Room Tax! No mention of use of water, or showers, or electric hookup, but *room* tax, and we'd been pitched on gravel ground with deer foraging among the desert scrub and stunted trees; however, we agreed that the tax on our 'room' was worth every cent, after all there was no extra charge for a room with a view, as is often the case in hotels, and apart from anything else we did see those star-laden skies.

Unlike the road west closed to tourist traffic, the road east of Grand Canyon Village leads to one of only two exits/entrances to the park's one million acres, this important region possessing five of the seven life zones attributed to the Northern Hemisphere. Having entered the park from the south, we were now heading out east. Distances between the scenic overlooks on the 25-mile-long East Rim Drive made driving necessary. From Yaki Point there was a tremendous panoramic view over the central section of the canyon. Instead of the dramatic reds and golden yellows ablaze at sunset, the gentle misty light of early morning painted the scene with pastel shades and pale shadows, making the solid rock formations seem light and airy. 'I said when I first saw the canyon that it looked unreal,' Jeff chortled. 'I was right. Look at it now, ghostly, otherworldly!'

A viewpoint called Grandview – an apt description – at a higher elevation than most places on the East Rim Drive, gets sufficient moisture to support large stands of ponderosa pine, as well as oak, pinyon and Utah juniper with dense vegetation softening the more usual stark rock edge of the rim. Between us and the stretch of river way below, a couple of turkey vultures circled, scouting for their breakfast. Resisting the temptation to explore what looked like a trail leading downwards from the viewpoint through the greenery, we took photographs knowing that they could never convey the mystic grandeur of the place. Native peoples are in tune with their environment in a way that is not easily understood by modern society. Speaking to a White Settler, a Native American is quoted as saying, 'Every part of this earth is sacred to my people. . . You must remember that it is sacred and you must teach your children that it is sacred. . .' Though no Indians now live within this area, the National Park Service is doing a good job with preservation. 'Yellowstone could do with emulating this place,' Jeff declared, the memory of the traffic chaos there engraved for ever in his memory.

Anasazi, Navajo for Ancient Peoples, were the prehistoric peoples of the American Southwest. At Tusayan, taking the spur road to the museum, we saw the remains of a small hamlet, where archaeologists think that a group lived in the twelfth century. Though 2,000 prehistoric sites have been recorded within Grand Canyon National Park these ruins alone are accessible to visitors. Utah juniper trees and pinyon pines, small, twisted, some clinging desperately to life with torn, bare roots, are the main trees throughout the park, growing at elevations between 3,000 and 7,000 feet. Juniper was used by the Anasazi for beams in their kivas (ceremonial buildings) also to make a type of gin, while nuts from pinyon trees formed part of their diet, and were just the thing to complement a pot of gin. I'm guessing!

From Lipan Point, named for a group of Apache in Texas, the widest spot in the canyon, there was a great view of the different ages of rock down to the Unkar delta and rapids. Prehistoric peoples used to winter down there, climbing out of the canyon to the North Rim during the summer. Along the east rim there are only three viewpoints from where the river can be sighted, as there were also three places along the west rim; the enthusiasm for even a peep at the river is the knowledge that the Colorado actually *created* this place by carving out the canyon while bowling merrily along. Is it any wonder that Indians have such reverence for nature?

Each of the viewpoints gives a different aspect of the canyon and from the last one, Desert View, twenty-five miles from the village, there were vistas of banded colourful rock and further away in the distance, the Painted Desert. Stopping once more, I took a picture of Jeff beside the National Park Sign. It was three and a half hours since we'd left the campsite and by driving out of the park we 'lost' another hour as the park doesn't observe Daylight Saving Time, but elsewhere in Arizona does. The sun had climbed in the sky and it was getting hot; we didn't change into lighter clothes, no time, then it was on to a good road, which descended quickly through a forest, a coyote at the roadside glaring belligerently as we passed. It was good to be on the move again in Harvi. A Navajo Reservation had: For Sale signs for 'Hand Woven Rugs' and 'Geronimo Moccasins', a reminder that we were back in the real world after our commercial-free sojourn.

In all directions there were Reservations. To be expected in Arizona as there are twenty Native American Reservations including those of seven of the best known tribes. The Hopi Reservation contains the oldest continuously inhabited communities in the United States, while The Navajo are the most numerous.

During the afternoon, we visited the Petrified Forest and Painted Desert National Park. The eastern side of the desert, within a Reservation, we'd glimpsed from a couple of hundred miles away, that morning. The National Park is only a small section of the desert. We paid the permit/entrance fee at the southern entrance. Stapled to the official map and guide there was a warning: 'A Zero Loss Tolerance Policy is in Force', if even the smallest piece of petrified wood was moved 'from its original location', violators would face 'a minimum fine of $270 and/or arrest'. Tough talking! A second slip of paper instructed: 'You Must be in your Vehicle and DRIVING Towards One of the Park Exits at 5.00pm Mountain Standard Time'. Not exactly welcoming, but at the bottom of the main Warning it read: 'Don't Destroy it. Enjoy it!' We intended to do just that. The temperature had climbed to 86°F and under a huge, cloudless sky we set off to make a self-guided tour.

Long Logs and Giant Logs in Rainbow Forest had a colourful concentration of petrified wood. The amazing range of colours in this wood-turned-to-stone was influenced by whatever combination of minerals was present during the process of petrifaction. One 35-foot section of tree, looking as if it had only just fallen over, was like all the other remnants: solid stone dating back 225 *million* years. Others appeared as if sawn into even segments. The petrified trees are of a genus now extinct, the nearest to them being Norfolk Island Pine and Monkey Puzzle. A marker propped against a small multi-coloured specimen read: 'Don't Touch' and sitting boldly on top of it was a green lizard, its tail hanging over the edge.

'The strict regulations don't apply to the park's creatures.'

'Probably he can't read!' Jeff replied.

Native Americans, who lived here once, couldn't have read either, but they communicated with each other, as well as recording their history, by using petroglyphs and pictographs. A petroglyph (symbols carved into rock) now called, for obvious reasons, Newspaper Rock, could be viewed from an overlook and there were others in a prehistoric ruin nearby.

The Painted Desert, mainly in the northern area of the park, had several overlooks with views over vast multi-hued land, barren and waterless – a bit like The Badlands. The museums, one near each entrance, had a wealth of information along with specimens of polished petrified wood; frustratingly, the clock allowed us only a brief visit. Feeling a bit like Cinderella as midnight approached, we didn't wait to find out what happened to those *not* in their cars by 5.00pm.

Shortly afterwards, we booked into a campsite and bought pieces of petrified wood in the small shop, all quite legally mined. It remained very warm after dark. 'It's snowing in The Rockies,' the girl in the office laughed, knowing that we were heading that way in a couple of days.

The next morning we left at 8am.

'Is that someone thumbing a lift?'

'Looks like it.'

'Is it a man or a woman?'

'Can't tell, unisex clothes, tall, lots have their hair tied back like that. . .'

'Should we stop?'

'There isn't another car in view. . .'

We were driving a long, straight, dusty road through a Reservation, desert scrub on all sides to the horizon, towards Canyon de Chelly National Monument.

By the time Jeff applied the brakes we had passed the figure, dressed in jeans and denim jacket, dark skinned, with long, straight, black hair in a pony tail. Jeff backed up a bit and waited.

'I think it's a girl,' I whispered, still not sure, as I moved back in the RV to open the side door. 'Do you want a lift?' I asked the round-faced, young woman.

'Please.'

I returned to my seat. She sat directly behind me. The seat belt restricting my movement, I had to speak to her sideways on. She avoided looking at me.

'We'll be stopping at the Hubble Trading Post (about ten miles away) and then going on to Chinle – will that be of any help?' I queried.

She looked flustered. Avoided eye contact. 'I just want a lift a bit of the way. . .' her voice trailed off.

'OK just say when,' Jeff intervened. 'I'll let you off. . .'

That seemed to calm her. She sat back in her seat, but she didn't reply. I wondered why she had thumbed a lift if she didn't want one! Harvi was plainly a motorhome and we hadn't seen any of them being driven by Native Americans. She made no attempt at conversation. The silence grew longer.

'Do you live on this Reservation?'

Relaxing a little she answered quietly, 'No, I live on one the other side of the highway, way back. I'm a Navajo Zuni,' she volunteered, smiling, showing beautiful teeth, her small black eyes looking past me. After a pause, she continued, 'My tribe are not friends with the tribe on this Reservation.' Much to our surprise she *did* use the word *tribe*, which we knew is considered offensive if used by whites. I knew that this was a huge Navajo Reservation; despite my curiosity, I refrained from asking what a Navajo Zuni was. We had come upon Zunis elsewhere, but thought that they were a separate group. She continued to chat. The inhabitants of this reservation she considered to be secretive and they wouldn't let her people 'join in their ceremonies or dances.' She didn't wish to be here, but 'had an appointment to meet her boyfriend,' but didn't say if he was the father of her two children. On the reservations school attendance was not compulsory, she told us, instead, children often preferred 'to herd their Grandma's sheep.' She had once visited Mexico, but, amazingly, hadn't been anywhere in the United States, though she would 'love to visit a friend, a grass dancer in Kansas,' if only she wasn't too nervous to go there.

Abruptly, in mid-sentence, she stopped talking. Becoming very agitated, as if she suddenly realised how far into the Reservation we had travelled, or maybe it was seeing construction workers on the road in the distance who might know her. . .

'We'll be turning off for Hubble in a moment,' Jeff soothed, watching her in the rear-view mirror.

A moment was too long, obviously. Throwing off her seat-belt she exclaimed, 'Oh! no! no! I *must* get out *here*,' and not waiting for the RV to come to a halt, she flung open the door and jumped down, slamming the door behind her.

Jeff drove around the construction gang to turn into the road towards the Hubble Trading Post. She was nowhere to be seen!

'Gee whizz, what was all that about?' he said with concern.

A few days later, relating the incident to fellow campers, we were told in no uncertain terms that we were crazy to pick up a hitch-hiker on a Reservation. 'What if you'd be threatened with a knife, or worse: a gun? You were lucky not to have been robbed.' Well, we weren't! It was a long time afterwards, however, on reading about etiquette when speaking to Native Americans, that I, on remembering this encounter, was mortified to learn that it is gross bad manners, an invasion of privacy, to look anyone in the eye. No wonder the poor girl glanced everywhere except *at* me!

The Hubble Trading Post at Ganado, a National Historic Site, had a display of crafts including examples of Ganado red Navajo rugs, everything of high quality – with prices to match. Two women were working at looms. A notice said that they did not understand English, but we could converse through an interpreter if we wished. Well we didn't wish! We hadn't yet recovered from our encounter with the hitch-hiker and, anyway, we were anxious to push on to Canyon de Chelly, thirty-two miles further north. The Cottonwood Campground there operated on a first-come-first-serve basis.

A pleasant young man indicated a space under the tall, cottonwood trees, some already showing their yellow autumn tint. 'There is no charge; donations are welcome,' he smiled. Leaving a 'Site Occupied' sign in our space, we set off in Harvi, stopping first at the museum to learn something about the area, which though owned by the Navajo, is administered by the National Park Service. Five periods of Native American Culture from 2,500 BC to the present day are represented within the region. For the past couple of hundred years the Navajo have lived in the Canyon. Outside the museum there was a nature trail through local-growing plants, also a model hogan. Constructed from logs and mud in a circular design with six (or eight) sides, a mud domed roof and dirt floor, a hogan is the traditional home of the Navajo people. The temperature indoors remains between 50°F and 70°F even if the outside temperature is very different. It was over 80°F; true enough it was cooler in the hogan.

Since entering Arizona we were never sure of the correct time! Much, but not all, of the state remains on Mountain Standard Time, but this Reservation observed Daylight Saving Time; therefore sunset would be an hour later than the evening before, which gave us time to explore. The two canyons: 26-mile long Canyon de Chelly joined at an acute angle with 35-mile long Canyon del Muerto are considered one of the Southwest's most extraordinary national monuments. A paved rim road with many viewpoints traverses both sides. 'We've time to do the South Rim today, and before we head off in the morning, we'll have a look along the North Rim,' Jeff suggested.

The dominant red of the sandstone contrasted with green vegetation. The sheer, heavily eroded walls vary in depth between 275 and 1,000 feet. Many families, some living in hogans, farm in the way of their ancestors along the canyon floor, the bottomlands, where small streams run. Ancient pictographs, one depicting running antelopes, decorate some of the cliffs. Two red sandstone pinnacles: Speaking Rock and Spider Rock rising 800 feet from the canyon floor can be seen from the last viewpoint on the South Rim.

The three-storey tower, at Mummy Cave, said to be one of the largest cliff dwellings in the United States, is where some well-preserved human remains were discovered. In different places there are ancient ruins built along ledges half-way down the cliffs. One ruin with eighty rooms and four kivas (for ceremonies) was inhabited between 1040 and 1275 AD. Another, occupied from 700 to 1200, had ninety rooms and contained a four storey section. America's first skyscraper?

At one of the overlooks a pretty, young woman, Pamela, had jewellery artistically laid out in the back of her open-doored van. We were already overspent, but I noticed rosary beads among a display of necklaces. 'Did you make these?' I asked, fingering the string of purple amethyst interspersed with silver beads.

'No!' she answered, shyly. 'My father makes lots of them.'

'Are you Christians?' I inquired, gently.

'*I'm* not. My father has always been one.'

I was amazed at finding Christian objects for sale in the middle of a huge reservation and longed to question her further. I didn't. I bought the rosary beads. I often think of Pamela.

After an early start to allow a couple of hours to view the North Rim, we pressed on through the High Desert Indian Reservation with its treeless scrublands dotted here and there with red monoliths. Any livestock or dogs that we saw were painfully thin. A sign near some buildings read 'Red Mesa

Redskins for Crafts'. Now if a *white* person had called them 'Redskins. . .'

We crossed the state line into New Mexico and took a side turning to Four Corners Monument in Navajo Tribal Park. It is the only place in the United States where four states meet. A circular concrete disc on the ground has the seal of each state: New Mexico, Utah, Arizona and Colorado. A woman had her photograph taken on all fours with a foot or a hand in each state. I just stood in the centre and looked happy, while Jeff clicked. There were stalls, some selling craft, others their famous fry bread, but we were on our way quickly – we had a long way to go. From now on it would be a case of driving from camping to camping, getting a little walking exercise and as much rest as possible at each stopover. Sightseeing was finished, except for whatever we could see from Harvi's high seats. We would need to drive alternately east and then northeast again and again diagonally up through the United States to the Canadian border.

After Four Corners, through the Ute Mountains Indian Reservation and we were into Colorado, at its southwest corner. We headed east. The desert now no longer of red sand but buff coloured – more as I had always expected deserts to look! Among groups of houses, surprisingly, there was a barn full of hay, then another and another. We hadn't seen much ordinary grass since leaving California, just different kinds of desert. Tree-covered hills ahead were such a welcome sight, that I took a photograph through the windscreen. Then it was like driving in Austria: buildings with balconies, firewood stacked against house walls, hillside after hillside arrayed in autumn glory, the range of hues truly magnificent, taller rugged mountains looming in the background, and signs for ski resorts. This was an aspect of driving: from country to country in Europe, province to province in Canada, state to state in America, that we enjoyed so much – the *sudden* change in scenery, sometimes after interminable journeys through mind-numbing, boring sameness.

In late afternoon it took an age to find a level pitch near hookups. At this elevation, still wearing shorts, Jeff was shivering by the time Harvi was set up. I made chilli and rice for supper. Then we prepared for a freezing night.

112

Chapter Nine

In the morning I had a headache. We're not skiing enthusiasts, but once, in St. Moritz, Switzerland, in summer, I suffered altitude sickness and had forgotten all about that until now in The Rockies, at an elevation of 8,000 feet. There was no time for self pity. It was snowing hard. Jeff, well-wrapped up, quickly did the outdoor tasks, and we left the deserted camping. I'm sure that US 160 was a scenic route with great vistas, but swirling snow blotted out everything, as the road climbed and climbed over mountain passes to 10,850 feet at Wolf Creek Pass. Harvi responded perfectly, as always.

Occasionally the blizzard cleared a little and we could *see* the mountains. A train with four locomotives pulling fifty-seven wagons trundled some distance away through the gloom. We changed to the I-25, with views of desolate rangelands. Despite the weather we covered over 300 miles.

The temperature nudging 33°F, it was dry when we trudged through slush into town in search of gloves, as well as groceries, after setting up on a near-empty campground, due to close for the five-month winter. The only gloves we could find were ones for gardening, in a hardware store. That was because there wasn't much town – it hadn't yet been rebuilt after a devastating tornado. Wearing our bright yellow flowered gloves, battered by a prolonged shower of pockmarking hail, we returned to Harvi. A woman from an adjacent motorhome told us that, though originally from this area, she had lived in Texas for many years and was now 'going back there, away from this awful, goddarn cold.' We felt tempted to turn tail to join her instead of heading north for Canada!

When Jeff finished tracing our return route on the big road atlas, I had a look.

'We're a few hundred miles directly south of Sturgis here.'

'Sturgis?'

'Yeah. Remember where all those leather-encased bikers were heading in the blistering August heat?'

'Was that really on *this* trip!'

A buffeting wind rattling the roof vent and violently rocking the RV kept us awake for ages. 'We've no water. It's frozen,' Jeff's voice wakened me from a deep sleep. It was 7am, one of the few times in two months that I was still asleep at that hour. I could have brained him! Everywhere was newly white. Snow had fallen, then frozen. The wind had piled the snow half-way up Harvi's windscreen, with frost patterns decorating the rest. My onboard 'Mr Fix It' discovered that it was only the water filter which had frozen. He removed it. Presto! We had running water. 'Good on you, Jeff. I can always rely on you!'

To fortify him to face the usual irksome outdoor chores, horribly unpleasant in this weather, we decided to have a big, cooked breakfast. With the fire switched on, taking our time, we savoured both the food and the snugness. Afterwards I could quite happily have caught up on my sleep. Fat chance!

'We'll have to get cracking. Need to drive 350 miles, or so, today,' Jeff puffed, struggling into warm clothes, before going outside. All his jobs took longer than usual. Then he cleared as much snow as possible off Harvi and did some de-icing. Thanks to his stalwart endeavours, we still hit the road before 9am to join the I-70 east.

A signpost informed us that Salina, Kansas, where we hoped to overnight, was 341 miles away. A train moved sluggishly across the flat, white land. A car towing a folding caravan with an air-conditioning unit on top, almost as big as the caravan, overtook us. 'Buddy, you're not going to need air-con now,' Jeff laughed. Frozen snow was lodged along the bottom of our windscreen, but as the road had a good surface and was ruler-straight, we could drive on cruise control. It soon became boring, boring, boring. Once again we were dependent on road signs to alleviate the monotony. The first one we saw read: 'Point of Interest next Exit'.

'There aren't going to be many points of interest along this route, if this level nothingness is anything to go by,' I mused.

'True. But I'm not *that* curious to make a detour,' Jeff retorted. 'Anyway, their idea of *interesting* mightn't be ours.'

Many advertisements made reference to Mid-America and a glance at the map confirmed that we were about equidistant from east and west coasts, the border with Canada and the Gulf of Mexico. 'Table flat and *boring*,' Jeff complained. Boring or not he wasn't going to be tempted to leave the road to see *anything*. '6-legged Live Steer, Large Dog, Rattlesnake jewellery', promised one sign. 'Live 5-legged Cow, Russian Boar' said another. He still wasn't tempted. Straight as a die the I-70E continued. So, too, did the signs: 'Largest Prairie Dog, Skunks, Raccoons, Peacocks, Fox – At Next Exit'. Why would anyone want a skunk? We'd smelled their stench a few times on our travels and were grateful to have survived the experience.

I switched on the radio. A medical programme was in full spate – well, the medical part lasted as long as the information part ever lasts on commercial programmes – about half as long as the advertisements. Would you believe the first one along was for animals: a pet contest. Not *deformed* creatures, not intentionally so. (I don't remember the connection between medicine and pets.) There were prizes for: the Scruffiest Dog; the Scruffiest Pet; the Pet who Looks Most like its Owner – a delicate way of saying a human resembled an animal. Ah, yes, but they made sure not to *say* that! While all this entertainment kept us from nodding off, we covered 250 miles, and for that 250 miles the world beyond the windows remained the same. Imagine driving from Liverpool to London on a straight road with nothing to see outside – except *occasional* advertisement signs?

Eventually the countryside became more rolling with a few bends in the road. I quickly vacated the driving seat. After another one hundred miles we arrived at an almost empty campground, with most of the soggiest bits cordoned off. 'Today's been the first dry day for ages,' the middle-aged woman in the office said disconsolately, handing me the receipt and a sheet of campground rules. Reading the instructions about what to do 'In the event of a Tornado', I remembered that we were in the land of the *Wizard*

115

of Oz. There was also a warning about the variable Kansas weather: we might experience anything from ice storms to flash floods. We didn't have any of those – just a marvellous prairie sunset.

A bright, clear, cold morning followed. There were many more trees than the day before. For miles and miles, hay rolls and large herds of cattle were spread across rolling countryside. The I-70 became a toll road through Topeka, the state capital. Our son from Canada was due here on business in a couple of days; by then we hoped to be 700 miles nearer Canada.

Now there was no call for advertisements for strange animals or only a *single* point of interest, because the numerous signs and memorials indicated that the area was steeped in history – Native American, Pioneers on various Trails, Civil War sites. . . There was no time for side trips to see any of them. In Kansas City, crossing the bridge over the Missouri River, we passed from Kansas to Missouri as the city is split between the two states. The interstate then cut across Missouri as it had done in Kansas. It became hot enough to change into T-shirts and shorts – we hadn't expected to do that again! – when we booked on to a campground and sat at a picnic table in the sun, while Jeff planned some more stopovers.

The next day we continued through countryside that was less open than on previous days with towns closer to each other. St. Louis straddles the Mississippi River with most of the city in the state of Missouri, and East St. Louis in Illinois. The interstate runs through downtown, alongside the Gateway Arch (erected to commemorate that the city of St. Louis was the gateway to the rest of America for explorers and pioneers) and over the bridge spanning the wide, mud-coloured Mississippi, busy with river steamers (had my maternal grandfather been here? I mused). Along the levees riverboat casinos were moored. An advertisement for one of the latter ran: 'My favourite 4 Letter Word is Cash'. Another sign read: 'Fried Chicken since 1892'. 'It should be well-cooked by now,' Jeff commented.

'Too bad we haven't time to look around,' I groused, not knowing then that, three years later, we would stay on a campground adjoining one of these riverboat casinos. There were extensive farms and beautiful wooded areas, but many built-up places, too, as we streaked across Illinois in a couple of hours and into Indiana; our 300-miles-plus that day taking us to a campground in east Indianapolis.

Monday morning, while having breakfast, the low sun's rays striking through the tree trunks transforming the dew-laden grass into a sparkling carpet, Jeff was in no mood for appreciating beauty; he was much too worried about the state of Harvi's engine. And rightly so. The previous day the oil pressure gauge had been fluctuating alarmingly. There were no garages open. Jeff had spent a restless night.

From the campground he drove to a garage for an oil and filter change, before continuing on the I-70 and, later, crossing the state line into Ohio. Alas! the oil and filter change hadn't cured the problem. The gauge flickered up and down as previously. Growing increasingly agitated, Jeff muttered, 'I'll have to find a Dodge garage, soon.' Not easy! After an age, driving in congested traffic, seeming to be going around in circles trying to follow conflicting directions from various well-meaning folk, we got to a Dodge garage. Nobody there would have time to do a full investigation that day. A mechanic suggested that it probably was the oil gauge that was faulty, because, despite driving several hundred miles the previous day with a dancing gauge, nothing drastic had happened – like the engine blowing up!

We drove around Columbus, the capital of Ohio, on the I-270 to join the I-71. After more than *1,100* miles we bade goodbye to the I-70. (Imagine driving across Europe on a single, straight road!) Not that that was any record for us on the same road – the TransCanada Highway, at more than 5,000 miles, is the longest paved road in the world, and we have driven it, not once, but twice.

In the late afternoon, we missed, well, *I* missed! the camp-ground we wanted, despite what seemed to be straightforward directions in the site book. It had been a long, tiring, frustrating day. Before our exchange of words got too heated, I found an alternative site. It was due to close for the winter in two days' time – saved by the calendar!

We were 'Ma'am-ed' and 'Sir-ed' every sentence by the elderly woman manager, but in a friendly way, not servile. The recreational park was lovely with great swaths of grass, two lakes and extensive woods decked in their autumn glory. There were rustic cabins tucked away around the edges of the wooded area, windows now boarded up, tarpaulins securely anchored over outdoor furniture, in readiness for the onslaught of winter. Only about half a dozen RVs remained. Three young kids happily pedalled bikes around the campground roadways. Their parents, Andy and Shelly, stopped by to chat. After living for four years in Iowa, where Andy had been at university, they had sold their house and were living in a small camper – more a tent than a caravan. This site was closing, but they had found another where they could stay for a couple of weeks, until they were due to return to Australia. Oh! Yes! they had visited England and Ireland – once, during a 'wet, cold summer.' Darkness didn't fall until 8pm. One of the few disadvantages now was that it got dark often as early as 6.30, which meant there were many times on campgrounds that we didn't talk to anyone.

In the morning, after just over 100 miles driving, we left Ohio and passed a big sign: 'Welcome to Pennsylvania – America Starts Here'. Not for us. We were nearing the *end* of our American trip. The road paralleled the shoreline of Lake Erie for some miles and continued into New York State and on to Niagara Falls, where we spent one night in America and our last two nights on the Canadian side.

Each time we visit the Falls we are thrilled anew. We first saw them when we lived in Toronto during the early part of our marriage, before we made our epic journey west; it was fitting, therefore, that this big trip to celebrate forty years of marriage should finish here. Niagara Falls is actually three cataracts – The American and Bridal Falls in New York state and the Horseshoe Falls in Ontario.

This year in the United States, we had covered over *8,000* miles; visited the three main places on our itinerary: Yellowstone National Park, California, the Grand Canyon, and much, much else besides. Our son in England and a grandson in Canada were celebrating birthdays. We toasted them and ourselves, when we dined in style that evening at a good restaurant.

Then from the sublime to the stark reality of RV living. During our travels we decided not to part with Harvi, as we had intended to do after this trip when we bought the RV – not for another year, anyway. We had grown to love Harvi! Our son had found a garage that would store the motorhome until it was needed again. Because of the severe weather for months on end in Canada the

118

vehicle would have to be 'winterised'. This meant that every single drop of water had to be drained off to prevent damage through freezing. The morning after our big celebration we tackled this chore. All the storage tanks had to be drained and dried. After disinfecting, the toilet had to be flushed through using a hose and left to dry thoroughly before closing. I dusted and polished. On the last leg of our journey, we stopped off at a truck-wash and had the outside spruced up.

Our Canadian family: our son (born when we lived in Vancouver all those years before) our English-born daughter-in-law, whose encouragement had prompted us to undertake this 8,000-mile trip, and our three grandchildren gave us a huge Welcome Back. They would see to Harvi until we returned!

A couple of weeks later, in England, where our other three children and three grandchildren and most of the wider family reside, there was a great celebration for two folk, who had not only supported one another through thick and thin during *forty* years of marriage, but had survived the trials and irritations of living in close proximity with one another for months, in a very confined space, and were not only still on speaking terms, but looking forward to many more years travelling together!

Chapter Ten

Within seven months we were back in Canada.

The excitement vibrating through the house was not because we'd arrived – no way! – it was for the large, newly-installed, blue-tiled swimming pool, which the youngest two were impatient to try out.

'Dad, is the water hot yet?' the goose-pimpled eight-year-old called, hopping from foot to foot.

'The heater's been on for hours. Check the water temperature. It needs to be at least 73 degrees.'

The ten-year-old knelt down to fish the thermometer, tied to the shiny ladder, from the water. Disregarding the reading, they'd had enough of standing shivering on the edge. At the deep end, feet first, they both plunged in, making a huge splash, to surface quickly gasping for air, spluttering, 'It's freezing!' They swam to the side ignoring the ladder in their haste to scramble out.

'It's f r e e z i n g! *F r e e z i n g*!' they chattered, swathing themselves in towels.

The well-wrapped up onlookers laughed loudly.

'Serves you right! That'll teach you to be patient. You should've waited till the water was warm enough.'

Whatever the water temperature, with the pool heating on it had to be higher than the air temperature. Leaving our blossoming garden – the daffodils long finished – we'd forgotten how chilly and still-late-winter Ontario is in mid-May. For many in temperate climates, springtime is the most popular season, whereas in continental zones spring is sandwiched meagerly between a long, harsh winter and a hot, humid summer.

With a visit to Washington DC planned, then to the southern states, we'd intended to begin our trip earlier, to avoid the punishing summer heat, but a special birthday party in Canada, scheduled for the beginning of August, and intending to stay till then, meant that we'd altered the *starting* date of our holiday.

Towards the end of May we crossed into the States at Niagara Falls, a pleasant young woman in emigration dealing efficiently with our papers speeding us on our way. It was decidedly cool on our overnight stop in New York. A photograph shows me sitting at the picnic table, hood up, jacket zipped tightly, watching a ginger cat on the prowl sending a multitude of little birds into a frenzy of chittering flitting between shrubs and trees, many still leafless. The guy in the next RV said that the season was up to six weeks later than normal.

There was lovely countryside along the Susquehanna River, in Pennsylvania. Then we crossed the Mason/Dixon Line, the former boundary between the slave and free states of America, into Maryland, our first 'new' state on this year's trip, everywhere green and flourishing. After much research, Jeff had located a site convenient for our approach, and the nearest RV site, to Washington. Meticulously I had written down his directions. Campgrounds can be elusive, even in open country, but in fast moving city traffic, would I see the signs in time to alert Jeff to make the necessary lane changes? I was more than a little apprehensive, I admit. Luckily, it was an easy find. No hassle! A good beginning to our holiday, we were all set up, sitting out eating lunch by noon.

On registering, a newsletter headed – A Monumental Experience, combining in words the extensive on-site facilities with the capital city famed for its numerous memorials, gave information on itineraries, and travel into Washington. This exceptional RV Resort was operated by the fifth generation of the family that had founded it.

After an afternoon spent in swimming pool, sauna and hot tub, a bus from the park took eight of us into the city to join a three-hour coach tour. The main buildings and monuments, well-known from pictures, looked attractive under floodlights, the Stars and Stripes fluttering at every turn. Founded in 1791, Washington – in

f

the District of Columbia – was the world's first planned national capital.

Making several stops, with hordes of school children, students, and tourists queuing and viewing, in some places it was a scramble to rejoin the bus at the designated time. Each time, as the passengers left the coach, the black lady driver was preparing to smoke, and she stubbed out a cigarette before swinging into the driver's seat to continue the ride and her spiel.

Making our own way by bus and metro, over several days we were able to explore. Washington is a city of monuments and museums. The 555-foot white marble obelisk, the Washington Monument, is the tallest and it, together with the Capitol Building and the White House, are probably the most famous. Among the myriad museums, the National Air and Space Museum is the most-visited museum in the world.

At the White House we got into conversation with a couple of fellow Dubliners on holiday, who were on a day-visit from Baltimore. 'Do you know that this place,' indicating the residence of the President, 'was designed by an Irishman. . . in the style of some buildings back home?' Yes, we did know!

Our friends are often amazed at the scores of *cities* we have visited in the British Isles and in Europe while touring with tent or caravan, a mode of transport not associated with city life. Now, on our travels in North America, in museums and galleries I could enjoy seeing the originals of objects and paintings previously only known from reproductions. On visiting St. Matthew's Cathedral, we saw a statue of St. Antony modelled on one in Padua, Italy, where we had seen the original; the mosaics around the walls had scenes from the life of St. Francis, copied from various places in Umbria, Italy and familiar to us.

'What a lot of places we've been to,' Jeff quipped.

'Yes, and all visited while camping!'

Washington is surrounded by the states of Virginia and Maryland (Maryland ceded land for the creation of The District of Columbia). The Pentagon, the *largest building* in the world, headquarters of the Department of Defence, is in Virginia, so too, is Arlington National Cemetery. The location of the grave of President John F. Kennedy, marked with an eternal flame, was decided on because only three weeks before his assassination, the President, on a visit to Arlington House, remarking on its peaceful setting added, 'I could stay here for ever.'

Robert Kennedy's grave is marked only by a small white cross. A cairn, donated by the people of Scotland, commemorates the airplane disaster at Lockerbie. There are memorials for casualties of various wars; the 600,000 who died (killing one another) in the American Civil War was the greatest loss ever in battle for the nation.

The names of more than 58,000 Americans who died in Vietnam are recorded on the Vietnam Veterans' Memorial (there is a separate Memorial for Women Veterans) located, not in Arlington, but in Washington.

One day, downtown, while waiting on a platform for a train, a tall, well-built man, casually dressed, wearing a baseball cap, edged towards us.

'You guys English?'

'Sort of. . .'

'Doya know how this here Metro works? Canya explain. . .'

The middle-aged man was making his *first* journey out of North Dakota and was totally mystified by subway trains.

'Probably picked up our accents,' Jeff suggested to me later, 'and didn't want to admit to a fellow American that he was bewildered in the Nation's capital.'

'Guess if you've spent your entire existence on a ranch in the wide open spaces of North Dakota, subterranean life must seem scary and claustrophobic.'

Returning late one afternoon, missing a train meant that we missed the hourly connection to the RV Resort by seconds – the rear of the bus only yards away from the stop. Much too weary to walk anywhere to fill in time, Jeff took himself off to sit in the shade of some trees, while I shared the bus shelter, the sun beating down, with a family, each of monumental proportions – no way as attractive as the statues in the city! – consuming junk food non-stop.

'Supper'll be late tonigh', with missin' the bus,' Mrs Fatso whined, offering a packet of melting, chocolate-chip cookies to Mr Fatso, who took a handful before passing them to Fatso son and Fatso daughter; all four then licking their sticky fingers.

'Like a cookie? Like a candy?' I was asked more than once.

Each time I declined with thanks.

'Sure?'

'I'm OK thanks.' I tried a smile.

Fatso boy, now sitting some distance away on the hot pavement, too lazy to pass the giant bottle of lemonade to Mrs Fatso, *rolled* it in her direction.

'Wotagoodidea,' she declared, stopping the bottle with a big foot.

Thereafter the bottle travelled back and forth until empty, when it was replaced with a bottle of coke.

It was a very, very long wait.

Harvi had been in situ for days. Our visit to Washington DC had been an enormous success, but Jeff, who tires of sightseeing more quickly than I do, and whose liking for city life is much less than mine, was ready to move on. He wished to spend a couple of days 'out in the countryside, doing nothing.'

The morning started misty, turned to drizzle, then it rained torrents, as we drove in Virginia passing a road aptly named: Dismal Hollow Road. It was Jeff's 65th birthday. He had clocked up his 25th in Banff, Alberta, during our epic journey across Canada. We reminisced about Banff *and* Lake Louise and the hair-raising journey through The Rockies.

'Remember those high, rickety, wooden bridges over The Kicking Horse River, in Yoho, and the way they swayed when we drove over them?'

'How could I ever forget!'

We talked about the intervening forty years. Where had they gone?

A long-held wish of Jeff's was to travel the scenic Skyline Drive and Blue Ridge Parkway, through Shenandoah National Park. During the day, marooned in the RV eating birthday cake, he plotted some stopping places along his proposed route.

'Ain't this just awful?' the woman in the office moaned, looking out at the downpour, when I braved the elements to ask if she had any literature on Jefferson's Monticello, in Charlottesville. She hadn't.

Fed up with the rain, which was forecast to continue for some time yet, we only stayed one day at Front Royal. *One* day doing *nothing* was enough for Jeff. That didn't surprise me. He finds it impossible to sit still. He was out of luck in fulfilling his wish regarding the Skyline Drive. We attempted it, but instead of the promised 'extensive views renowned for beautiful scenery', we were completely enveloped in cloud, as dense as fog, and had to abandon that, too. It was disheartening.

Stopping off for a couple of hours, Jeff caught up on rest in the RV in the car park, while I visited Monticello. America's third President, Thomas Jefferson, achieved many things from helping to write the Declaration of Independence to negotiating the Louisiana Purchase, that had doubled the size of the then United States, to introducing the neoclassical style of architecture to the country. Monticello, begun in 1768, took forty years to complete; the domed residence was the centre of Jefferson's private world.

The tours were guided. I much prefer to wander on my own; however, both the house and gardens were fascinating. Jefferson had up to 135 slaves, who helped with the construction of Monticello and worked the 5,000-acre surrounding plantation. 'He only freed two slaves in his lifetime and five in his will,' the lady guide told us, without any further comment. How did he square that with the Declaration of Independence and its self-evident truths that 'all men are created equal' and that among their 'unalienable rights' are 'life, *liberty* and the pursuit of happiness'? All very odd!

I hadn't previously known that four American Presidents died on the 4th of July. Thomas Jefferson, died on 4th July 1826, the *50th* anniversary of the signing of the Declaration of Independence just a few hours before John Adams, the second President, expired.

We drove under a leaden sky for another couple of hours. The single storey, 100-year-old, clapboard building, had the 'camp-ground office' at a table in one corner of what appeared to be an indoor village (the first shopping mall?) as it sold everything under its enormous roof from fresh milk to farm machinery. Except stamps! The ancient building had just been joined nearby by a smart, brick-built Post Office of America, complete with a damp, droopy flag. After the difficulty we often experienced purchasing stamps in towns, who would have expected a post office here? We had nothing to post!

The old lady in the camp office complained, 'Yesterday's rain was the heaviest I've ever seen. Real bad.' Our forlorn, squelchy pitch under dripping trees showed that she wasn't exaggerating. In good weather, the lakeside location would have been pleasant. Again, we stayed just one night.

To get to the highway we needed, we had to drive up to, and then over, the mountains and down the other side, a distance of about five miles. Descending, what was the first building we came to? A post office. We still had nothing to post. Continuing south in low cloud and frequent showers through green Virginia, crossing into similar lushness in Tennessee, stopping soon afterwards for lunch at a pizza place to give us a break from the RV, we then drove until 4pm to a small campground. The evening was warm and dry, which, along with the compactness of our individual pitches, contributed to a convivial atmosphere with cheerful conversation. A couple in a big outfit were also headed for Texas, then going to the Grand Canyon and Las Vegas. They were interested in what we had to say, and more than a little amused that we, from England, had visited these famous places ahead of them. While doing a mountain of laundry, I got chatting with Carol and Linda. Each was the sole driver of a motorhome. The husband of one was recovering from a stroke; the other's husband had advanced multiple sclerosis. Like ourselves, they were life-long campers and as their husbands didn't wish to give up just yet, the wives were stoically carrying on. I greatly admired them. There's no way that I'd be the sole driver!

The next morning, under heavy cloud cover, the mountains to our left looming as grey outlines, we joined I-40 west, which makes a diagonal across the state of Tennessee, a narrow rectangle, sharing borders with *eight* other states. Shortly, crossing a time zone it was 7.20am on Central Time. Passing through small towns, the numerous, usually brick, Protestant churches, white crosses atop small white steeples – all looking similar, as if bought through a catalogue. We were in the Bible Belt. Abundant trees, small towns with churches, and low cloud for mile after mile. . .

We stopped to buy groceries, and a take-out meal, which we ate on board Harvi. In the afternoon, the cloud lifting – but still no blue sky – the temperature 70°F and only a twenty per cent chance of rain, Jeff detoured to drive for a couple of hours along the Natchez Trace Parkway. As the roads and interstates in eastern United States were much busier than any of the routes we had followed on previous long trips, this scenic road, with many overlooks giving sweeping views, compensated a little for Jeff's earlier disappointments. Billboards are prohibited, and commercial vehicles are forbidden to use the Parkway. The quacking of geese and ducks from a distant farmyard way below us, cows grazing contentedly, turkey vultures circling, lots of birds, then two curious fox cubs by the roadside, all contributed to a pleasant detour.

A monument designed as a broken shaft marks the grave of Meriwether Lewis (dying aged 35 years) whose explorations with William Clarke in the 1800s had opened up America west of the Missouri River. We had encountered their names on previous journeys, first in Montana, last year in St. Louis, Missouri, and recently in Monticello.

Crossing into Alabama, there was the usual plethora of signs: 'Feed 8 for $13.82 at Funland' (we wondered what the *feed* would be at that price), 'Tattoo Artist & Body Piercing' and much more – all available in the next city, which was billed again and again as: 'Florence the Renaissance City'. Oscar de Priest, the first black man to serve in Congress was born here. Founded by an Italian, who possibly had never visited the other Florence, or whose plans for this place had gone badly awry, or who maybe just had a wicked sense of humour. . . The campground, though, in a leafy park some distance out of town, enticed us to stay for a second night.

On our free day there wasn't any sun, but despite the seventy per cent chance of rain forecast, no rain either. Other places were not so lucky. 'Just south of here, we'd *four* inches of rain in an *hour* this morning,' a couple, arriving on site, told us. The park, bordered on one side by the wide Tennessee River, where the occasional barge drifted by, had beautiful trees with lots of wildlife, especially birds, most of whose calls were quite unfamiliar to me from chuck, chuck, chuck, to moaning, moaning, to one that sounded like a rusty gate, to beautiful, sweet singing. The scarlet cardinals, which in the past I'd only seen as red flashes streaking between trees, were residents here, hopping around on the ground.

Alabama, Tennessee and Mississippi come together at a spot north-west of Florence. In heavy rain we drove for fifty miles along a narrow road through Alabama farmland, which widened to two lanes, when we crossed into Mississippi, the trees there standing in flood water. The relentless drumbeat of Ravel's *Bolero* on the radio coincided with roadworks which went on and on for forty miles. We could have been anywhere on the planet –

unbelievably, during that forty-mile stretch there were no road signs whatsoever! We emerged on to dual carriageway. The rain stopped. The clouds lifted. There were many huge magnolia trees, some still blossoming, when we crossed back, on the W.C. Handy Memorial Highway, into Tennessee and *sunshine*.

On bluffs overlooking the Mississippi River, Memphis is Tennessee's largest city, known for its music and the two men who introduced it: W.C. Handy, the Father of the Blues (who was born in Florence), and Elvis Presley, the King of Rock and Roll. In Memphis there is also the National Civil Rights Museum, formerly the motel where Dr Martin Luther King Jr. was assassinated in 1968. Much as we would have liked to acquaint ourselves with all this, we were anxious to get to Texas, as during the past week, even without sun, day by day, the temperature was rising.

We crossed the bridge spanning the wide Mississippi River into Arkansas, stopping at the Welcome Center to get more information and maps, answering the usual question: 'Where you guys from?' Driving on through flatter wider country, of diverse agriculture, than we had seen all week (though Arkansas has millions of acres of forest), under less leaden skies, despite the heat and the traffic, we made good time. On the banks of the Arkansas River, Little Rock, with its sister city North Little Rock, is the capital and also the geographical centre of the state. Maybe some other time we'd explore, but not on this trip.

Sweaty and weary having driven nearly 400 miles, we got to the campground at Arkadelphia at 4pm. After setting up, in the shelter of a stand of trees we sat at the picnic table and drank tea and more tea. When I recovered a bit I had a swim. Later, we called Canada; the family there was the conduit for the wider family's latest news, as our phone calls direct to anywhere else were governed by the time difference (7pm in Arkadelphia was 1am the next morning back home) – our daughter from England, visiting Las Vegas for a wedding, had enjoyed a helicopter ride over the Grand Canyon, before returning home to London. Everyone was fine. 'Where are *you* now?' We brought them up to date.

A giant roadside sign announced: 'Hope – The Birthplace of President Clinton'. Bill Clinton, then in his second term of office, was still riding high in the popularity stakes. Apart from its association with Clinton, Hope is renowned for its big *watermelons*, claimed to be the world's largest! In less than half an hour, at Texarkana, which straddles the state line (the post office building is half in Arkansas, half in Texas), we crossed into Texas (the President was almost a Texan!). It was 10am, murky, with the temperature a sticky 75°F.

Texas is big! With an area of 270,000 square miles (more than five times the size of England), it is by far the biggest of the lower 48 states. East Texas is famous for its pine forests. Our route took us through some of these, before giving way to extensive farmland with massive fields dotted with hay rolls. There were lots of horses. There were lots of cars driven by folk swamped by their outsize Stetsons. Along both sides of the highway there were wildflowers, any grass there and on the central reservation was already dried, unlike the lush green in other states, and only early sprouting in Ontario. An advertisement for a pawn shop promised: 'Cash for Anything Valuable (Except the Kids in the Back Seat)'. The terrain got flatter. The road straighter. The temperature hotter. The pawn advertisements continued at regular intervals until a sign said: 'OK It's Time You Told the Kids We Are Nearly There'. We were there, too, when we found the camping in Dallas, soon after noon, having driven well over 2,000 miles since leaving Canada.

When we climbed down from Harvi to cross the forecourt to the office, a Rottweiler – that we hadn't noticed – lunged, straining his chain taut, frightening the daylights out of us. Not the kind of welcome we were used to! We got one of the spaces reserved for small RVs on the Mobile Home Park.

Dallas, the eighth largest city in the US, is where President John F. Kennedy was assassinated in 1963. A memorial to the 35th President, designed as a place of meditation, has walls to shut out noise and is open to the sky. In a nearby part of town the author of a book, contradicting the findings of the official report of the death (long years before), was doing a brisk trade selling copies of the book, and also a video.

There are internationally known stores in downtown Dallas, but as in most American cities, the main shopping is to be found on malls elsewhere. 'Way outa city,' we were told at the bus depot. Taking a number 54 bus, transferring to a number 83, we travelled for fifteen miles to the indoor Galleria Shopping Center

– all that way for $1 each! Almost the only white people on the bus, the ride was interesting not just for what could be seen outside, but for the running news in lights on board the number 83, including the results of the General Election in the Republic of Ireland. 'More international news here than in daily newspapers,' Jeff laughed. The huge Galleria was interesting; it even had an ice-skating rink. The temperature outdoors was 88°F.

We have two abiding memories of Dallas, both seen from the RV park. One is of the evening sun reflecting on the glass walls of the numerous downtown skyscrapers, setting them ablaze; the other is of an electric storm over the city, the lightning competing with the neon lights to make a multi-coloured sky – a bit like the Aurora Borealis, which we'd often seen when we lived in Vancouver.

Having negotiated the snarl of traffic on the I-45 through the city, once we reached the campground, we decided not to endure the humid heat to venture back into Houston. Although it is situated fifty miles inland, Houston, the fourth largest city in the US, is one of its major seaports; however, the stocky character wearing knee-length, navy shorts, white collared T-shirt and navy peaked cap worn at a jaunty angle, who descended on us, 'to say Hi,' was not from some luxury yacht tied up in the port, but from an enormous outfit with a car in tow. So why was he dressed like that? He told us that folk in small motorhomes (like ours!) don't often 'get to talk' to folk in big units (like his!); therefore, he always makes the first move. How kind! Originally from Seattle, now retired, they wintered in South Arizona returning north just once a year. 'I never drive more 'an 200 mile a day.' Maybe that's why he's dressed like that, I thought: manoeuvring that colossus is akin to berthing a liner. I'm sure he would have been delighted to show off his home; we didn't ask. After a while he ran out of boasts and departed.

Despite the possibility of rush-hour traffic, because it was already very hot Jeff wanted to be on the road for 8am. Making a wide sweep around Houston to the I-45 south, we arrived an hour later at the Johnson Space Center, Headquarters of NASA. Rockets launched in Florida are controlled from here by Mission Control. Billed as 'The Closest Thing To Space On Earth – Man's Greatest Adventure', the fascinating five hours we spent there passed quickly. Amongst items on view outdoors were the three stages of a Saturn V rocket, similar to those which launched American astronauts to the moon during the Apollo programme. Indoors, there was a wealth of information and interesting exhibits. A spacecraft covers 100 miles in twenty seconds; circles the world every ninety minutes; the flight director is in overall charge; a doctor speaks to the crew on board for one hour each morning; and something that I had previously known – but forgotten! – GMT is always used for space travel.

Everywhere pleasantly air-conditioned, outdoors it was 93°F and Harvi's temperature when we returned was 110°F. We headed for Galveston on the Gulf Coast – well, actually, in the Gulf of Mexico; two miles off shore the island is reached by a causeway and a bridge. Would the heat there be more bearable? Though it stayed in the 90s during the day, bright skies and sea breezes were a great improvement on the liquid heat inland, where it is always several degrees higher than on the coast. We agreed that June was too late for Texas and the south and that, when we had changed our dates for this year's trip, we should also have changed our itinerary – we'd know better next time!

The campground being in a residential district, the walk to the bus stop took us past jungly gardens of cacti and exuberant flowers jostling for space. The hourly bus, on a circular route with a different number for the outward and return journeys, dropped us off near the cathedral. Oleanders bloomed everywhere, pink, red, white; various kinds of palms; hibiscus, yellow daisies. . . Working our way through restored Victorian neighbourhoods, Galveston was once the largest city in Texas, on to the Historic District known in its heyday as the Wall Street of the south. A devastating hurricane, with great loss of life, had trounced the island at the beginning of the 20th century. (Since then they had been less damaging, until Rita came along.) Going in and out of all the stores, we quenched our thirst with homemade lemonade in a barn-like building, selling a variety of imported drink and foodstuffs together with loads of ancient – though not quite antique! – paraphernalia, which looked as though it had been in situ long enough to take root. Like a set from an old movie, there was an ice cream soda place selling all manner of concoctions with ice cream, and also luxury chocolates. The ice creams we chose were delicious; chocolates, we reckoned, wouldn't make it past the door before becoming a mushy mess in the heat.

The timetable was only approximate we discovered, when the

'hourly' bus arrived thirty blistering minutes late. The front and middle doors flapped opened and, as if on cue, simultaneously out of each an elderly, white man on two crutches descended and struggled in unison across the sidewalk. We boarded, squeezing past a beautiful black girl standing guard by a big, box-like package, which was in the way of everyone getting on. A white woman with a folding zimmer was followed by two others, dark-skinned, with walking sticks; the next was a good-looking, middle-aged Mexican woman wearing a multi-coloured shawl, a cartwheel straw hat with various decorations dangling from the brim, an enormous birthday cake, on a stand without a cover, balanced precariously on her left hand, while with her right she fumbled with coins to pay her fare, the driver anxiously anticipating a faceful of creamy goo at any second! Sitting cautiously on one of the side seats, she was followed by a man carrying a huge, clear plastic bag full of toilet rolls. The large, oval, green plaque on the outside of the bus said: 'Galveston Island Adventure'.

Even with Harvi's air-conditioning working overtime, it was so humid each night that we only slept fitfully. One morning, the temperature 85°F, we set out early, carrying a canteen of iced water, to take the half-hour walk to one of the long, soft-sand beaches. I had a swim; though the water was too warm to be refreshing; even the stiff breeze was blowing hot. After an hour, I agreed with Jeff, who never cares much for the seaside, that today it wasn't much fun. On the way back to the campground we stopped at a cafe. At the cash desk we were told that the coffee was free for seniors. There were many of *them* at the tables, welcoming us into their chattering groups, well-dressed, well-preserved, the men balding, the women carefully coiffured. None looked in need of a free cup of coffee. All were white.

Galveston had been hugely enjoyable; however, it was time to begin the long return journey back north. Whichever way we headed it was going to be hot. Hot and *humid*. On our last trip, having driven the entire west coast of California before heading inland, we'd travelled home to Canada up through the centre of the continent. On the trip before that, we'd crossed the northern states. This time, why not continue along the Gulf Coast to New Orleans, then travel up the east coast?

Next stop New Orleans we agreed, hoping that we didn't melt away before we reached there. Jeff got out his maps. . .

Chapter Eleven

It was 83°F and humid at 8am, the air-conditioning in the office going full blast.

'Where y' headin'?' the dark-skinned woman asked, swiping the credit card.

'New Orleans,' I answered, as I signed the chit.

'Noo Orlins,' she repeated. Everyone in the south calls it Noo Orlins. (Does anyone know there's an *old* one in France?) 'That's on the 10 – 'bout 400 mile' east.'

'So I reckon,' Jeff agreed.'

'Bin there before?'

'No.'

'You'll like it. . . Good place. . . Nice havin' you folks stayin',' she smiled, handing over the receipt.

'Thanks. It was lovely being here.'

'You're welcome. Safe drivin',' she called after us.

Our drive from the island to the interstate, then west, took us past many petro-chemical plants. 'Rocket fuel's made there,' Jeff indicated one of them. 'The nation's life blood – a quarter of the oil refined in the US comes from Texas.'

A couple of hours later, in the middle of a bridge over the Sabine River, it was goodbye Texas/hello Louisiana. 'The road's equally bad in both states – corrugated,' Jeff complained, stuff on board rattling noisily, as we bounced along the ridged surface that went on for miles.

Unlike some previous long-day drives through unchanging

scenery, today the world beyond Harvi's windows, was interestingly varied; much of it of a kind we'd not seen before. There were paddle boats and canoes on the bayous; great areas of cotton and cane; expansive rice paddies; signs for casinos on Reservations; farmland; lush forests of live oak and soft, feathery cypress; a freight yard with miles of wagons. . .

Stopping at a rest area, we made tea and a cold snack on board Harvi. 'I couldn't face another burger, pizza, or whatever,' Jeff stated, 'no matter how hungry.'

'All fast food tastes the same,' I agreed.

With the dashboard air-conditioning blowing a gale, Harvi guzzling gas voraciously, we weren't even getting our usual eleven miles to the gallon. While Jeff filled up both tanks for a second time, I telephoned a campsite in New Orleans to reserve a space. The busy dual-carriageway was elevated over any swamp land and for the last thirty miles into the city it was carried on stilts. Trees growing in the water all around, what looked like tree stumps were roots through which they take in nourishment. How I wished that I could rest my feet and be recharged in that way!

The young, well-built, white guy in the campground office seemed irritably off-hand – maybe he didn't like the dripping heat any more than we did. 'If y' wanna tour you'll have to le' me know by 4.15,' he stated. Then, as we neared the exit, clutching a tour brochure, he barked, 'That's in forty-five minutes.'

Too hot and tired after our 400-mile drive to *think*, let alone decide what we wanted to do *tomorrow*, we set up speedily, acknowledging the smiles and hellos of a black family nearby, crowded under a giant fringed sunshade, not that shelter would alleviate the humidity. Nothing alleviates humidity. Except *fierce* air-conditioning. (Without *that* nothing alleviates *dry* heat either, as we discovered when caravanning, a couple of years before without any, in a desiccating 106°F temperature, in Extramadura, Spain.) For the rest of the day we remained indoors only venturing outside just long enough to make a 'phone call to Canada, and one to our son in England who was plotting our route on a US map.

The following morning, walking to the bus stop, we saw signs, repeated at intervals along the road (one just outside the campground gates), advising: Hurricane Evacuation Route. We were the only white people on the crowded bus into the city.

Thinking about the graves, in Arlington, of the assassinated Kennedy brothers, who had worked tirelessly for Civil Rights, and the memorial to Martin Luther King Jr., in Memphis, I recalled that when we lived in Canada forty years before, we heard frequently of the atrocities of the Ku Klux Klan and other bigots. In those days of segregation black Americans were not permitted on the same bus as whites. Can you believe until the mid-1950s, blacks weren't allowed to *play* on teams of that all-American sport baseball? That's true!

Jeff doesn't like hot weather; not that *I* felt cheery in sticky heat of 98°F. He was tetchy and non-communicative. At one stage, during the morning, I lost track of him, and had no idea where he'd gone. What if he's been taken ill? I panicked. He expects me to be a mind-reader – 'You knew I was looking for an English newspaper.' How would I know he was looking for an English newspaper? It was six weeks since we'd left England and he hadn't bought an English newspaper during that time! I won't say that he was happier, but he was less grumpy, once he'd purchased a week-old copy of *The Independent*. Despite this, we enjoyed our day in New Orleans, thanks to escaping often indoors and consuming vast quantities of iced drinks to cool down.

The carefully preserved French Quarter (also known as the Vieux Carré), founded by French Creoles in 1718, was more extensive than we'd expected. Jackson Square in the heart of the Quarter, a green park with huge, blossoming magnolia trees – I had no idea that magnolias grew *that* big! – is dominated on one side by St. Louis Cathedral, flanked by two 18th century buildings, the Cabildo and the Presbytere, both part of the Louisiana State Museum. Small two and three-storey brick and painted-stucco buildings, many with filigreed galleries, line the narrow streets.

Royal Street boasts an entire block of buildings with fan-light windows and beautiful cast or wrought iron balconies, so delicately worked they're called lace balconies, with exuberant trailing greenery and brilliantly coloured flowers. La Branche House with intricate double galleries, wraps around a corner. In contrast Bourbon Street, strident with ear-hurting jazz, has the small cottage, the former Lafitte brothers' Blacksmith Shop, (legendary pirates) dating from 1772, now a popular bar; and numerous stores selling less-expensive goods than the up-market and antique shops elsewhere.

Jeff has a knack of finding unusual souvenirs, usually bought with cash given as gifts – because 'he is so difficult to buy for'. We now have such a collection that to avoid our home looking like an overstuffed curio shop, from time to time, I have to change the objects on display. In north America any purchases had to be lightweight and easily transportable to avoid paying excess baggage on our return flight to England. His purchase in New Orleans was hand-crafted: The St. Louis Cathedral painted on a piece of slate measuring roughly five and a half inches by seven inches. Information printed on card on the back said that the grey roofing slate had been mined in Pennsylvania in the early 1800s, each tile hand-cut, before being transported by raft down the Mississippi. Jeff's plaque had previously been 'an old roof tile in the Vieux Carré'. The *orange* spires and details on the facade of the cathedral, though of course not an actual representation, nevertheless, for us, with its vibrant colour and surrounding rampant foliage, sums up our memories of that day – Jackson Square and the French Quarter, hot weather, exotic flowers exploding everywhere, and the mighty Mississippi River.

'Noo Orlins is the Nation's second largest port and this here River's our biggest,' a bulky black man, quite puffed up with pride, informed us as we stood on the high levee, our backs to Jackson Square, gazing across the wide Mississippi. 'Difficult river to control,' he said, removing and replacing his blue baseball cap. 'The level of the water changes as much as twen'y feet 'tween spring an' fall. In the past we've had *big* floods, 'cos in lots of places the river's higher than the land. Dija know that?'

'No. We didn't know. A couple of years ago, we saw the river near its source and there was flooding then from the Missouri/ Mississippi in the northern states.'

'Floodin' here too at that time,' he agreed. 'Not so bad as long ago 'cos they've built jetties and levees to restrict the overflow of water, also keeps out the ocean.' Removing and replacing his cap again, he went on, 'They say the levees are longer than the Great Wall of China. Isn't that somethin'?' Pointing to a great span to our right, he said, 'See that bridge there, a boat collided with one of them piers, few years back, and trucks and everythin' ended up in the ol' river.'

I thought of that black man proudly announcing to us that the high levee would not only keep out the waters of the mighty

Mississippi – *his* river – but also the waters of the ocean, when during Hurricane Katrina, a few years later, the whole of the Gulf Coast was inundated with such devastating consequences especially for the people, many of them black, living in the poor, run-down areas of New Orleans. We were in New York at the time, but only suffered days of drenching rain.

No visit to Louisiana would be complete without experiencing a Swamp Tour. Ours, near the West Pearl River, was led by a Wetland Ecologist. Sitting back to back along the middle of the canopied boat gave everyone a grandstand view, and being small it penetrated deep into the shallow backwater of the swamp interior. Eerily silent as we drifted between giant cypress trees, their trunks in the water, with wide-based tupelo, a type of gum, red swamp maple and to us the more familiar birch in crowded growth along the spongy water's edge, all festooned with Spanish moss, which isn't Spanish nor is it moss, but a type of air plant. With much to admire, fascination overcame my cringing dislike of the cloying, claustrophobic atmosphere created by the entrapping, gauze-like Spanish moss and the dense, damp greenery trailing into the dark, still water.

Among the jungly bushes there were a few cabins. Some had makeshift flag poles with the Stars and Stripes flying. A dilapidated one, clapboard shedding white paint, corrugated tin roof, with a blue, mock-historic disc which said: 'White House'. Another had 'My Hot Tub', on a rough piece of card propped against an old full-sized bath on the porch.

Our guide, knowing where alligators skulked, threw marshmallows into the water explaining, 'They prefer bright sun not this low cloud ceiling, but they'll always surface for food.' Sure enough, each time a head appeared with great jaws open to snatch the titbit, circled the boat a few times anticipating further morsels, and getting none sank below the water again without making a ripple. In all we encountered about a dozen of these swamp denizens. There was other wildlife too: water snakes, turtles, white egrets, a blue heron and, when we returned to more open water, great splashes of water-lilies, some white, some yellow.

As we left the boat, the guide indicating the leaden sky said, 'You've been lucky, folks. The afternoon tour's been cancelled; there's a storm comin'.' The clouds growing darker, our return by van to the campground was delayed when the vehicles ahead of us had to pull on to the verges to allow a full-sized bungalow on a low-loader to inch along, taking up the full width of the road. Throughout this trip we'd seen many prefabricated bungalows being transported, sometimes in an unfinished state; sometimes a finished half-house, followed by its other half; other times a family home, drapes on the windows, as this one was, being moved to a new destination.

It was past checking-out time, the sky ominous, when we arrived back. 'If you wanna be on your way, that's OK,' the black man in the office said, jovially. Jeff did. In record time we packed up and departed as thunder rumbled in the distance.

Soon we crossed the state line into Mississippi. And soon after that the heavens opened, emptying torrents of rain; drivers unable to see in the deluge, pulled off the road for about half an hour, until it abated. 'Thank God this didn't happen when we were crossing that lake,' I said, the coursing water obliterating the world beyond the windscreen. The bridge/causeway was *five* miles long, like driving on water.

The thunder storm continued all afternoon, and not having booked ahead, nerves were niggly when we found a campground. In reception, below the wall sign giving the fees, all payable in advance, with a special weekly rate, there was another in large print: 'No Refunds'. Jeff had been saying for days that he needed at least a week's rest, 'somewhere along the Gulf.' But it wasn't pouring rain then and it was now! Biloxi, noted for its mild climate, is situated part-way along a 26-mile, level, white-sand beach. (This entire stretch of coastline was flooded for *twenty-five miles inland* in the 2005 hurricane.) Disregarding the 'No Refunds', we paid for a week's stay. The only pitch that was suitable (because of water-logging in this resort, where it never rains!) was at the other end, furthest away from the swimming pool and amenities. Both jaded, we fell into bed before dark.

Sleep was shattered by a succession of loud blasts, the RV juddering with the vibration, as a train, on the other side of the high fence beside us, trundled and clanked past, hooter blasts every few yards echoing again and again and again for up to fifteen minutes, until the racket gradually diminished, to be repeated time without number during the night. I swear that all the 90-wagon freight trains that we had marvelled at on our travels throughout America, had followed us here to test their hooters while thumping across southern Mississippi. By morning we understood the 'No Refunds' sign in the office! Only another six nights to go. . .

Apart from the trains – there were few during the day, freight was moved at night! – ours was a lovely spot on a well-equipped campground. In the older part of town there were quaint stucco cottages and huge oaks festooned in Spanish moss, but it's the casinos, on boats, that account for Biloxi's popularity and, as previously, we found these good for meals. Vying with each other to look the most attractive, or outlandish, one building, viewed from across a wide road, looked like a giant wedge of pink-iced cake and seen from *that* casino: a large, white, circular domed-building with an identical, though smaller version one nearby, happened to be a catholic church with a separate baptistery. A separate baptistery, though common enough in Renaissance Italy, was quite unexpected here in Casinoland, quite apart from the strangeness of the two white buildings. God versus Mammon.

(During Hurricane Katrina all the casinos, being on water, were swept away. In pictures on TV, we saw that other buildings, including the church and baptistery, though badly battered, survived!)

We didn't get used to the trains. Every single one of them wakened us. Every one a mile long. We relaxed and rested in the daytime. Some days there were thunderstorms with dramatic lightning, often with prolonged rain; some days the weather was beautiful and with the heat less suffocating we could sit outdoors. On one occasion, while lazing under the sun umbrella, I watched a bird with beautiful blue plumage chase a tail-less cat several times, until the cat slunk away in disgust.

After a week *in situ* it was time for Harvi to hit the road again. In a couple of hours on the I-10 we travelled into and across Alabama. The heavily overcast skies belied the sign: 'Welcome to Florida the Sunshine State', when we crossed into Florida leaving the interstate for a scenic road giving views on one side of lush countryside with great magnolias, live oaks, golf courses, and on the other, stunning white beaches with aquamarine water fringed by lacy breakers. These beaches along the panhandle are considered the best in Florida; the white sand is ninety-nine per cent pure quartz. Further east, pine woods were being savagely uprooted by machinery making way for developers. Destroyers?

There's a striking contrast in the way in which American and British weather forecasters describe similar conditions. In the British Isles 'a cloudy day with some rain' might also promise 'occasional sunny spells' meaning: if you're in the right place at the right time you might get lucky. In the US – like this morning's forecast for instance – the 'partly cloudy skies' suggests that the rest of the sky will blaze with sunshine – but it often doesn't. Today the partly cloudy became full cloud turning menacingly black before drenching everywhere again for forty minutes. Losing another hour, it was 5.30pm eastern time, when we set-up on the edge of the private beach of a delightful, small campground.

'Only one night?' Bob, the middle-aged friendly camp manager, queried, thinking, no doubt, that having found this idyllic spot anyone with any appreciation of beauty would wish to stay longer.

' 'Fraid so,' we regretfully replied. There weren't many on the site, no big yokes; it couldn't have been more different from the one in Biloxi – if only we hadn't spent a week there.

We had a long chat with Bob, who had an Irish surname, about Ireland and all things Irish. In particular he enthused about the natural beauty of the Island, ruefully accepting that its emerald glory depended on THE RAIN. Afterwards, while I cooked dinner, Jeff got out the campsite books and maps to see where we'd go next. As dusk fell we watched, through the windows, sea birds on long legs striding along the shoreline scouting for their evening meal. Later, lulled by the rhythmic rise and fall of the waves, we slept well. No trains!

I wakened at daybreak to the swish of the sea. Jeff is a morning person. I definitely am not! On this occasion instead of turning over for a further snooze I opened the curtains and looked out. There wasn't enough light to see much. This was a first for me, a walk on a beach before sun-up and that the beach was a deserted one – apart from Jeff, a tiny figure in the gloomy distance – and on the Gulf of Mexico was thrilling.

'Didn't expect you at this time of the day,' Jeff greeted me, grinning broadly. 'Are you not well?'

'Isn't it just beautiful,' I murmured, looking around, ignoring his teasing.

Four egrets, a flutter of white in the half-light, flew in to strut in single file along the high water mark scrabbling for breakfast.

'There was a big grey heron here earlier,' Jeff said. 'Pity it's so cloudy. Don't think we'll see the sunrise.'

'It'll be at the far end, the other side of Harvi. I'm going back for my camera.'

I have bored everyone to tears with my photograph. But I love it! The bottom almost black, showing in silhouette Harvi, a small tree and the slender handrail of the fishing pier, beyond that the sun rests on the water throwing a narrow band of orange/red along the horizon and backlighting, with glowing colour, a triangular mass of loose dark clouds, which magically – only an instant before – had lifted off the water in deference to the rising sun. But after breakfast I didn't have my camera to hand when the grey heron, that Jeff had seen earlier, returned. Standing to his full height on a wooden stump, his left foot grasping a still-struggling, large fish, the heron, motionless for many minutes, cruelly disregarding the thrashing death throes, gazed impassively out to sea. That was the *picture* that got away.

Reluctantly we said cheerio to Bob and his beautiful stretch of beach. Leaving the coast the highway cut across the top of Florida from the Gulf of Mexico to the Atlantic. Knowing that we had booked a site for the next few days meant that we could relax a bit and enjoy the 250-mile drive through lovely countryside: luxuriant trees festooned in Spanish moss, flowering yuccas, palms, with lots of cattle egrets and other birds pecking along the lush roadside verges.

At Jacksonville we headed south to St. Augustine, the *oldest* city in the United States. New Orleans was founded by French Creoles at the beginning of the 18th century; St. Augustine is two hundred years older and is Spanish. It's reputed to be the place where the Ponce de Leon expedition came ashore in April 1513, subsequently calling the locality: La Florida. Spain was then set to confront England on the North American continent as Ponce de Leon claimed for Spain all the land from Florida to Labrador. St. Augustine became the first permanent European settlement in the continental United States.

The campground on Anastasia Island was reached by the long Bridge of Lions, a-flutter with flags, so called because of the two huge beasts of white Italian marble at the western end, and on past the Anastasia Light, famous for its black spiral design.

'March and April are the best months in Florida,' various, well-meaning folk had told us. Too bad, we'd mis-timed our visit – it was now nearing the end of June. *Hurricane* was the title, in lurid print, of a newspaper in the camp office, with underneath: *Learn to Survive*. It informed us that the Hurricane Season was from 'June 1st thru November 30th'. Very specific! Was May 31st guaranteed safe or December 1st?

'No worries,' the young girl laughed when we registered. 'The Emergency Operations Cen'er gives plen'y of warnin' of an approachin' storm. There ain't any forecast. Not yet.'

The newspaper gave advice on everything from: *A Survival Kit Checklist* to protection for pets, under a heading: *Is Your Pet Ready For A Disaster?* We were glad that all we had to contend with were late-afternoon thunderstorms, because, apparently, even in moderate winds, not a hurricane, vulnerable tents and motorhomes 'could be blown away'. With good amenities and two pools, the campground was within reasonable walking distance of a beach; it also, for a modest fee, ran a van into town each morning, with a pick-up several hours later.

St. Augustine, tucked away in north-east Florida, tootled happily along quietly minding its own business for more than 300 years, when in 1885 a pioneer developer, Henry Flagler, realising its potential as a nice spot for his wealthy associates to relax, (under the pretext of honouring a chunk of US history, no doubt) built a railroad south from Jacksonville and two hotels in the town. The former Ponce de Leon Hotel, now Flagler College, is regarded as one of the best examples of Spanish Renaissance architecture in America (though not like any architecture we'd seen in Spain!); the former Alcazar Hotel, now The Lightner Museum, also an unusual building in lovely gardens, houses a vast collection in its 300 rooms. Nearby streets are named: Cordova, Granada and Sevilla (again, with nothing evocative of the actual places). There were Anglo names too: King, Charlotte (after a queen) and St. George to acknowledge the British presence in the area from the 1700s.

The oldest city lays claim to many other 'oldest', or 'biggest', or 'first' in the US: The Castillo de San Marcos National Monument is the oldest fortification; the oldest Spanish House; the oldest wooden School House; the first Mission; the 208-foot stainless steel cross, which can be seen from twenty miles out at sea, stands in an attractive park, with a modern church dedicated to world peace, marking the place where Christianity was first permanently introduced; the citrus trees planted in Florida were the first in North America; the first long highway ran between the Missions of St. Augustine and Pensacola. All interesting, as were the huge City Gates and a magnificent, long, green, tunnel of towering live oaks. The restored Spanish Quarter, however, was a bit too much like a Theme Park, too sanitised, to feel historically authentic; though the Spanish masonry construction practices, keeping as close as possible to tradition, used in the restoration of some buildings was commendable. Coquina: shellstone – shell fragments compressed over thousand of years which, though soft in the ground, harden once exposed to air, used years before in the fort, was now used in a boundary wall in the restored district. Tabby: ground oyster shell mixed with lime, could be seen in a house dating from 1750. It is not as durable as coquina, nor is it resistant to fire.

When we'd had a surfeit of this spotless showplace and its well-off visitors, we took to the wide, empty beach backed by sand-dunes dotted with wild palms and giant cacti, and flocks of pelicans dive bombing in the ocean. On our return to base either from town, or the beach, we were relieved to find that the campground hadn't been strangled to death. A leafy, green vine, called Kudzu, was rampant in the south eastern states, defying all attempts to eradicate it. With tenacious tendrils needing little support, a single plant can creep 100 feet in a season. In hot, humid conditions it grows at the rate of a foot a day! Draped profusely, Kudzu was smothering shrubs and hedges on our route to and from the beach. Maybe by now it has taken over the whole island.

At night we could open windows to enjoy gentle Atlantic breezes and, for the first time in weeks, sleep without the racket of the air-conditioning. Apart from the usual laundry and cleaning, I did a big sort-out in the RV. There was bulky, cold-weather clothing, some of which was used at the beginning of the trip; also we had thought that we might do the Polar Bear Express journey in Canada later, but had now changed our minds. There were blankets and a sleeping bag, which we'd needed earlier. All this clobber, and items we'd bought as gifts, I stowed away in the least accessible corners freeing space close at hand for everyday things. I recall that, during our stay on Anastasia, we ate bananas 'til they came out our ears, because after buying a big bunch we then remembered that they go off quickly. Ah! For the joys of motorhome living!

The July 4th holiday weekend was looming. Jeff was busy surveying maps and the availability of campgrounds, always very time-consuming. One place we tried with 1,200 pitches had been fully booked for weeks. Giving up any hope of getting anything on the coast, booking a week ahead, we got three nights on an inland site in North Carolina, about 800 miles away. The evening before we left the island there was another massive thunderstorm, but this time Jeff's handiwork with a tube of sealant, bought at a small general store, kept the rain coursing down the *outside* of the window and not creeping in around the edge soaking the bedding. Several families had joined forces to have a celebration, the long table set with dishes, children already seated, when the storm broke. Rain is rain wherever it falls. In our travels in Europe and North America we have come to know that it isn't only in the British Isles that rain is WET!

We crossed into Georgia and headed for Savannah, a place I'd always wanted to visit. The Sunday traffic was light. We made good time. Frustratingly, we couldn't find the campground listed in the book, nor any campground, anywhere. There was nobody about to ask. We eventually spotted a small sign: 'Camping', and a directional arrow, repeated a few times along the route, which led us for miles seemingly out into the wilds. It wasn't really a camping, more a hobos' encampment. There were no amenities. But no fee either. A scruffy man, impeccably polite, indicated where we could park on a level bit of rough ground. I was not comfortable in those surroundings. Didn't feel safe. Jeff was crankily overtired and disinclined to continue driving looking for somewhere else, especially as we hadn't a clue where we were! It was the worst afternoon, evening, night of this trip, or any trip. In the morning, we – rather I – was relieved to find that we hadn't been attacked in our beds; nobody had bothered us; we were safe and well. 'I told you there was nothing to worry about. You always make such a fuss about nothing.'

Savannah is a place we'll remember even though we didn't *see* much of it. On the 'camping' we were eighteen miles out of town.

Nearing sunset at Grand Canyon Village.

Leaving Grand Canyon – reluctantly!

Hubble Trading Post, Navajo Reservation, Arizona.

Wood changed to stone in Petrified Forest, Arizona.

Cacti at Boyce Thompson Arboretum, Arizona.

The Old Mission, Sante Fe, New Mexico.

St.Louis' Cathedral, Jackson Square, New Orleans, Louisiana.

Music Hall of Fame, Nashville, Tennessee.

Baskets made only by descendants of slaves,
Charleston, South Carolina.

Wooden School House, St.Augustine, Florida.

Gateway Arch and downtown St.Louis, Missouri.

Pilgrims' Landing, Provincetown, Cape Cod, Massachusetts.

Jeff stopped off at a garage to have an oil change for the RV. Afterwards he toured around some of the reputed twenty beautiful squares and avenues with lovely old houses and moss-hung trees arching over wide roads in the city. Truly romantic! Remember *Gone with the Wind* and Scarlett O'Hara? The manure-like miasma pervading for miles all around was, 'from the sewage treatment works,' a guy at the garage explained. The 18th century mansions authenticated by 18th century smells!

Leaving Georgia we got brochures and camping listings at the Welcome Center in South Carolina. Hot, with cloudy sun, the busy single-lane highway towards Charleston, without stopping places, gave me no opportunity to look at the literature we'd picked up. I endeavoured to peruse it as we sped along through vast areas growing cotton and tobacco, interspersed with marshlands. Any campgrounds listed for Charleston were way out of town. We missed the first one we aimed for, but soon after 11am, ten miles south of Charleston, pulled on to another and got a space, a long, long way from the entrance and the swimming pool. (Later when I had a swim I was almost dry by the time I walked back to the RV.) There was no public transport into the city. We would have to travel there in Harvi.

The woman in the camp office said, reassuringly, 'It's an easy ride in and there's plen'y of parkin'.' (Oh, that it were true!) 'There's two-hour *free* parkin' at the Information Cen'er.'

In town we followed the directions to the Visitor Information Center. Of course, there were no empty spaces. It was sweltering – after all we were still in the deep south. Everywhere was busy. Jeff began to rant because I didn't know what *exactly* I wanted to visit or the *names* of the streets on which the buildings were, that I *might* want to visit. Now was not the opportune time to remind him that it was his idea to drive into Charleston without first delaying on the campground to have lunch, or read our few leaflets which I'd not had a chance to look at because I'd been searching for a campground, and as we couldn't park at the Information Center to get any information how could I know what I wanted to see? Many bickering circuits later, on a one-way-system, the gods were with me and I directed Jeff to *indoor* parking, reserved especially for RVs and large vehicles. I still had no idea what was to be seen in the city, but at least we'd arrived and parked. We took the Dash trolley (25c each for Seniors) to the

Old City Market and had lunch there at a restaurant.

The market, with indoor and outdoor sections, covers *three* blocks selling everything imaginable. Once again, succumbing to temptation, we bought items for gifts. We resisted buying any baskets – awkward for transporting to England – and if we did buy, what would we use them for? By an entrance to the indoor market, two beautiful black women working intricate designs with rushes and grasses, and two tiny boys, all shaded by a large, colourful parasol, were surrounded by a great display of their wares. The sweetgrass baskets are unique to this area. The craft, originally introduced by slaves from Africa, is carried on by a handful of their descendants.

The centuries-old city, the setting for *Porgy and Bess*, is regarded as one of the South's best preserved. In the sultry heat we wandered up and down streets admiring the sympathetically-restored, beautiful old houses and commercial buildings. The first shot of the American Civil War was fired in Charleston Harbour on April 12, 1861 and from landscaped gardens along the palmetto-lined waterfront, we looked across to Fort Sumter National Monument, where there's a museum commemorating this, but extreme weariness washing over us – we'd started the day ten hours before, hundreds of miles away in Georgia – instead of taking a boat out to the museum, we walked back, legs buckling beneath us, to retrieve Harvi and return to base.

The next morning we reserved a space on a campground twelve miles north of Charleston before heading into the city. On the way we stopped off at a grocery store to reclaim my reading glasses' case, left by the till yesterday. It was still there. The teenage assistant's mystified expression that anyone would admit to *owning* something so shabby (though the hand-beaded decoration on the scuffed suede remained intact) was fully justified – it probably was as old as she was! I'd bought it long ago in Yugoslavia when the country was still communist. Uniting my specs and their case, we drove straight to the indoor parking and paid for a 3-hour stay.

In one of our leaflets, Charleston was referred to as the 'Holy City'. Incredibly, it has more than 180 historic churches. St. Michael's Episcopal church, dating from 1761, looking familiar to us, was modelled on St. Martin-in-the-Fields, in London's Trafalgar Square. It and many others have tall spires creating a most unusual skyline for an American city. Across the street from a Jewish synagogue, outside St. Mary's Catholic church, built in Greek Revival style, we got talking to some people awaiting a funeral. Though few of them had visited Ireland, they knew a lot about the place and here were members of the local Irish Club, as was the gentleman to whom they wished to pay their last respects.

Charleston was delightful! From there we headed out of town to Boone Hall, originally a cotton plantation of some 17,000 acres, established in 1676 by an early English settler in South Carolina. First, after our busy morning, we went to the Gin-House Cafe for some lunch. In my ignorance, I thought that gin was an alcoholic drink (which, being a teetotaller, I've never tasted, anyway!) but it was a machine for separating the fibre from the seed. At one time, Boone Hall produced handmade bricks and tiles and these could be seen in various buildings (including the cafe), paths and boundary walls. Doubtless making bricks kept numerous slaves occupied for their entire lifetime, though *they* were not the 'chosen' ones to live in the nine brick cabins, which still stand on *Slave Street*. These were 'reserved for the house servants'; the others, including the brick makers, lived elsewhere on the plantation, their quarters long disappeared. I don't suppose slaves were much concerned with what to do in their 'leisure' time judging from the brick cabins 'reserved' for the house servants, which were little more than dormitories of bunks. Let's not be too self-righteous! Today, there are many kinds of slaves, not least those working in the Third World to satisfy our consumerism; and there's no excuse for not being aware of their appalling working conditions and rates of pay. Also, I recall a conversation that I had once with a South African colleague in London during the era of Apartheid. I remarked that white South Africans appeared to regard their black servants in the same way in which an English family might treat a favoured pet dog. Looking thoughtful for a brief moment, she nodded, matter-of-factly, 'Um, I suppose you're right.' And *that* was not all that long ago. Little changes!

Dating from 1743, the three-quarter-mile avenue of moss-draped live oaks leading to the handsome mansion are world famous, known from films and television. Alas! Hurricane Hugo in 1989 felled some of these oaks. No way can you drop in to a tree nursery to buy 'some 250-year-old trees, please' to fill the yawning gaps. We spent an enjoyable, informative afternoon there and then drove to the campground, where we had a reservation, just as a thunderstorm broke overhead. With using Harvi for transport and being parked outdoors all day without the air-conditioning running, the temperature on board was 100°F. After being hooked to electricity on site for a couple of hours we got it down to 78°F and the humidity down to 55.

At Boone Hall there was lots of feathered activity, including a grey heron and several egrets, on the peaceful stretch of pond near a huge field of colourful wild flowers. Here, on a campground noted for its family-oriented facilities, there was a lake where kids could launch their rubber dinghies from a small wooden dock. A notice said: 'No Swimming in the Lake'. Fair enough, we thought, as there were two swimming pools on site. The earlier thunderstorm had cleared and, for the first time on this year's trip, we watched a sunset reflected across water. Dusk fell. 'What's that humpy thing with those two little lights up front?' I asked. The humpy thing was a ten-foot alligator, soon joined by a mate, and the 'lights' were beady eyes shining in the near-darkness. On our swamp tour in Louisiana we'd been told that 'Alligators move very fast. They can strike as quickly as a snake. Dogs often end up as snacks.' What about kids, we wondered? There were no warning signs, nothing in the camp literature about these creatures, just 'No Swimming in the Lake'.

We were up and away very early. The grass sodden, it must have rained heavily during the night. With the air-con blasting we hadn't heard it. It makes the most awful din, but with the humidity bad it was the lesser of two evils. The two-lane, straight road carried on and on through swirling mist. Flowering magnolias, tree nurseries selling shrubs and palmettos, everywhere green, green and drippy. 'It's so wet there are water lilies growing in the roadside ditch!' I told Jeff. The dreaded smothering Kudzu was galloping through this state, and when a few hours later we crossed into North Carolina it was rampant there, too.

Outdoors there was no air. The humidity and heat made me feel faint. Jeff had been suffering quietly – sometimes not so quietly! – for weeks. By early afternoon we'd had enough and pulled off the road. The grossly overweight woman in the camping office, rivulets of sweat plastering her hair to her forehead, sighed wearily, 'It's not usually this humid, not this bad.' Later, we could have added, 'Not many campgrounds are this bad: overcrowded and unkempt, the swimming pool so dirty I can't use it to cool off.' We felt rotten. Not having the energy to leave to look elsewhere, we suffered it for one night.

The next day's four-hour drive inland in North Carolina delivered us to the big, well-managed campground that we had pre-booked for three nights, bedecked with flags and bunting, and the promise of fireworks. Blue skies and a temperature of 100°F on July 4th – resulted in a jolly Independence Day for all on the campground. The following day there was a massive thunderstorm, knocking out the power and telephones for several hours (no air-conditioning! and the pools were closed). Later, when the rain eased, but there was still no power, a temporary telephone line was fixed up. There was a scramble to use it. Having arranged to call England, we took our turn at the small table in the open grassed area. They were having a soggy time back home, too, *without* decent temperatures – it had been the wettest June on record! After hearing that we didn't grumble about the lack of air-conditioning, well – not *all* the time. July 4th was an important date for us, being the fifth anniversary of Jeff's stay in hospital, in Italy, which at that worrying time I was convinced would mark for us the end of decades of *independent* travel with tent or caravan. Yet here we were, in our own RV, camping in North Carolina, our 37th American state – all but two of them visited since then! – surrounded not by a Tuscan landscape of needle pines and ancient cities, but by rolling farmland of enormous fields growing corn, tobacco and abundant peanuts.

Appropriate? Many of our mystified friends think so. 'For what you spend on each RV trip,' they say helpfully, 'you could have a holiday in a Luxury Resort.'

When we decline these suggestions explaining that we love the *freedom* of *camping* and being in the great outdoors, their abrupt response invariably is, 'You're nuts!'

Peanuts to you too!

Chapter Twelve

Virginia Beach – why on earth go there? Let me explain. There's more to Virginia Beach than the 40-block boardwalk along miles of golden sand, some of it crowded, true. There's the interesting Virginia Marine Science Museum, one of the most-visited museums in the state; also the Adam Thoroughgood House, dating from 1680, claimed to be the oldest non-Spanish brick house in the US. Yes, I know there're more T-shirt outlets than anywhere else on the planet, but shopping's not compulsory.

We'd intended to visit New York City and Boston on our return journey. In this heat? No way! While *in situ* in North Carolina, we planned an alternative route back to our family. From Canada we'd visited different areas of New York, though never the Thousand Islands region. We hoped, now, to do that.

After leaving Virginia Beach, we passed on our right the Cape Henry Memorial, where a stone cross commemorates the landing in 1607 of the first English settlers; and on our left Seashore State Park, where a fact of nature assures that Blue Spruce grows no further south, nor Spanish moss any further north, than here. Then US 13 continued across the mouth of Chesapeake Bay on the Chesapeake Bay Bridge-Tunnel. In the British Isles and Europe, we've driven over long bridges, in tunnels through mountains or under stretches of water; this was unusual in having, in its 17.6-mile length, different types of major structures: bridges, tunnels and four man-made islands. On one of these there was a parking area, a restaurant and an observation pier giving great views over the ocean including, up close, a couple of ships. Among the myriad shops in Virginia Beach there was a post office. The first time we stopped it was closed and the machine outside didn't have stamps of the kind we needed. When leaving town, driving past in Harvi, it was open, with nowhere to park. Here, surrounded by the waters of Chesapeake Bay, the machine indicated that its stamps were *exactly* as we required. Just one snag – it was out of order. I bet our folks have no idea how appreciative they should be when they receive our postcards from the Greatest Democracy in the World.

From the northern end of the bridge, rail tracks running alongside, US 13 continued through flat countryside, the fields dotted with people picking crops. A small McDonald's was the lone building. We needed a coffee. Afterwards, as we walked towards Harvi, a long shunter-train came to a halt. The driver and his mate scrambling down from their perch gave us a 'Hi there!' and a cheery wave. Abandoning the train, they disappeared into McDonald's. Was this a new kind of Drive-Through?

For Sale signs along our route offered: hams, peaches, corn-on-the-cob, cucumbers, soft crabs, onions, watermelons, fireworks, building lots, shrimps, hot crabs; and in the middle of extensive farmland there was a Christmas Shop. Would the train crew stop off to buy any of these goodies? Nowhere offered stamps.

US 13 left Virginia delivering us into Maryland, where apart from the nuisance of having to move pitches a couple of times to enable Jeff to reach all three hookups, then juggling Harvi level, we enjoyed a pleasant lakeside stopover. The next morning, still on US 13, soon after 9am we crossed into Delaware. There was no State Line as such, no difference in the surroundings, just a big board declared: Welcome to Delaware. We had never been in this state before, nor, come to think of it, on our extensive travels had we ever met anyone from here. It was our 38th American state and the last 'new' one on this trip. From the Welcome Center we detoured to a post office. Would you believe the counter clerk didn't have the required denomination stamps and had to ask another clerk. Neither had airmail stickers. At last the cards I had carried through *three* states thumped into a mail box.

Delaware is small: 2,057 square miles. Only Rhode Island is smaller. What it lacks in size it makes up for in importance – some say mockingly: self-importance. Signs for: 'Delaware 1st

State' abounded. In 1787, it was the first to ratify the Constitution, and boasts significant historical sites and many restored ancient buildings. There were pleasant homes in leafy, flower-filled gardens. In the countryside near Dover, the capital, the Amish way of life was evident and we saw a few of their black buggies clip-clopping along past hedgerows and verges sprouting hibiscus, a trailing bright orange creeper, and banks of sweet-smelling, yellow lilies, all growing wild. Delaware doesn't have a state sales tax, making it a mecca for shoppers from other states.

We got chatting to a young woman who previously had been stationed with the US army near Oxford, in England. 'When we were returnin' after two years, I couldn't cajole my *wonderful* nanny and her husband to come to America. Nothin' we promised would coax her here. The husband was keen to come, but not nanny. Know why? She was too scared to fly,' she laughed. In another store a man asked me if I lived near Huddersfield – which we don't, though we know the area. 'I liked that place and all round Yorkshire, real nice.' He seemed pleased to reminisce.

Shortly it was goodbye to Delaware. It was goodbye, also, to the ocean, which had never been far away from us on our coastal journey of *2,500* miles through *eleven* states. In Pennsylvania, more than anywhere else in North America, the rural landscape always reminded us of the terrain in northern Europe. We were in Dutch Country, which of course is not Dutch, but Deutsch: German. In the 18th century German and Swiss immigrants, escaping religious persecution, came here. Maybe the landscape reminded *them* of home? In Lancaster County there are more than 700 Amish farms, mostly dairy, but also producing corn and hay to feed their herds. The Mennonites in Ontario, with whom we were familiar, have similar beliefs and customs. They attempt to live the simple life of the pioneers. They don't use electricity or motor-propelled vehicles of any kind, making for severe hardships, especially considering their ferocious winters; nor do they allow the use of alcohol or cigarettes. Their clothing is plain, often black. Women wear bob caps, because their heads must be covered at all times, and long, enveloping skirts, which in the daytime heat must be most uncomfortable. Apart from farming, then selling their produce at Farmers' Markets, the women make attractive quilts, a tradition going back more than 200 years. We saw many hand-made signs advertising these along the narrow lanes and back-roads.

One afternoon there was another tremendous thunderstorm thrashing the tall trees under which we were parked, with torrents of rain continuing for ages, before gradually petering out. Much later, the storm banged around again more viciously than before, suddenly knocking out the electricity, marooning another camper and myself in the small, two-machine laundry – more a glorified shed – at the farthest end of a near-deserted campground, with the washers full of wet clothes, in pouring rain and pitch darkness apart from the zigzagging lightning.

'Not a predicament Amish women would find themselves in,' I bellowed above a crash of thunder.

My co-prisoner nodded in agreement mouthing, '*They* are not reliant on newfangled inventions!'

Neither of us had a flashlight. I wondered if the Amish used them. Probably taboo. They, like the *sensible* ones in the bible, would have lamps *and* oil at the ready.

Next day bowling along through beautiful, rolling, wooded countryside we took a turning for Reading. Parking on a street, we meandered around the attractive 19th century town. Though it promoted itself as the 'Outlet Capital of the World' we realised that the 'Outlet' must be *out* of town. Harvi needed gas. A sheriff was filling up at the next pump. Jeff asked him for directions to The Mall.

'Come on. Follow me. I'll take y'there.' Scything a way through heavy traffic taking many twists and turns, Harvi keeping up close, we arrived some fifteen minutes later. (Those many twists and turns proved to be a problem when we tried to find our way back, afterwards.)

'Thanks ever so much.'

'No problem guys. You're welcome,' he smiled, giving a wave.

Strange as it may seem, it wasn't the first time that a police car *rescued* us. A couple of years before, in Spain, on a baking hot Sunday morning, we were looking for the listed campsite for Seville. With sparse traffic, taking our time, we followed the directions carefully. Twice we did so. Twice we ended up driving right past the doors of Departures, at Seville Airport. Twice we were surprised that any folk getting out of taxis, or trundling their baggage across in front of us, showed no surprise at seeing us in a laden car towing a *caravan*. Back out to the highway again from there to scrutinise our surroundings. This time we could actually see behind the airport terminal a row of flags fluttering. The campsite? The only snag was we couldn't fathom out how to reach it, useless to take again the only side road, the one we'd already used, twice. Jeff drove on for a few minutes.

'There's a police car parked on the wide verge ahead. We'll ask them. Oh nooo,' he moaned, 'it's pulling away.'

Then, disconcertingly, Jeff flashed his lights frantically – on off on off on off. The stop lights of the police car glowed red in the distance; then the reverse ones came on.

'Good, they're coming back,' Jeff said with satisfaction, as the distance between us narrowed. Two young officers got out and walked in a business like way towards us.

'Gee, I hope they don't get mad with us for flashing the lights,' I thought, trying at the same time to phrase in Spanish what we wanted to ask them.

I needn't have worried. Courteously, they led the way. And yes, it *was* necessary to drive through the airport Departures. The small camping had everything except peace and quiet – we'd never previously seen, at eyeball level, the wheels and under-carriages of so many aeroplanes!

Enough of that. Back to Pennsylvania. With daytime temperatures in the high 80s, we had some surprisingly cold nights down to the low 50s, enabling us to trade the racket of the air-conditioning for a couple of blankets, and sleep. On one campground I was intrigued by humming birds at a special feeder. The humming sound is made by the vibration of their wings as they hover. Really they look like gorgeous butterflies with long, long beaks. The titbits laid out on a separate bird table were usually snaffled by an acrobatic chipmunk, hanging upside down to reach the goodies.

It was time to move north. The up and down winding road through rolling countryside of farms, forested areas, lovely individual houses on big lots, took us into New York, the Empire State, one of the thirteen original states. New York City, tucked in the south-east corner, was the *nation's* first capital. We stopped at the Welcome Center, a lovely building on a rise, giving a panoramic view of green landscape and wooded hills – a world away, not only in distance, from New York City.

We continued north, passing away to our left the Finger Lakes (so called because the Iroquois Nation considered that God had placed his hand here: creating their home) where, nearly twenty years before, with our two daughters, we had our very first camping experience in North America.

'What luxury we enjoy now compared with then,' I laughed.

'Too true,' Jeff agreed, remembering the clapped-out car, riddled with rust, that we'd borrowed for a couple of weeks.

'The tents were too small to stand up in. We had to do all our cooking and eating, everything except sleeping, outdoors,' I reminisced. 'Not that we did much sleeping – the tents being almost too small to *lie* down in!'

'Ah! For the good old days. We were young then.'

'Young? Younger, maybe, I wouldn't swop the years to go back to *that* kind of camping!' I retorted.

In mid-afternoon, near Syracuse, we spent an interesting couple of hours at the Onondaga Nation Territory's reconstruction of the Mission Station, Sainte Marie among the Iroquois, a living history museum documenting trade between French and Iroquois cultures in the mid-17th century. French settlers, from Quebec and Montreal, wanted fur, especially beaver pelts for fashioning into gentlemen's top hats. The Iroquois (composed of five nations), whose territory spread across present-day New York State, exchanged furs for valued metal tools to replace their stone and wooden ones. Frequent skirmishes between the various native cultures – vying for this trade – as well as with Europeans, abated following a peace treaty. As part of the truce the Mission, the first European settlement within Onondaga territory, was established in 1656.

Costumed interpreters, portraying the actual people who lived there all those years before, were kept busy answering questions, not that many – like none! – could understand the *medieval* French spoken (there being no Quebecois present, they in the 21st century still use it), nor the various American Indian dialects. To be fair, everything was available in American English, too. Rosaline, a teacher on the nearby Onondaga Reservation, explained, 'I'm accepted as Indian, because my mother is a Native and our culture is passed down through the female line. So my children are. My father is not, nor is my husband. He's Irish!' she giggled. None of them lived on the Reservation. Bonnie, darkly beautiful, a social counsellor, was full Mohawk as was

155

Paul, a student teacher.

We carried on for some time past apple orchards, fields with livestock and hay rolls, clumps of orange lilies and sumachs with their brilliant red, upstanding, cone-like flowers lining the roadsides, and were lucky to get the last available place on a small campground sloping down to the St. Lawrence River. *Eventually* we enjoyed the great views and a spectacular sunset. Before that, there were heated words as we juggled, tired and sweaty, to level Harvi on such a steep slope. And after all that effort, we could only stay one night because the campground was fully booked. The next morning we had to shove off and look for somewhere else.

Discovered by Jacques Cartier in 1534, the 800-mile long St. Lawrence River drains the Great Lakes to the Atlantic Ocean. It took the US Congress a great many years to ratify a bill authorising the joint Canadian-US construction of the St. Lawrence Seaway, in which the Canadian Government had been interested since the end of the 19th century. Today the 2,342-mile Seaway, constructed between January 1955 and June 1959, from the Atlantic Ocean to Duluth, Minnesota, in the heart of the continent, carries more shipping each year, from all over the world, than either the Suez or Panama canals. The Thousand Islands' 68-mile section of the Seaway, lies east of the Great Lakes, about 1,000 miles from the sea. We spent several steamy days (and nights, the air-conditioning banging away) exploring, in temperatures up to 100°F, with some dramatic thunderstorms thrown in for diversion, to say nothing of being attacked by hordes of marauding mosquitoes.

Our three-hour cruise was billed as: 'A Two-Nation Tour', though there was no opportunity to go ashore in Canada. The exact number of islands is debatable, but the tanned, long-legged, girl commentator stated with such conviction that, 'There are 1,793 islands,' you would think she'd *counted* them herself. To be considered an island, the requirement is that one square *foot* of land, or rock, must show above water at all times, and they range in size from that meagre measurement up to ones that have an area of forty to fifty square *miles*. When the boundary was established between Canada and the US, following the end of the 1812 War, it was decided that no island should be divided, resulting in the international line zigzagging crazily, because it had also been agreed that the *land acreage* should be divided equally between the two countries and, of course, those stipulations weren't known a million years ago, when the mile-thick ice sheet melted away leaving islands strewn haphazardly.

Each year the Seaway is open for nine months and ice-bound for the other three, the tideless fresh water freezing in this stretch to a depth of two feet. There are no restrictions on clearing trees on the US islands. Canada has much more stringent laws regarding conservation, their islands are considerably more green and less inhabited. There are some spectacular summer homes, the most sumptuous being the famed Boldt Castle on Heart Island, built at the turn of the 20th century by rags-to-riches George Charles Boldt for his adored wife, who tragically died, aged forty-two years, without ever setting foot in the place. Our boat – the reason we chose that particular trip! – *didn't* stop at Heart Island, but sailing quite close we could see people streaming off gangplanks, no doubt to exclaim rapturously while touring the castle. One of the few American traits that we don't like is the way in which many of them judge the worthiness of anything and everything by its *worth in dollars*: how much it *cost*, how *big* it is. . . They pay homage to success of any kind, but especially if it has a high price tag. The more opulence on show the more awestruck with admiration they are. On one occasion, in the Royal Palace in Monaco, we got trapped in the middle of a bunch of American tourists who, suitably impressed with the surroundings, exclaimed loudly about how well 'Our Grace' or 'Our Gracie' (the actress, Grace Kelly, married to Prince Rainier of Monaco) had done for herself, as if these fellow countrymen knew her personally and expected to be invited to dinner. Here, in New York State, *mock* castles would have to suffice.

To maintain even a modest house on an island is hugely expensive. Strict laws, with massive fines for any infringement, govern water speed limits and the dumping of any rubbish.

'Sewage from each island goes into septic holding tanks and periodically a barge comes visitin' to pump them out. They call it *The Honeybarge*! Guess Why?' Our pretty, young guide was enjoying herself.

When, a few days later, after our eight-week trip to Texas and back, we returned to Canada, it was not by the towering 8.5-mile 'island hopping' Thousand Islands Bridge, under sections of which we had cruised, but by a shorter, less busy one east of Massena, a direction sign pointing: *Ottawa Canada's Capital*. In fact, we came upon the bridge so swiftly, that we missed the gas station we were looking for on the US side, and then had to fill up at much greater expense as soon as we arrived in Cornwall, at the other end. It was back to litres, kilometres, Celsius, instead of gallons, miles and Fahrenheit and some changes in spelling, for instance: centre instead of center and, of course, everything written in English *and* French, and I mean *everything* – from road signs to the labels on sauce bottles – and that's just the day-to-day differences. I won't venture into the huge differences in Laws. Or Politics. To us, much as we always love the United States, Canada feels like home.

From Cornwall, Ontario, the Headquarters of the Seaway Authority, to the western limits of the province is *1,000 miles*; the area of Ontario is almost four times that of the UK – having travelled extensively in the province, we know! Driving west from Cornwall, wildflowers: purple, blue, yellow, white along Highway 2, farmland – and its smells! – some marshy areas, and attractive, well-scattered, individual houses contribute to this area of Ontario, north of the St. Lawrence Seaway, being much quieter, more rural, with less tourists than in New York.

We parked at Iroquois to watch a tall ship going through the lock, before carrying on through the pleasant town of Brockville, where we started to look out for our overnight campground. Thinking we were 'lost', and with no traffic passing, or anyone to ask for directions, Jeff pulled up near a vehicle-repair garage, and I was dispatched to get directions. Inside the dimly lit, hanger-like building there was a solitary figure – a guy welding, wearing goggles and ear muffs, sparks flying around as if from the anvils of hell, amid an ear-splitting din. Fully focused on the dangerous task in hand, how was I to attract his attention, while keeping out of range of the sparks? Jeff would be none too pleased if I rejoined Harvi without finding out about a campground; the sparks here would only be a forerunner. Jumping up and down, my gesticulations growing ever wilder, perspiration breaking out all over me, at last, before I collapsed, the guy caught sight of my flailing limbs. He shut off his machine. In the eerie, ensuing silence I walked towards him. He removed his ear-muffs, but not his goggles.

'Hi there! Wotcanado for you?' he queried, his lips faintly smiling, the upper part of his face a blank behind his protective mask, surprised, no doubt, to see a 'strange' woman in this kind of place.

The small campground, with a pool, was tucked away among trees, near the river, less than a kilometre further along the road. I had a swim, and afterwards while showering an unexpected thunderstorm broke. I raced back in pouring rain across wet grass, too late to assist Jeff, who had rolled away the awning single-handed. We were glad to bang on the air-conditioning for a while to have some respite while making supper. Later the storm cleared and we enjoyed a tranquil, sunlit evening with nobody about, just plenty of lively bird life.

Gananoque means a place on the river by the rocks, the river being the St. Lawrence. When we stopped in town for some lunch, rain was tumbling, not just straight down, but also blown sideways by a buffeting wind, ensuring that we got drenched from all directions. Giving up, after thirty minutes, our sheltering doorway, we dashed, as fast as the steep incline and running water allowed, up a hilly road to wade through deep puddles to a cafe entrance. A man threw open the door.

'Do you wanna eat inside, or out at the picnic tables?' he grinned, mopping up the water dripping from our clothes.

Our shoes squelched as we crossed to a table to join others, equally soaked, seeking refuge from the storm, with the mop-wielding guy following close behind cleaning up our muddy footsteps.

The next couple of days we spent in a beautiful heritage building (the stone house feeling like an enormous castle after nearly nine weeks in our dinky motorhome), appreciating the hospitality of cousins of mine, sleeping (indoors again!) in a huge room with floaty, gauze drapes on floor-to-ceiling windows, framing views of wide, sunny skies, colourful fields and a long grassed runway. I enjoyed the delights of their gardens adjoining the house, declining the offer of a flight in one of their private planes, but Jeff was game to be taken aloft to do a sweep over the Thousand Islands, covering in an hour the area it had taken us a couple of weeks to see.

We had a look around Kingston, which we knew from previous holidays, on our way through to a campground near Brighton for a couple of days – our last stop 'on the road'. On the last morning we completed the cleaning; drained off all the water; and winterised the RV in readiness for storing it. We weren't going to relinquish Harvi – not just yet. He had a reprieve for another year!

We headed west. A couple of hours later there was no way of avoiding the hectic, fast-moving traffic, when we joined the multi-laned highway around the top of Toronto, then home to a great: Welcome Back.

Preparations for *the* birthday party were in full swing – the event which caused us to reschedule our trip, resulting in our enduring the gruelling mid-summer heat in the south, because we hadn't altered our itinerary to suit the temperature as we should have done. Hindsight is great! Despite the melting heat, we'd had a fantastic time. Apart from not visiting New York City and Boston as planned, we'd visited many places, including the Thousand Islands region, which had not been on our itinerary *and* we were keeping Harvi for another year!

With family arriving from England for the festivities, the big birthday party was well worth the delay, the swimming pool very popular with all the guests. Now there was no standing on the edge shivering, no jumping in feet first; while we'd been away, our grandsons had perfected their diving skills.

Chapter Thirteen

Red roses rioting up a fence beside us, was an unexpected bonus on a campground in New Jersey, situated 'only 15 minutes from Times Square in New York City'. During our winter planning of this year's trip, Jeff had got a leaflet for the site including travel directions which we'd found easy to follow, after a two-day drive from Canada with good stop-overs, apart from time spent for repairs. Although Jeff had a full service done on the RV, including the fitting of a new oil pressure switch, within a couple of hundred miles the gauge showed a fault, yet the engine was running normally – not overheating, or getting noisy.

'I'm not going on like this. The *new* switch must be faulty,' he hissed, in annoyance. 'We'll have to find a Dodge repair-shop.'

Quicker said than done! When he found a garage that had a switch in stock there was further delay.

'I *know* the job will only take ten minutes to do, but the guy says he can't do it for another three *hours*,' Jeff whined, exasperated.

Patience is not one of his virtues; however his frustration was understandable. Before his heart problems, he did all his car maintenance and repairs himself. In fact, he was working on my car on our driveway at home, when he had his first heart attack! Now, waiting for someone else to do a job that he could do himself, he found stressful.

To visit New York City and Boston, 'left over' from last year because of the heat, and to wander around the six states of New

England was our plan. We had five weeks, from Memorial Day, (Veterans' Day) for the US part of our holiday.

We set our alarm clock for an early pick-up from the campground, for a 10-hour guided coach tour of New York. Forty years before, Jeff had spent a week there, but for me to visit The Big Apple was a long-held ambition. It was a marvellous day giving a good introduction to the major sites, with lots of stopping places from the John Lennon Memorial, in Strawberry Fields, Central Park, to the Empire State Building, not the *tallest* building in the city – that was the World Trade building – though still the ultimate symbol of Manhattan, its mid-town location giving a great panorama, when we finally reached the observation deck after a lengthy time queuing.

We'd two hours at Ellis Island, in the shadow of the Statue of Liberty. Ellis Island, called the 'Gateway to America', was the main immigrant receiving station for over sixty years, up to 1954. Considered to be one of the 'greatest migrations in human history', during the peak years prior to the First World War, as many as 5,000 people a day were processed here. It is claimed that 100 million Americans can trace their ancestry back to this 'one tiny portal'. To be eligible for entry to the US the immigrant had to prove two things: that he/she (i) was disease-free (ii) would be able to make a living. Over the years about two per cent of those eager to enter were rejected and *deported*. For some of them the harrowing disappointment led to suicide.

In the stark, lofty halls there was much written material about the immigrants. These walls had echoed to the babble of as many as twenty-five spoken languages. There were hundreds of sepia photographs; some showing people with their entire worldly possessions contained in straw baskets, or just in a *single* cloth bag. Although he 'found' his uncle (lately deceased) who had arrived in the 1920s, and whom he had visited in New York, Jeff soon became overwhelmed by the atmosphere of the place.

'I've had enough of this. . . our stop here's much too long. . . could have done with this time at the Empire State. . . I'm going outside.'

He 'escaped' outdoors to restlessly await our boat pick-up that wasn't due for ages. Not wishing to join him fidgeting and complaining, I remained indoors and found the place fascinating, though I offered a silent prayer – many silent prayers! – that I hadn't been an immigrant here.

On subsequent days, we left our rosy pitch to take a bus from outside the campground, on through the Lincoln Tunnel arriving in the heart of Manhattan twenty minutes later, giving us long hours to explore. I love big cities! I found the 'buzz' in New York quite exhilarating. Jeff is much less keen; and as he doesn't share my liking for museums and galleries I enjoyed their glories, while he, good-naturedly, found interests elsewhere.

The Metropolitan Museum of Art must surely be one of the world's greatest, and my idea of heaven would be to live in the place! Two half-days had to suffice. Something new for me there, which I really admired, was the amount of Tiffany glass on display. I also made a couple of visits to the MoMA. There was an abundance of art and artefacts from the 1880s onwards; some of the paintings I appreciated; some I didn't, probably because I didn't *understand* them. I won't go as far as saying – like some of the kids I used to teach, who, impatient when they didn't understand something, stubbornly gave up all attempts to learn, loudly protesting – 'It's *rubbish*, Miss!'

Unlike other places where all public buildings close on the same day, this city that never sleeps has the good sense to have varying closure times, so that I always had a museum or gallery to visit for a few hours in between meeting up with Jeff. On one occasion, while waiting for him under the clock at Macy's, I watched, fascinated, as a young woman, standing in the middle of the sidewalk, holding a small mirror in her left hand, applied eye make-up, the procedure taking a good five minutes. She took a long look at the finished result; smiled at her reflection; then putting her paraphernalia into a smart, leather bag, slung it over her shoulder and clicked away on her high heels.

Jeff joined me grinning broadly, 'Sorry I'm a bit late. I've been watching a group on the street giving a performance with singing and readings and distributing leaflets. Not only did they call themselves: "The Twelve *Black* Tribes of Israel", but they endeavoured to prove that Black Americans originated in Israel,' he laughed.

When aloft in the Empire State Building, we'd a bird's-eye view over Fifth Avenue with its multitude of skyscrapers dwarfing the neo-Gothic Saint Patrick's Cathedral, and the famous yellow taxi-cabs diminished to strings of yellow beads.

We had another view of busy Fifth Avenue from the steps of Saint Patrick's when, at the end of the vigil Mass for Pentecost, the great front doors were opened to allow the congregation of some two and a half thousand people to emerge into bright early evening sunshine. This prestigious building on one of today's most famous streets began life in much different surroundings – in the mid-nineteenth century *poor* Irish immigrants scraped cash together to purchase a small piece of land *cheaply*, because then it lay well outside the city.

The Frick Collection of mainly European art, at Upper East Side, was delightful, quite breathtaking. Furniture, pictures, objets d'art are displayed in what used to be a private house, built just before the First World War, looking every inch an 18th century residence with its beautifully proportioned rooms lined with silk wallpapers, high ceilings with gilded mouldings, heavy drapes, chandeliers. . . To preserve the ambiance of a home there were few ropes or glass cases, no barriers. Though, from time to time, there was a disconcerting kerfuffle – if anyone stood too close to scrutinise something because the lighting was rather dim, an alarm buzzer sounded loudly, shooting the uniformed attendant out of his chair to investigate what was going on.

Designated a New York City landmark, the Solomon R. Guggenheim Museum on Fifth Avenue, was designed by Frank Lloyd Wright. (I saw several drawings of his in the MoMA, and a few years later admired examples of his architecture, and furniture, in Chicago.) What a building! Across from Central Park, next to the Church of Heavenly Rest (yes, that's its name) stands the 6-storey, spiral rotunda created originally to house a collection of avant-garde art; a much later addition of a 9-storey tower greatly increased the gallery space. Early in the day, the place was not busy apart from lots of young school children, impeccably behaved, viewing an exhibition of art on loan from China – nothing avant-garde about that – some of it dated from 600AD. I marvelled at objects, from various dynasties, in different materials. With audio earphones in place, a neatly dressed, dark-haired boy, he couldn't have been more than eight years old, listening intently to the commentary, was gazing transfixed at an exquisite, startlingly white, porcelain, five-petal-flower dish; its shape and crispness more usually seen in something fashioned from metal. What was this child thinking? I wondered, but I didn't wish to intrude by speaking to him. Why break the spell?

In contrast, on an upper floor, outside one of the picture galleries, a man, aged about fifty, wearing shorts, trainers, T-shirt, and a baseball cap back-to-front, using an elegant column for support was doing leg stretches. Surely his antics were more suited to the running track around the reservoir in Central Park? A gate to there, at the top of some steps, was directly across the road from the Guggenheim.

With only a sprinkling of people in the cafe, the notice on each table saying, 'Please be so kind as to *share* your table with others who are waiting', didn't apply, but at a table near me two old dears – well, to be honest, they were probably *my* age, I liked to think that they looked older! – dressed to the nines, heavily applied make-up, dripping flashy jewellery, were *sharing* one small square of carrot cake. Eyes fixed on the single plate, silently, first one then the other took a minute scrap on her cake fork, making a little go a long way. The food was overpriced – maybe they were being prudent rather than parsimonious.

While I was museum-hopping Jeff spent time on the opposite side of the Hudson River, exploring in New Jersey. On the morning we were leaving he took me to see one of the places he had found. 'You're going to *love* this,' he promised, as we drove. Parking Harvi, we crossed a small, flowering shrub-filled park. 'Take a look at that!' he declared.

There was an extensive view of the river, busy with boats and a long barge chugging past, and strung along the water's edge the full length of Manhattan Island: the famous New York Skyline its buildings a-twinkle in the sunlight. What a view! What a wonderful city it is!

Heading for Cape Cod we had an overnight stop inland from Mystic, in Connecticut. The campground was waterlogged in places. Having settled the RV with some difficulty, deciding not to move it again, we set out on foot to have a look at the tall ships at nearby Mystic Seaport, a re-creation of a 19th century fishing village. Well, that was our idea. And that's what it remained: an idea. Yet again, we were the only people who thought feet were for *walking* – the narrow, twisting road had no sidewalks and we soon grew weary of jumping into the thorny hedge out of the way of horn-blowing cars. A fortuitous gap in the hedge enabled us to escape from the road to wander in a small, overgrown graveyard. Several of the headstones had long collapsed into the rough, weedy grass. The surname Williams, with the ages of the deceased given as: 25, 33, 59, 78 years. . . and the dates of their deaths, all long ago, male and female, barely decipherable now on the moss-covered, crumbling stones still standing, prompted me to say, 'I wonder if this was a family graveyard? There's no space here for there to have been a church, but there might once have been a house.'

'Maybe,' Jeff mused. 'The family probably died out. Looks now there's nobody responsible for maintenance.'

In the morning we headed north along the coast. Leaving Connecticut we crossed two long bridges, Jamestown and Newport, to the smallest state in the US: Rhode Island, Little Rhody. Officially called Providence Plantations; two colonies were combined – giving the smallest the longest name of any state. Newport, regarded as one of the great sailing cities of the world, home to the America's Cup races, during the 19th century was the summer playground of filthy rich families vying with each other in building grandiose mansions. Were they aware that the first settlers on Rhode Island were pirates? Apart from filling up with gas, and shopping for groceries, near Newport, we didn't delay, just carried on into Massachusetts and to a campground on Cape Cod, arriving there at noon.

'That's three states in as many hours,' Jeff said. 'Makes a change from driving for days and days in just one state.'

'Well, Texas could swallow up the *whole* of New England and have lots of space left over,' I replied. 'In fact, the area of Texas is four times that of New England.'

Jeff's query in the office, when booking in, whether it would be possible to *walk* into Falmouth, was answered with one word: 'No!' The town was quite close. 'You guys wanna *walk*?' the youngish manager asked, puzzled, as if he'd never met anyone who voluntarily *walked* anywhere. 'There's no sidewalk. Much too dangerous.' He went on to explain, helpfully, where the parking lot was in town and added, 'If you're wan'in' to take a boat-trip any day to Martha's Vineyard *I'll* drop you at the ferry at Woods Hole and collect you later.' We thanked him and agreed we'd do that.

After lunch we set out in Harvi and parked in Falmouth for

166

several hours. With two museums, colonial homes, inns, much rusticity and a green sward – Falmouth's Village Green is a National Historic Landmark – reminiscent of a village green in England, it was very pleasant, though we didn't find it much like Falmouth in Cornwall.

The next day we went to Martha's Vineyard.

When the ferry docked, most of those on board transferred to a rather battered, small tour bus on the quayside. We scrambled on. So, too, did the two young women from Tennessee, who had followed up their, 'Where y' from?' with 'How sad about Diana,' as if sympathising with us on the loss of a relative. The group from the Azores, with whom we'd chatted about Portugal, and Lisbon in particular, also squeezed on. The bus rattled to life, as did Jock's commentary. With only one stop for half an hour at Gay Head Cliffs, we were bounced all around the island for three hours, while being bombarded with details of countless wealthy celebrities who own estates, all of them tucked away out of sight of prying eyes. . . and prattling bus drivers.

Jock went on, 'When President Clin'on and his family drop in, 200 secret service agents travel with him.' Pointing, he added, 'Four outa the las' five years Clin'on stayed on that farm over there.' We all looked over there – not a sign of a farm, just acres of dense woodland forming a screen. Nobody got a word in edgeways to ask Jock where the 200 secret service agents stayed. In tents, the lucky ones in RVs?

The area around the foot of the striking red cliffs of Gay Head is known as Aquinnah, meaning The Land Under the Hill, to the Wampanoag Nation, the only Federally recognised tribe in Massachusetts, who have lived there for generations. In a shop selling native craft, a gorgeous dark girl with long, straight, black hair, explained that Wampanoag means: People of the East, as she swaddled in copious amounts of bubble wrap the terracotta bowl we bought, decorated all over with an intricate design, painstakingly accentuated with delicate paintwork and signed on the bottom, not by a Wampanoag, but by the Navajo girl in New Mexico who had created it.

At the end of the tour Jock delivered us back to the town of Oak Bluffs, famous for its 300 gingerbread cottages. As we were starving, a fish and chip lunch at the Hungry Whale was good. Methodist Revival Meetings began at Oak Bluffs in 1835.

Thousands used to flock there annually, living in tents. In time the tents were replaced by wood-frame Victorian cottages. Now these are prized candy-coloured summer homes. The outdoor Tabernacle and the park-like grounds are open to the public and an information sign said that this was how it looked, 'Over a hundred years ago, when Harriet Beecher Stowe and President Grant were here'. In a shop, near where the bus dropped us, we bought a couple of table mats for the RV, decorated with a doll's-house-like dwelling. Wandering around the warren of cottages, each different, I said, surprised, 'Look! There's the actual doll's house shown on our table mats!'

We got chatting with the owner; in red-checked shirt and black baseball cap, touching up the white paint on his fence. 'We're in Florida for eight months of the year and here for the other four,' he said with pride. What a nice way to live!

'Anywhere on Cape Cod would be a nice place to live,' we agreed, during our week's meanderings on the 62-mile long peninsula. We felt quite at home there. With its clapboard houses and little towns with narrow, winding streets, the *smallness* of everything was very un-American. The scale as well as the English names – even the variable weather! – were familiar, and we found places where we could *walk*!

We strolled the beach at Hyannis Port, viewed the President John F. Kennedy Memorial and toured the museum dedicated to him. That is, I visited the museum. Afterwards, when I caught up with Jeff, he greeted me with a triumphant grin, 'See what I managed to get by rummaging in a chandler's shop tucked down a side street. Just the thing I've been looking for, for ages. Well, in the past week or two. . . '

'What is it?'

'A locking nut.'

'A locking nut?'

'Yes, for your front seat in Harvi, to keep it rigid, so that it doesn't wobble about when you turn it around to sit at the table.'

'Oh, good!'

Hyannis Port provided the nut; the repair job was undertaken a few days later in another famous place: Provincetown, when we moved to a delightful, wooded campground: Camping Dunes' Edge Campground, at the far end of the peninsula. (Among purchases in that town, one afternoon, were safety pins, when the zip broke on Jeff's trousers!) The outer edge of the Cape, with its white sand beaches and nature preserves, is sparsely populated, apart from artists who treasure its light. Provincetown, known as P-town, is where the Pilgrims came ashore from *The Mayflower* in 1620 and a 252-foot Italian-style monument commemorates this event. Built wholly with stone from Maine, it is the tallest all-granite structure in the US.

Relaxing, reading under a shady tree, swimming, lying stretched out on sunsoaked sand-dunes nearby – all of which I enjoyed, are not Jeff's idea of bliss. No way! Hours spent dismantling the front passenger seat, fixing the locking nut, checking the seat runners, then putting it all back together again – not golf or yachting – is his idea of an 'activity holiday'. I readily admit: I was truly grateful to him that the seat was much more comfortable after his handiwork.

The Center for Coastal Studies, a non-profit making research, rescue and education organisation, is based in Provincetown. Well-wrapped up, we boarded the *Prince of Whales* to go on a whale-watch trip, on a cool, overcast morning. There was a squally shower as we cast off. Not everyone had come suitably attired for the weather; in particular there was an assortment of headgear, including a small man dwarfed by his big, straw boater with blue and orange ribbons, obviously intending to stay inside, or maybe he was more used to cruising in the Caribbean. Anyway, once at sea, I didn't see him again, as we braved the elements and remained on deck.

'Too bad we've no sun. We should see lots of whales, though,' Shelly, one of the on-board, enthusiastic conservationists trilled into her mike. And we did. During the four-hour trip, we saw as many as five at a time swimming close by, sometimes on each side of the boat at the same time. There was a mother with twin offspring. 'Other females accompany a mother, staying with the family all the way from the Caribbean,' Shelly explained.

There was plenty of participation among the watchers as they moved around the boat from side to side.

'Look over there!'

'Here, this side!'

'Oh, there's one blowing, now there are two. . .'

'*There's* a bubble cloud.'

'A bubble cloud?' Shelly queried. 'That means it's a humpback.'

h

Humpbacks can grow in length to seventeen metres (fifty-five feet). They have distinctive feeding behaviours such as making bubble clouds; they also have distinctive markings on their tail flukes, by which they're identified (a bit like our finger prints). Finback whales are even bigger, growing to eighty-five feet. When one of them surfaced it blew a jet of vapour twenty feet into the air, repeated four or five times. Heads or tails – there was plenty of excitement. I wondered what the consequences would be if one of these monsters arched a back *under* the boat.

These trips are not just for the pleasure of the passengers; the scientists on board collect and record data. 'On our trip we saw eighteen individual Humpback, Finback and Minke whales, some of them more than once,' Shelly reported, as the Pilgrim Monument, which could be seen from miles out at sea, grew taller and taller, as we approached. A famous landmark now, but all those years ago *The Mayflower* could have done with such a marker. The pilgrims didn't *mean* to tie up here. They were looking for Jamestown, Virginia, 600 miles to the south!

Cape Cod is famous for its cranberries. It is said that the first export from Massachusetts to the Mother Country was cranberries – not for juice or sauce, but as ballast in ships. Nowadays, they are cultivated commercially, but in the wild they grow in low-lying, damp places. One of our walks took us through a forested area, which then opened out, the trail traversing marshy ground, which later we discovered was a wild cranberry bog. Large flies clouded around Jeff (but not me) settling all over his shirt and bare arms. Persistently, they returned again and again, despite our swiping at them continually, until we got well clear of the marsh. Poor Jeff was covered with large, red, painful weals for days afterwards, even on the skin which had been covered by his shirt.

Driving Historic Route 6A, the old King's Highway, listening to the car radio, we bemoaned for the umpteenth time, how much we always miss the BBC when we are abroad. 'This is The Cape's Number One for Talk Radio; I'm Joe Bloggs and you're 'tooned' to the garden hotline. . .' yack, yack, yackidy yack, on and on – no denying that it was *talk* radio. Short spurts of news about forest fires, the gun lobby, distant wars, deaths of famous people, were interspersed with long advertisements, some done as two-way, fatuous dialogues. Parking in Sandwich, the Cape's oldest town, we abandoned Joe Bloggs to his 'potoonias', to visit the Glass Museum with its fascinating collection.

Afterwards we headed for Plymouth. *Mayflower II*, an exact copy of the ship which brought the pilgrims from England, was sited at the waterfront. Nearby, enclosed in a protective glass case, is Plymouth Rock, claimed to be the very stone they stepped on when coming ashore after leaving Provincetown, because they hadn't found that area suitable. However, it was many years after their arrival (after they were all long dead!) that this hunk of rock became a show piece; therefore, we found it difficult to share in the fervour of those swarming around it taking photographs.

We set off for Boston. When registering in the campground office, we also booked a day-long coach tour of the city. Early next morning Steve picked up ten of us and then stopped at another couple of places for others. Boy could he talk! As he drove into the city, and there negotiated hoardings around giant holes in every street, 'There are always more construction workers than tourists in this city,' he complained in an aside, facts and figures tumbling out seemingly effortlessly. Nobody disputed any of it; therefore, it must have been accurate, after all, we were the only non-Americans. Much later in the day, the rest of us flagging, when Steve, still vibrating with zeal, declared, 'Now I get to ask you questions,' it was Jeff, who first with correct answers to questions on their history, won a cup. No! Not that kind of cup! Not the sort made of metal with an inscription on it; his was a pottery one for coffee, adorned with Boston place names.

We had an interesting day with many stopping places and, apart from all the historical events, we learned that the city had the tallest buildings in the north-east; in south Boston seventy-five per cent of the inhabitants are of Irish descent; the city had the first botanical gardens in the country; also the first public library to lend books free, though I don't know if the Irish influence was especially responsible for either of those, but for Steve's loquacity? Maybe!

Another day, cool and showery, venturing into Boston on our own, gave me the opportunity to enjoy the extensive Museum of Fine Arts and, not far away, the remarkable Isabella Stewart Gardner Museum, designed in the style of a 15th century Venetian palace, surrounding a courtyard garden. While in The

Frick Gallery in New York, I had written in my notebook, 'I *love* Vermeer!' not the man, you understand – he's been dead for centuries – but his paintings on display there. Here, in the Isabella Stewart Gardner there used to hang a very famous Vermeer, *The Concert*. Now a notice in the centre of a blank space on a wall said that it had been stolen and never recovered. Another painting, Rembrandt's *Storm on the Sea of Galilee* was taken in the same raid, on St. Patrick's Day, in 1990. Whatever happens to these stolen works of art that are so well-known they can't be sold on the open market? When I was traipsing around a mock-Venetian palace, fretting about missing pieces of canvas, Jeff, escaping from a sudden downpour, was tucking into fish and chips in a pub, while watching on television a soccer match between Brazil and Morocco.

But he'd had enough of cities. Especially rainy cities. 'Let's go up to Maine,' he suggested at supper that evening. 'Doug, at the garage (where we left Harvi over the winter) says Maine is his favourite state. It's got *everything*: a dramatic coastline, sandy beaches, pine forests, even historic towns.'

I didn't interrupt Jeff's eulogising to point out that *he* wasn't fussed about beaches, sandy or otherwise; he thought that *pine* forests were boring and as for history, well. . . However, we'd come to see New England and Maine was one of the six states. I agreed to go there next.

In the morning we said goodbye to Bernice and Tony in the adjacent RV. From Vancouver Island, both retired, we had long chats about the beauty of British Columbia and had told them of our experiences there on a recent visit and also that, long ago, when newly-married, we'd lived in Vancouver. 'You're heading *north* in this cool, showery weather?' Bernice queried, concern showing on her face. 'We're going south to Florida where rain is *warm*,' she laughed. We still exchange Christmas cards.

Gloom pervaded everywhere from the ground to the sky, when we set off. We quickly covered the 18-mile stretch of New Hampshire's *only* coastline and on through Portsmouth, the state's *only* working port. 'Expect a grey day with a high of 65°F' was the forecast on the radio, as we crossed a bridge from New Hampshire into Maine, passing signs, one of which said: 'Fireworks are Illegal in the State of Maine', and another: 'We have tough Drink Driving Laws'. Though neither fireworks nor drink driving featured on our agenda, the warnings along with the weather didn't promise a jolly time; nor did the plethora of outlet stores, which stretched for miles. We gave up trying to park in York and then Ogunquit to have a look around, just kept driving north hoping the weather would improve.

With a light drizzle falling, a breeze ruffled the water of the deserted swimming pool and sent leaves scurrying from our path as we approached the office.

'There's a new section just been opened on the far side of our park,' the young girl at the check-in said helpfully, drawing a ring in pencil indicating the area on the campground map she handed us.

We set up Harvi in a choice spot. There wasn't another outfit in sight. It would be quite a hike from there to the pool, laundry, telephone. The privacy and peace in such pleasant surroundings would be compensation, we agreed, 'Though if this rain continues it won't matter where we're parked,' I groused.

'In Maine we say, if you don't like the weather, wait a minute,' the girl in the office told us, 'it changes frequently.' Changes to what? Does the sun ever scorch the sandy beaches? Would we be taking refuge from heat in a shady pine forest? We should have asked, but didn't.

'I'm going for a walk,' Jeff declared, donning a waterproof. 'Though the rain has eased a little, I'll take an umbrella.' I didn't wish to explore the neighbourhood. I'd felt rotten all morning and longed for a snooze, but two argumentative flies, which had buzzed in the door as Jeff left, put paid to my dozing. I was restless and miserable. God, it was dreary! It was only 60°F in the RV with daylight so dim that I abandoned my desultory attempt to read.

Late in the afternoon Jeff returned. 'We're quite close to a beach, if this downpour ever clears,' he said, looking around our compact motorhome for somewhere to spread his big, dripping umbrella and then, peeling off his wet coat, somewhere to hang that. The weather didn't clear. In the nine hours between our arrival and going to bed I ventured out of the RV only twice – both times to the new Amenities Block, for the sake of a change of surroundings!

All night the rain drummed relentlessly on the roof. In the din, we didn't hear any trains passing; there had been many during the day. Now their vibrating rumbling and shrill hooters would have been welcome as an assurance that we were actually on land and not adrift on an ocean.

In the morning it was still raining. Bleary-eyed from disturbed sleep, we peered out to discover in alarm that the tarmac on which we were sited was criss-crossed with cracks. 'We better move, and quick!' Jeff's voice rose several notches, as splits rapidly widened prior to chunks breaking away. He flung open a door, hopping out to disconnect the power and water, clambering back in again, the rain plastering tight curls of hair to his forehead. He drove Harvi to another pitch. Then it was a struggle to get it level on blocks – my turn to get drenched – before re-connecting.

About 9am (2pm in England) we trudged through torrents of water the third of a mile to the office to telephone our youngest grandson.

'Sorry! That number is not available,' the English operator said sweetly.

'That's their old number,' I said, not so sweetly, squinting at the scrap of paper in Jeff's hand.

Wordlessly, grabbing the big umbrella, he stomped out to tramp back the third of a mile.

'You'll need the *flowered* address book,' I called after his disappearing back.

He didn't bring the flowered book, but another one. It had the same number as before. He insisted on dialling it again. Same sweet reply, 'Not available'. We tried our son in Canada to get the correct number from him. There was nobody at home. Thoroughly soaked, loudly 'discussing' whose fault it was, we returned to Harvi.

It was 11.30am. We needed some tea. I located the flowered telephone book. Bearing the correct number we returned again the third of a mile. After contacting our grandson, who had been waiting for *hours* for our promised call, we telephoned our other kids in England and Canada. As we finished a wisp of paper from Jeff's wallet floated to the floor. In *his* hand-writing there was our grandson's correct number – in his pocket all the time during the past four hours. In Canada the weather was fair, the same in England. With us it had rained non-stop for a full day and night.

On returning, we were dismayed to discover that an area of ground behind Harvi in his new location had disappeared completely taking with it a couple of trees, which now lay in a tangled mass leaving a gaping chasm just feet away. Abandoning our umbrellas, we scrambled to disconnect again. Jeff started the engine and gingerly moved off slowly for fear of dislodging any more earth. We re-sited some distance away on higher ground, hoping it would remain stable. With difficulty we jockeyed level; then plugged in yet again to electricity and water – though with an ocean emptying from the sky all that was required was to hold out a pan from the doorway and it would have filled in seconds.

After that elemental encounter, we needed showers, hot ones, and a complete change of clothes, especially shoes. 'Might as well try out the new shower block,' I suggested. 'These soggy clothes will have to wait 'til tomorrow. I'm not fagging all that way back again. The laundry's beside the office.' Back on board Harvi, somewhat refreshed, the umbrellas spread to dry, two large plastic bags full of muddy clothing, we decided to make dinner. We ate about 4pm: grilled steak, potatoes, mushrooms, mixed vegetables, followed by dessert and coffee.

The radio was our only contact with the outside world. All of the north eastern states were being pounded by the storm sweeping in from the Atlantic. Everywhere was inundated. Seven – *seven!* – inches of rain had fallen during the past 24 hours. In Boston sewers had ruptured. Being cooped up in Harvi, for what seemed like eternity, I greatly appreciated Jeff's repair job on my no-longer-wobbling-about seat, which he'd done in sunny Provincetown. What was it like there *now*?

During the evening, dishes washed, tidying done, I wrote up these notes, then settled to do some postcards. I'd just written on one that we were marooned, 'as if on The Ark,' when a loud rat-tat-tat on the side door caused me to jump a foot in the air, all wobbly – me, not the seat – (unexpected sounds always startle me) jerking my hand sending a long streak of black pen across the white surface of the card.

'Who on earth's *that*?' I stuttered, my voice just a squeak.

'Neptune, who else?' Jeff replied, mockingly, getting to his feet and noisily swishing open the side door.

In the half-light of dusk, it wasn't Neptune trident in hand, but a campground warden dwarfed by an enormous umbrella on which rain danced crazily.

'Are you guys leavin' in the mornin?' he asked, from under his canopy, spouting water on our carpet, making it a darker shade of pink where it splashed.

'No! We're booked on for a few more days.'

'We've opened up a gap through the boundary fence at the back,' he went on, pointing. 'You'll have to bounce across the uneven ground to get there, if you're goin'. The main campground road's collapsed, washed away,' he went on dejectedly. 'Lots of folk got out 'fore that happened. You're kinda isolated. All by yourselves,' his voice trailed off as if he couldn't bring himself to admit that in the scramble to evacuate we'd been forgotten. 'Crater in the road just there,' indicating the other side of some bushes. 'If you decide to go the back way don't try it in the dark – too many big pot holes.'

'We've already moved *twice*,' Jeff replied. 'Hope we'll be OK here.'

The lower part of the guy's wellingtons had disappeared in oozing mud, which made a slurping noise as he lifted one foot, then the other, to tramp heavily in small steps all over our pitch, 'Should be OK. It's only soft on top. Quite firm underneath, quite firm,' he said, with an assurance I didn't share. Bidding us 'Good Night,' he squelched away holding his streaming umbrella aloft, to be quickly gobbled up by the gloom.

It was only at bedtime, after I'd dried the sodden carpet by the door, that we discovered that water had seeped in through the rear window. It was still raining making it impossible to apply sealant on the outside. Jeff packed around the inside of the frame, as best he could, while I mopped up with towels, then used the hairdryer to dry the wet patch on the bedcovers. It had been quite a day!

Chapter Fourteen

Jeff mooching in the kitchen wakened me at 7am. The drumming rain boring holes in my skull, 'the only thing we can do today is sleep,' I thought, miserably. 'Instead we're up at *7am*!' Marooned on our mud-covered rock ledge, we made breakfast last for hours, while listening to the radio news and weather forecast. A great storm was lashing coasts from the south northwards. As a consequence, New England was experiencing 'one of the fiercest rainstorms of the *century*.' A warning that winds were gathering strength was followed by a Flood Alert; rivers in several states 'were rising alarmingly.' Mercifully there was no loss of life. Details of extensive damage were given – though we were affronted at not being mentioned! – homes evacuated, lightning strikes, bridges washed away, floating cars. 'Seven inches of rain fell, Saturday,' the announcer said, 'and a further three inches are expected today.'

'Thanks pal,' I said, looking at Jeff, expecting agreement; none was forthcoming. With the urgency of a man setting out on an important mission, puffing a bit from the exertion of struggling into his waterproofs, he declared, 'I'm going out to look at the broken roadway. I'll get some photographs,' he added, gathering up his camera bag.

'Great!' I replied. 'And I'll see to all that stuff waiting from yesterday to be washed,' I added, sarcastically. That fell on deaf ears. He'd already departed. The rain growing heavier gave me an excuse to postpone the excursion to the laundry until later in the day, by which time the muddy clothes were augmented by a heap of bedding that had got wet when Jeff opened the rear door to put away tools he'd used. It was one of the few occasions during our long years of travel that I missed church on a Sunday and it was the first time, ever, that bad weather was the culprit.

Throughout the US and Canada we'd had jibes about the rainy British Isles, but at no time previously *anywhere* had we experienced a non-stop deluge lasting *forty-nine* hours! Considering that 'an inch of rain an hour' doused southern Maine on Saturday evening, Harvi stood up well to the onslaught – with the only ingress of water being that leak in the rear window. Of the ten million uninhabited acres in Maine, plus all the beautiful scenery visited by tourists, all we saw was the *inside* of our motorhome. I ran out of books and took to reading the labels on packets and jars – some of which, complying with Canadian laws, gave extra material, being written in *French* and English. I got to know every rivet, mark and scratch on the RV's interior. Not since invigilating examinations – and they were only of two-to-three hours duration – have I suffered such boredom.

Heavy road-building equipment moved on to the campground early in the week. As the forecast warned of unsettled conditions with heavy showers continuing for some time, there was no point in staying. Three days later, we made our getaway. Whatever delights of scenery, or history, that Maine had to offer would have to wait for another visit. Maybe!

We took off for New Hampshire. It wasn't raining – yet – but would be before long, the sunny spells being shorter than the cloudy ones. The road climbed gradually all the time towards wooded mountains. Saying that there are quite a few trees in New Hampshire is a bit like saying there are a few pebbles on a 10-mile stony beach. Big signs warned: 'Brake for Moose – It Could Save a Life', and they didn't just mean that of the moose. The unprecedented rain had caused extensive flooding, when rivers burst their banks in this state of many rivers.

Arriving at our chosen campground in the afternoon, we drove through the entrance before noting with alarm the crudely constructed sign – 'CLOSED'. Parking at the gate, looking around us it didn't take long to know why it was closed. There just wasn't any campground! What had been until recently an extensive park of individual pitches divided by hedges for privacy, with landscaping, trees, a children's play area and a meandering river along the far boundary, was now a scene of total destruction, deep pools of water everywhere. At the top of a flight of debris and mud-strewn steps, the office door was ajar. We went in. Two women and a man, all wearing boots, were endeavouring to restore order to soggy surroundings.

'Hi, how are you today?' the man asked, cheerily. Did he really care how *we* were in the circumstances?

We commiserated with them. While we had been entombed in Harvi with just a slight leak in one window, their entire campground had been inundated when the meandering river swelled to a roaring torrent.

'All happened very quickly. Luckily we got everyone off site,' one of the women said.

'Including the ones in the cabins,' the man intervened, 'before the water rushed in. Then, as we watched, stunned, all was swept away. Everything. Trees. Bushes. Hedges. The cabins. The kids area. . .'

'All the picnic tables, too,' the other woman cut in.

'Not only the dozen dinghies that were tied up, but the *dock* as well!' the man's voice rose in disbelief.

'You wouldn't believe the force of the water. The speed it all happened. . .'

All three of them were talking at once, as they remembered.

'Swooshed away! Smashed to bits as they bounced along.'

'Then we'd to make a run for it ourselves.'

'That's for sure!'

'Had to get out real smart!'

'Took several days for the water to go down,' the man continued.

'Just come back here today. There's nothing to salvage,' one of the women added, shaking her head disconsolately, while dumping a bundle of water-soaked leaflets into a giant, black, plastic bag already bulging with destroyed brochures.

'Was the water in *here*?' I asked in surprise, remembering that we had come up a flight of steps to the office.

'Yeah, you bet,' the man answered, crossing to a wall to indicate the dirty water mark.

'If the water was over two feet in here, how deep was it on the campground?' Jeff exclaimed.

179

They were amused at our consternation.

'Deep!'

'We're just glad we got everyone away safely.'

'Worst rain I've seen in my 35 years.'

'Scary!'

Theirs wasn't the only campground to be flooded. We found one after much searching, which not being near a river, had been only partly submerged. All the RVs were parked cheek by jowl, higgledy-piggledy, around the perimeter of the park, looking out at the expanse of water – now being enjoyed by ducks! – which had swamped their previous camping area. Good-naturedly, space was made for us to squeeze in. Once, returning in Harvi, during a thunder shower, a magnificent rainbow arching over the campground was reflected in the 'lake'. A magical moment, some compensation for the continuing unsettled weather.

A state of emergency was declared for New Hampshire. Throughout the entire Mount Washington Valley, not just campgrounds, but golf courses and farmland had been swamped by the monsoon weather. The local newspapers were replete with accounts of rescues. The most bizarre described how one minute a man and a woman were kayaking down a river, the next, they were swept thirty feet sideways into a wood, as the river became a sea, where the woman was deposited high in a tree still in her kayak, while the man, being tipped out of his, was left hanging on for dear life to a bending branch within feet of the white-capped water. The survival of farm crops, strawberries and vegetables was dependent on how soon the waters subsided.

We attempted various 'walks' as the scenic countryside was delightful – when it could be seen through rain or mist. Then, determined to experience the novelty of staying dry, one day – and that one day was enough! – we spent hours at the Factory Outlet stores, with their lure of no sales tax, on numerous plazas, stretching for three miles along the highway. During a brief sunny spell, eating at a table outside Dunkin Donuts, we watched in amazement a girl balancing a tray on her left hand, bearing three cups of coffee, as she cycled nonchalantly along the busy road with motor bikes and cars whizzing past her. 'Maybe she's practising a circus act,' Jeff quipped.

On a day of cloudy sun, with no rain forecast, bidding goodbye to our campsite neighbours, we set out to explore the White

Mountains, beginning on the 32-mile long Kancamagus Highway. There are no private homes, service stations or buildings, just surroundings of unspoilt landscape with rivers, rocky gorges, forests, and wooded mountain slopes; the Kancamagus is the only designated National Scenic Byway in all of New England, yet it was surprisingly devoid of sightseers. Maybe others didn't trust the weather forecast as we did! We took our time, lingering at each viewpoint and overlook, then on to Lincoln, the ski resort of Loon Mountain. I bought a pair of shoes, before finding a good place to have a substantial lunch.

During the afternoon, stopping at a large parking area near the famous Franconia Notch, the best known high pass in New England, we joined a cheery, chattering throng in shorts and T-shirts, revelling in the unexpected warm sunshine, while enjoying snacks, or ice cream, with many taking photographs of the Great Stone Face, or Profile, or the Old Man of the Mountains – seemingly he had many names. Measuring forty feet from forehead to chin, weathering of five ledges of granite had sculpted the silhouette of a man's face.

'I think he looks like. . .'

'No! I think he looks like. . .'

'No he doesn't! *I* think he looks like. . .'

Now it no longer matters whom he resembled. He's gone! Four years after this jolly afternoon, on holiday in Canada, perusing a newspaper at the poolside at our kids' home, hundreds of miles from Franconia, I read that this 'face' was no more. Quite suddenly it had crumbled and fallen off! I, too, have photographs, if anyone has an opinion about who he *was*.

We pressed on to Twin Mountain, where we got a spot on a lovely campground deep in woodland encircled by mountains. And there was no overnight rain. A day and a night without rain. . .

Next morning we continued on through the White Mountain National Forest. We passed Bretton Woods, not much more than a famous hotel and a ski lift. The Mount Washington Hotel with its enormous, odd-looking, *red* roof was where, in 1944, the International Monetary Fund and the World Bank were set up. On past Crawford Notch, another well-known mountain pass, through Bartlett to Glen (where, some days previously, we attempted a 'walk' in poor weather) back to the beginning of our big loop along the Kancamagus and on through wonderful scenic country. In picture-perfect Jackson with its clapboard buildings, we parked briefly to have a look around and to photograph a particularly lovely covered bridge. Covered bridges, often painted red, are now recognised as historic landmarks and reputedly there are about sixty in New Hampshire.

The Presidential Range (nine peaks named for nine presidents) is the most famous part of the White Mountains, with Mount Washington, at 6,288 feet, being the tallest mountain in New England. Lots of energetic folk climb to the top. We passed Tuckermann Ravine Trail one of the most popular paths. Jeff was tempted. Being an avid walker, accompanied by my brother-in-law, back home, though none of their treks was totally uphill, I'm sure he would have succeeded. He agreed not to try it alone, because I certainly wasn't going to puff my way anywhere! Rumour had it that on the eastern face of the mountain a long toll road went to the top with the opportunity of a tour by van taking the strain. That would suit me fine.

Stage rides to the top date back to the opening of the road, built by Irishmen, in 1861. The winding, more than 8-mile, road is called America's first man-made attraction. In the early days it was an all-day event when a 12-passenger wagon was drawn by a 6-horse team. Fifty years later horses were replaced by mechanical horse-power. The guided van-tour that we joined, still calling itself a stage service, one of a modern fleet of large vans, took one and a half hours. The family who ran the stage in 1861 was deeded the rights to the summit and today their descendants alone run trips. Keeping it in the family?

It must be a surprise to those who labour up on foot to find that on getting there it doesn't feel like being on top of a mountain. There is a terraced car park – of all things – several buildings, radio and TV transmitters, an observatory, and a museum. Everywhere crowded. But at least those trudging up under their own steam can stay as long as they wish, while for us it was a case of choosing how best to spend the brief half-hour we were allowed. On the reverse of our ticket it stated, 'This ticket guarantees you a ride down only on the stage you ride up on. If you choose to stay on the summit longer than the period of time announced by your stage driver, you do so at your own risk.' So there!

Well, I didn't feel like walking a winding eight and a half-miles downhill. . . Luckily it was fairly clear, not misty, with good views. Our driver had told us, 'Today's a good day. Sixty per cent of the time the top's in cloud. In winter it's buried under twenty feet of snow.' One year they had an amazing forty-seven feet. And boy is it windy! Even on a 'good day'. It is reputed to have the worst weather in all fifty states with winds up to 150 miles per hour, the record being 231 miles. Because of the severe weather, the timberline is at 4,000 feet, whereas in The Rockies it is about 10,000 feet. Deaths on the mountain can number a dozen a year. In the Information Center, the first name on the list, begun in 1849, of people who had died, was that of a man from Bridlington, Yorkshire. Storms in the treacherous seas off *that* coastline have claimed countless lives there.

'Bet he thought he was safe up a *mountain*,' Jeff said. 'Just goes to show. . .'

The coal-fired steam train, the Mount Washington cog railway train, grinding along at about four miles per hour, climbs the western flank of the mountain. Belching clouds of black smoke, it noisily came into view, then slowly chugged to a halt, disgorging more people. Built in 1869, the world's *first* mountain-climbing railway has to contend with gradients of up to thirty-seven per cent.

Back on board Harvi we drove on to Gorham, where we stopped to have a meal, though we resisted the invitation to book places on the advertised dawn, or dusk, guided, two-hour, explanatory moose tours. Despite the frequent information boards throughout the state warning about the dangers of running into one of these great beasts, we hadn't seen any in the forests, and we weren't going to go hunting now – it had been a long day; clouds were gathering: we needed to press on to find a campground.

Dusk falling, in Lancaster, we found one at the rear of a gas service station on a river in the last few yards of New Hampshire. The other bank of the River Connecticut is in Vermont. We set up speedily, jittery at being beside a river, as it was obvious that flooding had only recently receded. Returning to the entrance to contact Canada from the phone on the outside wall of the shop, it took longer than usual to get through. 'Hello. . .' 'Hello. . .' was drowned by several motor bikes vrumm vrumming on to the forecourt and none of us could hear a darn thing! The sky emptied itself once more. Jeff, declining to take his umbrella saying, 'I'll be OK; it's not going to rain,' squeezed under mine. We got soaked. Again!

Leaving early, mist rising off the river, we crossed the bridge into Vermont, our sixth New England state and the last one in the US for this trip. The winding, up and down road carried us through soft, rolling hills and fertile valleys in this, the most rural of New England states. We'd exchanged the White Mountains, named for the white bark of birch and poplar trees growing on their slopes, for the Green Mountains, which are, well, green, because dense forest covers them, as it does much of Vermont. The traditional image of old-fashioned America, of small dairy farms with red barns and villages with a covered bridge and a white church amid a group of clapboard homes, each with a great woodpile stretching along the side in readiness for a withering winter, now offering garden produce and maple syrup for sale, here was a reality, and all bathed in warm sunshine – quite charming. Warning/Beware signs for Moose alternated with those for Cattle, depending on the terrain. There were others, too: 'The Farmer's Daughter, Gifts' over a barn/shop; an alliterative sign said 'Area Agent on Aging Office'.

We stopped in Montpelier, Vermont's state capital, the smallest capital in the nation – the name indicating the influence of nearby Quebec and French Canada – for a look around the city with its golden domed capital building in leafy gardens. We had lunch in a pleasant cafe. Afterwards we hit the interstate: I-89. Everywhere green, green, green, with range upon range of hills, their summits lost in misty murkiness. It became sultry; the kind of day you'd like to take a shower every half-hour. The only rest area warned: 'No Facilities'. We parked, briefly, as the RV would overheat without the air-con on, to have a cold drink. It was possibly the first occasion since leaving New York City, weeks before, that we complained about heat!

Both the founder of the Mormons, Joseph Smith, 1805-1844, and Bringham Young, his successor, 1801-1877, were born in Vermont. It was a time much later than theirs, which came to mind, when we passed a direction sign off the interstate for Route 100, indicating Stowe, a venerable ski centre, further north.

'I think the Von Trapp Family lived in Stowe,' I volunteered, brightly.

'Who the heck are *they*?' Jeff asked, his voice rising. 'Do we know them?'

'Well, we don't actually *know* them. . . they're all dead now, anyway,' I answered, sheepishly.

'Well who *were* they then?' Jeff retorted, irritated.

I wished that I hadn't blurted anything, but thought that I'd better explain, or he'd get more annoyed. 'It's the family that the *Sound Of Music* was based on.'

There was a long pause, then, 'Oooh Nooo! Not that Julie Andrews' film that's been on TV every Christmas since the Talkies were invented?'

Ignoring his sarcasm; 'Yes, Julie Andrews played Maria, and she only died in Stowe in 1987,' I replied, warming to the topic – briefly! – before Jeff cut in.

'Not all those nuns, and that damned song, "The Hills are *Alive* to the Sound of Music" for heaven's sake?'

'Yes,' I said. And shut up.

Finding the campground in Shelburne easily, we registered for two nights on a good site, our pitch opposite the gate to the swimming pool, which I readily tried out. It made a change to be wet, other than from rain. Later, in the laundry – always a good place to get into conversation with fellow-campers – I chatted with a family from Minnesota, returning from visiting New Brunswick and Quebec. Though enjoying Canada, but not finding the Quebecois friendly, or helpful, they seemed glad to be back south of the international border. I told them that we'd been in Minnesota, and explained about our travels in the US. 'Vermont is our 44th state.'

'You're from *England* and you have been in forty-four states in *my* country!' Judy exclaimed. 'I don't think I've ever met any *American* who has been in *forty-four* states,' she went on excitedly.

While we transferred our laundry from washers to dryers, we continued our chat. Lots of questions from Judy began, 'Have you seen. . ?' or 'Have you been to. . ?' Most of my answers were in the affirmative.

'Gee what do you know! Wouldn't I love to see all that. Wouldn't I just? Enough to make me *wish* to be older, to be retired,' she laughed. 'We'll buy a motorhome. . .'

'I'll come too,' her young daughter, Cindy, chipped in.

'You'll be over twenty. You won't want to come with your

Mom and Dad.'

'Oh yes I will!' she replied, emphatically. A born traveller, I thought, mentally acknowledging how compelling the urge is to see what's around the next corner, or on the other side of that hill, and if the only way to do it is to hitch a ride with Mom and Dad so be it. Good for her!

The 100-acre Shelburne Museum has an outstanding collection of American Art housed in more than thirty buildings, moved here from locations all over New England. Despite our mode of travel, we could hardly have seen each of them in their previous places. It was a great idea to put them all together in one area. Among the many things I learned was the fact that, for fourteen years towards the end of the 18th century, Vermont was a republic with its own coins and stamps.

Two years later, thousands of miles from here – on the other side of the continent! – we met a couple, celebrating a special wedding anniversary, who were from Shelburne. To their utter astonishment, we discussed with them the wonders of their museum. 'Can you believe that. . ? Amazing!'

Vermont is the only one of the New England states without a coastline, but it does have Lake Champlain, 120 miles long and varying in width from a mere 400 yards to twelve miles, named for the explorer Samuel de Champlain, its recorded history dating from 1609. We visited Burlington, situated at one of the fattest parts of the lake, a university city and a centre for water sports. It was a perfect summer's day. A day to be treasured by the locals, too, I would think, because in some years it has been known for their winter to be nine months long.

'Wonder what that funny-looking building is?' I said. Set in the centre of a great, green lawn it was like a barn, with a high pointed roof. We walked across. It was the Catholic cathedral. On the inside, too, it was unusual – makeshift, almost.

'Looks like a temporary building,' Jeff suggested. 'Strange.'

The air-conditioning was going full belt in the restaurant at lunchtime. It was cool to the point of being shivery. 'The first decent weather we've had in weeks,' I complained, 'and now we're going to catch pneumonia.' Regardless of the time of year, the one thing you can be certain of in the US and Canada is the indoor temperature will be the complete opposite of that outside. The colder it is outdoors the higher the heat inside – stuffy, airless heat – and a pleasantly warm day comfortable in T-shirt and shorts, leaves you with teeth chattering, wishing you could cover up exposed flesh, once you move inside. Crazy!

Apart from the weather, which had been more unpredictable than anything we had ever known in the British Isles – honestly! – New England had been interesting. But it was time to move on again. Time to bid farewell to the US for this year. A gentle rain was falling, when we left the campground at 8am to travel north along Lake Champlain, through sparsely populated countryside. Later, the drizzle eased allowing us to detour to Saint Anne's Fort, in a picturesque setting alongside the waters of the lake. There, we discovered the reason for the strange cathedral in Burlington. Arson caused a fire which destroyed the cathedral in 1972. The 14-foot, one and a half ton statue of the Madonna, standing on the tower of the cathedral from 1904 until 1972, then languishing in a warehouse for nineteen years, had been restored with gold leaf applied to vulcanised copper. It stood now in this ancient, beautiful place.

Raining again, we crossed into Canada heading for Montreal, the surroundings as sodden as they had been in New England, but in places looking most odd as great swathes of countryside were bare, yet right next to them were areas flourishing lushly. There were many big trees, which appeared to have been split down the centre – nothing at all on one side of the trunk, but fully branched with leaves on the other, or denuded places in otherwise dense forests. This extensive destruction had been caused during *one* night the previous winter when, instead of their usual snowfall, there was heavy rain which turned to ice as it fell. The weight of the 'solid rain' split trees in two, or worse: caused them to fall destroying everything in their path. Pylons and power lines were brought down plunging half the city of Montreal together with much of the provinces of Quebec and Ontario, and places in the US, into darkness. *Millions* were without electricity; some for a couple of weeks! Imagine? We recalled seeing it on TV in England, and having experienced, long ago, the unimaginable depth of cold of a Canadian winter, we had shuddered in sympathy.

The campground we had pre-booked was in the process of being rebuilt. The ice storm felling many trees, ripped up the road and demolished the amenities block and the warden's bungalow,

187

fortunately vacant during the winter.

Intermittent rain continued over the following days, curtailing our sightseeing; however, visiting during a bright spell, enabled us to admire the glories of Notre Dame cathedral with its wonderful stained glass. I had visited Montreal a few years before with my daughter. Much to the hilarity of family and friends, I stayed with her at a youth hostel. No! I wasn't the oldest guest. There was an Australian woman, travelling around the world *alone*, who was older – OK! – only a bit, just a few months. . .

'I stay at youth hostels in preference to hotels,' she explained. 'It's much safer for a woman on her own.'

I expressed surprise.

'Oh yes! I assure you it is.' Her voice did that Australian upward sweep, which makes all of them sound youthfully lively, regardless of their age. 'I travel light, just with a back-pack. Don't carry much cash. Often join up with others. It's such great fun,' she went on, her voice doing that endearing sweep again. Almost (but not quite!) making me envious.

Jeff had never been in Montreal before and in the drenching conditions he proclaimed loudly that he didn't wish to be there now. Anyway, we'd been on tour long enough and were eager to see all our gang, still 400 miles away. With better weather than previously, we'd a couple of pleasant stop-overs. On our last one we winterised the RV, which we always did with mixed feelings – the end of explorations with Harvi for this year, but it would be good to have a couple of weeks by the pool enjoying the Canadian tribe – who informed us that *their* weather had not been wet like ours! – and then to England to catch up on life with our families there.

We had visited New York City and Boston, 'left over' from last year and – despite the rainfall! – greatly enjoyed touring all six New England states.

After a spruce-up wash and polish, we delivered Harvi to storage – all ready for the following year! Where would we go. . . ?

Chapter Fifteen

After four and a half days, driving almost 2,000 miles, and four nights spent in motels, since waving, 'Cheerio. See you later,' to the kids in Canada, we were set up on a campground in San Antonio, Texas, eager to begin this year's exploration in earnest. It was the first week in April. No way did we wish to be in Texas ever again in the heat! Anyway, we were here, at this time, to see their renowned spring flowers.

In four days we'd come from snow making mysterious white shapes of everything outdoors, Ontario not yet released from winter, crossing the international border at Niagara Falls, boulders of ice, reluctant to thaw, bouncing about in the torrent, soon afterwards, battling bitter winds in Ohio, where, later, a Tornado flattened 200 houses in Cincinnati, killing four people, to Kentucky, the temperature warming: coaxing trees to leaf and greening the countryside. Pyrotechnics by way of an electric storm lit up North Little Rock, our second time there. Reaching Hearne in Texas, our last night 'on the road', springtime was exuberant everywhere. This is an aspect of travelling long distances overland that greatly appeals to us: experiencing changing topography and climate. For *me* having a map in my head is often more easily understood than one on a page, as anyone will testify who has overheard the exchange of 'endearments' between us when *I* am navigating.

Travelling in Europe, we've often covered sections of the same roads several times. Now, much of our route to Texas was familiar from an earlier trip; however, Kentucky, one of the four original commonwealth states, was a *new* one for us. Deciding on this year's route, during the winter back home, I'd suggested that three states not yet visited could be included.

'How many have we seen so far?' Jeff inquired.

'Forty-four, can you believe?'

'Gee, have we? How did that happen?'

'Might as well add another three. . .'

'Yeah, it's no problem including them at the planning stage.'

Kentucky was as I'd always imagined: an extensive lush region of gently rolling fields as emerald as Ireland's, wooded hills, farms, white paling-fences, magnificent thoroughbred horses, Baptist churches with little steeples and slogans: 'Jesus Saves', 'Praise the Lord', 'Jesus is King'. Passing through Glencoe, Warsaw and Sparta in quick succession, far-flung places in Europe, I fell to day-dreaming, as I frequently do when I'm not driving, about the folk who had settled areas and named towns – were they homesick for their birthplaces, or endeavouring to recreate the familiar? Louisville was named for a *king*: King Louis XVI of France, no less a person than Thomas Jefferson having signed the city's charter in 1780. (By the time he became the 3rd President of the United States, poor King Louis had been beheaded.) Nowadays Louisville is famous as the home of the Kentucky Derby.

'It takes place next month,' Jeff said, 'the country's most important horse race. Can't imagine, though, that the entire continent closes down to watch gee-gees, as Australia does each November for the Melbourne Cup!' he laughed.

Jeff's not interested in horse-racing, but is partial to a drop of Jim Beam, the prolific ads reminding us that the bourbon whisky is produced in the area. Driving south, there were signs for The Blue Grass Parkway, My Old Kentucky Home State Park, Jesse James Riding Stables, with a huge mural of three race horses on the side of a building, to historical matters: a sign for the birthplace of President Abraham Lincoln. Gaining an hour on changing to Central Time and not having to set up Harvi on a campground, allowed more time for driving. Carrying on to near Portland, we got a room in a motel, but not much to eat at 6.30pm in the only cafe within walking distance and we'd had enough driving for that day. It was still three hours till closing time, yet much that was listed *on* the menu was, 'Off'.

'I'll never again turn my nose up at a fast-food joint,' Jeff groused, struggling to quell his rumbling stomach. 'We're in Kentucky for Pete's sake. The least I'd expect is a Kentucky Fried Chicken place.'

'There'll be one in town – you don't want to go there.'

'Is there anything in the RV?'

'Nothing that would be hot,' I replied swiftly, visions of him in the *dark*, on the motel *car park*, banging around noisily, fiddling with the propane to light the cooker – and that would be just the start. . . In truth, there wasn't any food for a cooked meal in the fridge, as we'd delayed stocking up until we were set up on a campground. He survived, though not silently.

Next day into Tennessee, it was 76°F and humid, when mid-morning we took a break in Nashville, capital of Tennessee and home of country music. Reminders about the latter were everywhere and the slogan 'Honor Thy Music' – an addition to the Decalogue? Music Row is the centre of several country music attractions, including the recording industry. On Music Square East, we visited the Country Music Hall of Fame and Museum. 'You will see more than 3,000 items related to country music' the brochure promised. No time for all that, instead we followed a directional arrow to 'See Hank Williams 1948 Packard, our newest exhibit'. Jeff and I laughed aloud. It was the exact age, also made by Chrysler, as the Dodge we'd traversed Canada in, all those years before. . .

'Why didn't we donate our car to a museum?' Jeff joked. 'We'd made that epic journey across Canada in it.'

'Our car was *never* shiny like this one!' I retorted. 'It was almost *ten years old* when we bought it. . .'

After nights in motels with heat blasting, we now slept comfortably in the RV, windows open savouring gentle breezes. Literally *tons* of wildflower seeds are sown yearly in Texas. They were rioting everywhere. Fields repainted deep blue by bluebonnets, the state flower, at their best in April; others turned golden; others fiery red; miles of roadsides planted to mimic nature in multi shades of mixed flowers and grasses; the open land adjoining the campground had drifts of prickly poppies, their greyish-green foliage a foil for their frilled petals, snow-white and fragile as tissue paper, a drop of pure gold in the centre of

191

each bloom. There were gardens, great ornamental urns, hanging baskets all awash with vibrant colour. Away from habitation, nature too put on a grand show, unaided. It's claimed that there're more than 5,000 species of flowering plants *native* to Texas. We saw them all!

A long, hot Sunday in San Antonio proved to be great fun. Not that the Alamo (the name means cottonwood), our first stop, is regarded by *anyone* as a place for levity, we quickly learned, being a repository of Texan history's Spanish/Mexican colonial past and a monument to the heroism of the 189 men who died there in 1836, during the 13-day siege. Bristling with guns the building is festooned with paraphernalia belonging to these people. A wall-mounted wooden board lists the name and nationality of each, including James Bowie, William Travis and that hero of song and legend, Davy Crockett.

The crowd milling about outdoors was augmented by those spilling from a service inside the building honouring the Scots who had perished in the siege. There were scores of men sporting Scottish regalia, blithely unappreciative that Texan temperatures are kinder than Scotland's to kilt-wearers, because not one, that we spoke to, had ever visited Scotland. Looking as if kitted out in fancy dress, a lone figure, attired in green white and orange with a striped hat to match, striding stiffly, wide-legged trousers flapping about his legs, so thin and long he could have been on stilts, proudly announced from way above us, that he was the President of the Irish Society.

'Should've been here last month,' he drawled, his hat wobbling precariously. 'Every St. Patrick's Day is *real* big here. No, I've never been to Ireland,' he answered. A pity, I thought; if he had he'd know how daft his costume looked.

'Of course, I'm Irish,' he spluttered, peevishly. 'Don't have to be *born* there. My folks came from those parts way back.' Not as long ago as the Irish who died at the Alamo, I bet; now *that* would have been something to talk about.

You soon realise the significance of this place for Texans. 'We love the Alamo – we love Texas' was emblazoned everywhere. (Another prevalent, threatening-sounding slogan 'Don't Mess with Texas' is only their way of requesting us not to litter.)

All other states complain that Texas is too boastful. In reality, I think that The Lone Star State has plenty to brag about! Apart from Alaska, it is the USA's biggest – 800 miles from east to west, more than that from north to south, with great diversity of landforms: mountains, lush plains, dense forest, a sea coast, and baking desert. Ample natural resources, especially oil, cotton and timber, provide wealth as do tourism and oil refineries. Apart from their 5,000 plant species, three quarters of all American birds are represented here, and three of the ten largest US cities. Texas has it all. (And, shamefully, the death penalty, too.) Anyway, not courting public opinion, they don't give a damn what others say about them. Texan children pay allegiance to the *Texan* flag and the American flag everyday in school.

Midway in this state The West begins in earnest. Cowboy gear: ten-gallon hats (Stetsons), checked shirts, jeans were worn by both sexes. At lunch, amid a throng of big-shouldered, noisy Texans, we wrestled with mammoth-size steaks plus all the trimmings, in an establishment that quite obviously eschewed fancy decoration or pernickety refinement. Afterwards, in an attempt to walk off our over-indulgence, we waddled down a stairway to the River Walk, Paseo del Rio, several miles of stone pathway on both sides of the San Antonio River. Regardless of the local pride in the city's number one tourist attraction, it's no competition for Venice, that's for sure, not a single mock-palace in the conglomeration of hotels, restaurants and bars. Nor, by any stretch of the imagination, can the magenta-coloured, small barges, crammed with people, diligently following every gesticulation of the guide, be considered romantic.

'What can that guy be talking about?' I asked Jeff, 'the one pointing this way.' While watching the boats plying the San Antonio River (Spanish, I know, but it's also *Italian*) we were sipping coffee on the balcony outside Starbucks, where else?

As the temperature soared (an earlier phone call to Ontario informed that it was snowing!) so did the racket from a Mariachi band. Dressed in white suits, all amply proportioned, one, without doubt, was the fattest person we'd ever set eyes on. At least, while performing, we were spared the sight of them wearing their sombreros. One type of Mariachi band plays mainly string instruments, including many guitars; the main instrument in the other type is the trumpet. Too bad for us we had the second kind! Not understanding any of the lyrics bellowed above the din, becoming deranged by the decibels, we were convinced that all

j

Mexican songs sound the same.

After the exhilaration of San Antonio, intent on a few days relaxation, we drove south to a campground near Corpus Christi, on the Gulf, for our only view of the sea this year. Alas! The weather curtailed our visit. Parking alongside the ocean gave us a grandstand view of flocks of ravenous pelicans plunging into the water, rising in an instant, their wings iridescent, the lucky ones with dinner in their beaks, others trying again and again without success, and a great grey heron, scorning such frantic activity, standing motionless, biding his time. We returned after a long beach walk exhausted from being knocked about by the stiff breeze which had sprung up from nowhere. Jeff, who assiduously avoids being outdoors in such conditions, said that he didn't feel well.

'Think it's goin' to blow *real* bad,' the pretty, young woman from reception came over to warn us. Harvi was shuddering and shaking. 'You best move. You'll get covered in driven sand. Go over there. Squeeze in between those two big ones. They'll give you a bit of shelter.'

The wind whooshed around all night gusting up to seventy miles an hour. Each blast sent Harvi into a rocking frenzy and only for the protection of our hefty neighbours, we would have been whipped over, or sucked out to sea. Scary!

After a sleepless night, we exchanged ocean for desert, driving west from Corpus Christi, then north along a two lane highway with sparse traffic, close to the border with Mexico. For much of the time, away to the far horizon, there was nothing except scrub and stunted trees intermingled with cacti. Thinking of my dinky pots with three-inch prickly plants on windowsills back home, the variety of flowers and *size* of these cacti in the wild amazed me. A large placemat printed with named pictures of desert plants, bought in San Antonio, together with a book on desert flora, helped me to identify the great splashes of golden poppy and the clumps of yellow brittle brush among the familiar cream spiked soap tree yuccas and red-flowered prickly pear, the oldest of all known cacti. Another prevalent one, a close relative of prickly pear, is called: teddy bear cholla. The paradoxical name a joke surely? The thick, fleshy, brown stems look furry, but like every other cactus they're covered in barbs – some cuddly teddy bear!

Overwhelmed by a nauseating stench, in trying not to breathe we began to cough and choke, making us gasp for breath all the more. 'Whew! *That* smells like skunk,' Jeff stuttered, quickly shutting off the incoming air. Too late! The combined stink of a gross of rotten eggs, boiled cabbage, ripe manure, plus all odours offensive to the olfactory nerve permeated the RV.

'Didn't know skunks live in the desert,' I said, grabbing my nose. 'It'll take ages to clear.' And it did!

'If ever a stink stank, that skunk stunk,' Jeff trilled, when it was safe to breathe.

'Is that original?' I asked, surprised by his facility with language.

A sign at a filling station, 'Next Service 60 Miles', was a reminder to top up with fuel, but Jeff always started off each day with both tanks full; however, we pulled in briefly to clean the windshield, thickly encrusted with desiccated insects. Further on, a Picnic Area was nothing more than a table under a small shelter, without space to get off the single lane road. We had to drive on to park, for a quick lunch on board Harvi, by the gateway to a lone house. From a window, a woman gave a cheery wave.

'I read somewhere that Texas is derived from an Indian word meaning friendship,' I said. 'Where else would you be welcome to park in a private gateway?'

'Don't suppose she's ever had anyone park here before.'

'Certainly not a motorhome with *Canadian* number plates. We're right near *Mexico* here, as far from Canada as is possible in the US.'

On the outskirts of Laredo we were stopped by a couple of Border Patrol Officers with dogs, checking if we had any 'illegals' on board. 'Illegals' is what they call the half million Mexicans who cross to the US each year without permits or proper documents. One burly man climbed aboard the RV, opening cupboard and bathroom doors while quizzing us; the other kept both dogs on a short lead. 'That's OK folks,' they said pleasantly. Driving on, we kept an eye out for a Dodge service as the fridge wasn't working efficiently on propane, only when plugged in to electricity. When we located one, they were unable to help.

Joined to Nuevo Laredo, Mexico, by two bridges across the Rio Grande, Laredo, since being founded in 1755, has been under seven flags, even, at one time, being the capital of a separate republic. We didn't attempt to cross the border – far too much hassle and time consuming on a baking, blue-skied day. Disappointed by no available parking, we had to be content with a quick circuit of the town by RV, which at least had the advantage of giving us a view from high up. Congested, the many one-way streets were very narrow, their names mostly beginning with San. Nowadays, largely an immigrant town, retaining much of its Spanish colonial atmosphere, though somewhat decayed, it was a tonic for the spirit in contrast to the characterless uniformity of so many places. We saw the approach to one of the toll bridges, crossed a viaduct over a long, hooting train, marvelled at the abundance of exotic flowers and shrubs, passed a great white cathedral, and most importantly: avoided colliding with anything.

On an exit road from the town back to the highway, patrols were stopping all vehicles before allowing them, after examination, to proceed.

'Canadian?'

'Irish.'

'Oh!' both of our pair said, in surprise. One young man checked our passports and paperwork, then asked a few questions. We could truthfully answer that we hadn't stopped in Laredo. The other taking the dogs on a sniffing turn around the exterior of the RV, I hoped the animals relished the miasma of skunk lingering there.

During our years touring the USA, particularly in the southern states, we were well acquainted with the ongoing problems along the Mexican border with hundreds of immigrants every day intent on entering illegally. There were complaints of theft, or damage done to property. Often we'd heard news items giving tragic accounts of bodies being found in deserted country, or mountainous areas, where Mexicans, attempting to get into the States undetected, died of hunger, thirst, or more commonly, exposure. Unprepared for the length of time it takes to *walk* to populated places to get food or drink, or ill-clad for the often huge difference between daytime and night-time temperature, they die a lonely death. Wetbacks (mojados), describing those who splash across the Rio Grande, are frequently involved in smuggling narcotics. Serious clashes with the authorities are commonplace.

Parched, sweaty, our eyes aching from the desert glare, badly in need of a break, it was a relief soon after 4pm to pull on to a campground offering good amenities, but with only scrappy trees. Aided by the pitch's level concrete base, we set up quickly. With no shade, in a temperature of 94°F, if we wanted any comfort we'd no choice but to put up with the racket of the air-conditioning. This we gladly did, and, despite the noise, even managed a siesta.

The brush covered hills away to the east of us were where the 1959 film *The Alamo* was filmed, the good-looking woman had told us when registering. I'd no wish to go there now, or, for that matter, ever. A stroll around the scrubland adjoining the campground, as sunset neared, was sufficient exercise for me, though it held no attraction at all for Jeff, who was very out-of-sorts.

'I've seen enough desert for today, thanks,' he uttered sharply, his mood an indication that he wasn't well. I hoped that it was only tiredness or heat exhaustion. . . He adamantly refused to drink the copious amount of water needed to cope with these conditions. There was nothing I could do except fret in silence.

A strange creature bounding across my path made me gasp, frightening the daylights out of me. Later, describing its grey body and brown face and ears to Shelly and Greg in the adjacent RV, I learned that it was an antelope jack rabbit.

'I've never seen one before; much larger than I'd expect a rabbit to be,' I explained.

'Comes out in the evening. Only see 'em in *these* deserts,' Greg said. 'Weighs about eight pounds, twenty-five inches, or so, long. Able to outrun a dog, you know.'

'Guess that's why it's called an *antelope* jack rabbit,' Shelly laughed.

The big, big sun fell towards the horizon, and the small trees at the perimeter of the campground transmuted to filmy, black lace against the apricot afterglow as it faded slowly. On one side of us it grew fully dark, yet the light in the west lingered for ages.

Harvi's eastern windows bathed in brilliant light from the newly risen sun woke us. During the hours of darkness we'd slept as if anaesthetised. To my relief, Jeff declared at breakfast that he was quite restored. When camping, in tune with nature's great outdoors, I share his *habitual* delight for the *early* part of a new day that, very definitely not being a 'morning' person, I *never* relish anywhere else.

On a deserted road, soon after setting out, we were startled when suddenly from behind a jumbly jungle of tall prickly pear to our left, three enormous sombreros, dwarfing their occupants, popped up for a split second. Then quickly sank from sight. Curiosity, (or courage?) got the better of them and all three swarthy Mexicans stood up again to peer at us through the cacti. They seemed uncertain what to do. Should they 'hide' again, or walk to the road towards us?

'Poor guys. Must have been *listening* for an engine; obviously didn't expect *us*.'

'Yes, the quizzical expressions implore, "Are *you* the truck we're waiting for?" '

'In that headgear they don't exactly blend into the surroundings.'

'Their hats are big enough to camp out in – maybe they did.'

'We won't stop. No wish to alarm them further.'

'Hope we don't encounter any patrols asking awkward questions.'

Not all landowners object to 'illegals'; many are content to employ cheap labour on their ranches and sort out the documentation when, or if, it is required. Leaving the three colourful characters hovering among the flowering cacti for their 'employer', we hoped that he would be compassionate.

The road was mainly straight mile after mile, but up and down. Each climb being longer than each descent, resulted in too much loss of speed to stay on cruise control, as we headed away from the international border towards the distant, soft-outlined, brown-velvet-draped mountains. Spread across the rolling sandy hills, flowering cacti interspersed with green-barked palo verde, small trees with feathery, greeny-yellow foliage, the showiest of desert flowering trees, which we were seeing at their best in April and early May, and always in the vast azure dome a vulture circled languorously, or swooped suddenly to earth on spotting a meal.

We pitched up much later than usual because of difficulty finding a camping, even one like this with few amenities. After sunset it quickly grew cool.

'No need for air-conditioning or open windows tonight. We'll need extra bedding,' I said, rummaging for all the bedcovers that I'd stashed away weeks before, back in Canada, and hadn't yet needed.

'Yeah, it was gradual ascent, but we've climbed about 2,500

feet during the day. We're in The Picos now, at probably more than 3,000 feet, not surprising it's cold.'

Despite the layers of clothing on *me* and the *bed*, I was miserably shivery all night when the daytime 84°F dropped to below freezing. In the darkness, I thought of the Mexican trio we had seen and the 'illegals' we *hadn't* seen, who, no doubt, during the night, were hopping the border in numerous places, and I wished them all safety.

'El Paso – 238 Miles', read the first signpost we passed soon after 8am, with underneath: '64 Miles to Next Service'. Continuing across the high desert, we stopped in Van Horn for gas. Outdoors, it was decidedly chilly. Shortly we joined the I-10, and gained an hour by crossing into Mountain Time Zone. Heading west across the desert along the southern fringes of the Guadeloupe Mountains, still climbing, after a couple of days on near-deserted roads, the interstate in comparison seemed busy, though it carried only light traffic. The I-10 is the most southerly interstate, running from Jacksonville in Florida to Los Angeles.

'We've driven most of this interstate on previous trips,' I said, looking at the road atlas to check where we were. 'Now we'll do the bit that's left. We did the same on the I-90 – drove right across the north from coast to coast.'

'Not once but *three* times,' Jeff quickly added. 'Much of it prairie not unlike the sameness of desert. *And* great sections of many others. I don't really like driving interstates, but it's a good way to cover distances quickly. Anyway, we've no choice now: there's no other route to El Paso from here.'

Months before, when we had been planning this trip to Texas, I got the notion that, seeing that we were next door to Mexico, I wanted to visit a world-famous religious shrine in Mexico City. We'd seen replicas of the Image that's retained there in various places on all our trips in North America.

'Next door to Mexico, maybe,' my son mimicked, 'but not next door to Mexico *City*.'

'I know that,' I answered, defensively.

'It's about 1,000 miles from the border,' he went on.

'Umm, I know,' I nodded. *Silently* I acknowledged that it was the same distance as that from London to Moscow, with a similar gulf in language and culture.

'Well, if you're daft enough to go, don't even *think* of taking

Harvi over the international border. Vehicle insurance for Mexico is not straightforward and it costs the earth. Much better still, don't go!' He then quoted various mishaps, and worse, that had befallen colleagues of his on different occasions in Mexico City. 'They had to go on business – you don't *have* to go, so *don't*!' He was quite emphatic.

I decided to wait and see – until we reached Texas! We had inquired in San Antonio about flying from there, but even that seemed complicated and costly, with no inclusive short-stay packages. By now I was reconciled to not going. Then I came upon a couple of ads in a guide book for El Paso. One was for a campground, stating that motorhomes could be *stored* there when not in use; another for the AAA, said that visits to Mexico could be arranged through their office. I cheered up. Maybe a visit to Mexico City was a possibility after all? In the event, one ad had a bearing on the other.

It was well past midday when we located the AAA office.

'Mexico City is no more dangerous than any other city,' the good-looking woman behind the desk, Norma, retorted (but she looks Mexican, I thought, so she would say that). 'If you take care, as in other places, you'll be perfectly safe,' she assured us, her bristles subsiding a little.

She gave us two quotations – one travelling by an American airline from Texas (but not El Paso), staying in an American-owned hotel; the other flying with a Mexican airline from Juarez, just over the border from El Paso, and staying in a Mexican hotel of similar 4-star rating, just across the road from the American hotel. There was a considerable difference in price. Our choice of the Mexican one – the cheaper! – visibly pleased Norma. 'You'll like it there,' she smiled broadly, showing perfect teeth. 'Everyone in the hotel will speak English. It's in the Zona Rosa area where all the good hotels and tourist facilities are. There'll be no problems.'

'Before we book, I'll have to check with a campground that they've a vacancy and that we can leave the RV there while we're away,' Jeff explained.

Norma indicated the phone on her desk. The affirmative reply from the campground was encouraging. For some reason, that I've forgotten, there had to be a lapse of at least three full days between booking and travelling. The tickets would be ready for collection three days later. We paid, and decidedly hungry, went in search of food.

I was quite elated.

'Wait 'til you hear what The Canadians say,' Jeff cautioned. In a reversal of roles, they had plenty to 'say' – but the deed was done!

El Paso, short for El Paso del Rio del Norte (the pass through the river of the north), the name given by a conquistador, dates from the end of the 16th century. It was fitting I thought that, before seeing anything of the town, we had first booked a trip to Mexico.

It was late afternoon when we scouted for the campground that we'd arranged to stay on for ten days. We don't usually book ahead, well, not for that length of time, without first knowing something about the place. What if it was awful? It wasn't. It was the end of their high season. Most of the *Snowbirds* had already set out for cooler destinations, not to return till winter, leaving plenty of space. Days on site were peaceful to spend time as we felt inclined, which was mostly doing nothing more strenuous than having a swim, afterwards lying in the shade, while listening to the pong pong of tennis balls being whacked by energetic souls, some of them as old as ourselves. 'They're crazy playing in this heat!' Jeff commented one day, retreating indoors to the air-conditioning.

Every evening we'd a grandstand view of the sun setting fire to the heavens (the conflagration more appropriate, maybe, to the other place), making slim silhouettes of the tall, needle cypresses, surrounding the campground.

The temperature in the RV rose to 100°F, when we parked it on the Cielo Vista Mall for a couple of hours, and boarded a bus from there to downtown to go to the Mexican consulate, where we sorted out visas, and to the AAA to pick up our tickets from Norma. Instead of parting Harvi from his air-conditioning lifeline again, at other times we took transport organised by the campground to see some of the sights in El Paso and neighbouring Ciudad Juarez.

'Hello. I'm Jesse,' the driver-guide said on stepping out of the car, one morning. Tall, heavily built, attired in black: shirt, trousers, long leather jacket (in that heat!), his facial expression obscured by dark, black-rimmed glasses, he looked every inch a movie gangster.

'Just two of you?' he drawled, turning the chewing gum around in his mouth. Disappearing briefly into the office to check, 'Yeah, just the two of you,' he said, bouncing out again. 'Hop in.' He held a rear door open for us.

We were off. So was the spiel. Boy could he talk! (And we'd no one to share him with for the entire day.) Could he boast! There was no forgetting that we were still in Texas and that, although he was an Anglo-Mexican, he was a Texan first. However, despite his youth – a mere twenty-two years – he was knowledgeable about El Paso and Ciudad Juarez, where we went first. Juarez, once a stop on the Santa Fe Trail, is now together with El Paso, the largest binational megalopolis in North America. It is full of small factories and assembly plants (maquiladoras), 'many owned by Americans, the Mexican workers paid as little as fifty cents an hour,' Jesse informed us flatly. As time went on, we wondered what his role was in the scheme of things; driving taxis wouldn't account for his apparent affluence.

We were glad we hadn't ventured across the border by trolley, as we could have done, finding it quite unlike Tijuana, visited from California. At a market, pestered by vendors intent on selling us something – anything! – resulted in us buying *nothing*, it being impossible to look around, or even to think! At the touristy shops, packed mostly with mass-produced, tawdry goods, after some searching, we found well-crafted, individual pieces of jewellery and a Native Indian wall-hanging beautifully painted on tree bark. Every stop gave Jesse, cigarette in hand, time for a sotto voce exchange with each manager. Afterwards, he took us around different districts of the town, 'poor, middle class and rich,' he said, the latter having beautiful homes within landscaped gardens. 'There's no point in taking you to see the area of the "filthy" rich,' Jesse laughed scornfully, 'because all their properties are behind high security fences *with guards at the gates*.' In this place – armed, no doubt.

Pulling up near the cathedral, he introduced us to a man waiting for us there. Angelo, long grey hair in a ponytail, an elderly, dignified Native, took us on a tour of the new cathedral after first showing us around the adjacent Mission church, dating from Spanish times. In excellent English, with a long, bony finger he pointed out details encouraging us to cherish their beauty, or age. The Mission's original ceiling beams and woodwork were similar to ones we'd seen in Mission churches in California and elsewhere. The modern stained glass windows in the new cathedral, 'Look their best at sunset,' he said quietly, 'not at this time of day.' Though obviously not impressed, not only with the windows, his demeanour was respectful because *this* building was currently the active church.

We rejoined Jesse, his long frame leaning against the van, legs outstretched displaying his expensive black shoes, chatting earnestly with another man, both blowing smoke rings. Bidding us a polite goodbye, Angelo, beaming broadly, indicating the old Mission church, said in a reverential whisper, 'That's my favourite!' It was easy to imagine his ancestors worshipping there when it was newly built.

Back across the Rio Grande, there was time for a jaunt up Scenic Drive as far as the adobe buildings of the Fort Bliss museum, near the famous Fort Bliss military base, the large air defence centre. An overlook gave a view of El Paso and Ciudad Juarez, an extensive ugly sprawl of rail tracks, buildings packed tightly with few open spaces, the mountains on the Mexican side defaced by slogans cut into their slopes.

'That's the end of the Rockies,' Jesse pointed to mountains in the US.

The *end* of the Rockies? The *end* of a *mountain range* wasn't something I'd ever deliberated, though mountains have to end somewhere. Here, it looked as if they'd been brought to a halt by the density of construction – quite sad, really.

'We've seen the Rocky Mountains for much of their length,' Jeff enthused, 'from Canada south through the States – in numerous places.'

'Yeah, they begin in Alaska.' (The following year we'd see those, too!) 'But you've seen them in so many places! Well, that mountain chain is *3,200 miles long*,' Jesse declared, obviously impressed by our travels.

We'd hit on something that *we* could boast about.

Our sojourn in Mexico was fascinating. There were no upsets. Well, apart from a visit to a pharmacy that is, when my allergy itch, which I'd had for a couple of weeks, worsened to the point where I could have shed tears of frustration at not being able to soothe my raw skin. And that wasn't really an upset – more an entertainment. . .

'Picazon, erupcion, picar, un sarpullido,' I babbled, the words falling over each other in my haste to remember them from the phrase book, while simultaneously giving a display of scratching vigorously around my middle. (I didn't think he'd appreciate my stripping to show him. If I'd been 40 years younger, maybe. . .)

'How long have you had this itch?' he asked politely, in perfect English. The cream that he prescribed calmed the problem for a while.

It was the first occasion in our long years of travel that Jeff and I remained together *all the time* for the duration of our visit. It was a new experience for me, quite strange: not exploring on my own; I mutely hankered to visit museums, which are anathema to Jeff.

'Remember, the signs in the museums are in Spanish/Mexican only,' Jeff said.

I'm sure I could have interpreted some of them if I went on my own, but I didn't press the point. Norma may have been right in saying it would be no different from any other city, but discretion being the better part of valour, we were taking no chances.

We spent a rewarding day at the shrine of Our Lady of Guadalupe, The Lady of Tepeyac, justifying our effort in coming to Mexico City. In many places throughout North America, not just in the southern US, we had seen replicas of the Image, which dates from December 1531, of the young Nahuatl (Aztec) woman, in a blue-green mantle over a flowered pink dress, that is preserved there. Representing beliefs, both pre-Hispanic: Tanantzin, mother of the Aztec gods, and Catholic: the dark-skinned, black-haired Virgin of Guadalupe, 'The Eternal She', links together a society as varied and heterogeneous as that of Mexico, where, incidentally, discussion of race is a taboo subject. Regarded as a symbol of national unity, copies of the Image can be seen everywhere throughout Mexico. Millions of pilgrims (about 15,000 daily), travelling from even the remotest parts of the country, come to the shrine each year, making it one of the most visited sites in the Christian world.

Opened in October 1976, replacing an older building, the magnificent Basilica with its lofty Canadian pine ceiling, accommodates 20,000 people. Supported by 1,000 subterranean pillars, with none in the interior, there is nothing to obstruct the view of the white Carrera marble altar, over which hangs the Image. Despite the Basilica's proportions, it doesn't look like a sports' arena and regardless of the numbers attending, mostly Mexican, but American and others, too, the place was almost silent, with an air of reverential devotion.

At various times scientists have scrutinised the representation, on coarse cloth, of the 5-foot-tall young woman. It appears to be painted, yet it 'sits' on the surface of the loosely woven fibres, but does not permeate them. Neither the fabric nor the colouring has deteriorated with age. The pattern of stars, on one side of the mantle, is an exact representation of the northern constellation; and on the other side, is of the southern constellation, in the sky over what is now Mexico City, at 10.30am on December 12th, 1531. . .

Using reputable taxis for transport, the other hectic days flew by seeing as much as possible in the city and the surrounding area. In the centre of the Zocala, the world's largest square after Red Square, atop a tall flagpole hung the most enormous national flag we've ever seen.

'From Europe?' a young Mexican man asked us.

'Si.'

'Where?'

'Irlanda,' I heard myself reply. More than forty years since we lived there, true, however, I did have our Irish passports in my waist bag, so I didn't give my usual convoluted explanation of who we are and where we live.

'Ah! Gut country. Gut country,' he replied smiling. 'Hava gut time.'

Roberto, our driver, one day took us to visit The Pyramid of the Sun. 'At the spring equinox, 21st March, the sun aligns with the western face of the pyramid,' he told us. We have visited Newgrange in Ireland, where the sun shines through the entry door at the winter solstice, and Stonehenge which celebrates the summer solstice. How clever were these ancient peoples. Roberto was visibly relieved that we didn't require him to accompany us when we climbed Teotihuacan, The Pyramid of the Sun – all 700 metres. The stone steps are very steep. Only the lower section has a rope handrail, after that it's a scrabble – sometimes on all fours for people like me with short legs (and an achy hip) – to reach the step above, slow progress, but it gave ample time to view the surrounding countryside and, nearby, The Pyramid of the Moon and the ruins of the ancient Aztec city.

Depending on whose version of history you read, the 16th century conquistadors are portrayed on a scale between: being extremely cruel tyrants down to – some of them! – not being such-bad-guys-after-all. The temple that used to crown The Pyramid of the Sun had long disappeared, when restoration began in the early 20th century. On the unfenced plateau at the top (when, breathless, I finally arrived to join Jeff, having climbed its 248 steps), a young woman teacher with a group of school children, aged about six years, hands clasped ring-a-roses style, was chanting happily. What about, we had no way of knowing, but it is a chilling fact, in any version of Aztec history, that this is where *human* sacrifice took place, as it was believed that the shedding of human blood was necessary to make their Sun God rise each day. In 1487, a little more than thirty years before the arrival of Hernan Cortes, *20,000* captives were sacrificed by King Ahuzotl. Today's carefree bunch of kids and their teacher could at least acknowledge that the conquistadors, whatever their faults, had abolished the practice of human sacrifice.

While Harvi had been in storage, a mechanic had replaced the outside wonky door on the propane compartment for the fridge; thereafter, we'd no more trouble with the supply shutting off while we were in transit. (These big RV sites in the southern states cater for travellers who live permanently in motorhomes.) A few days afterwards, more than a little self-congratulatory, we headed out of El Paso to begin the return journey to Canada. Our second visit to Texas had been a great success; we saw the wild flowers that we'd come to see and so much else besides and, despite the lack of any encouragement from anybody, our visit to Mexico City was wonderful, with no altitude sickness, only mementoes and memories to sustain us for a long, long time.

Shortly we crossed the state line into New Mexico. The plan was to return to New Mexico later in the trip, now on this glorious Sunday morning we were intent on driving the 162 miles into Arizona. It was a long, slow climb across the high desert with scarcely any road traffic; sometimes across scrubland of cholla and yucca, with an occasional oasis of greenery surrounding a dwelling; other times there were trees and cultivation and hand-written For Sale notices for: Pecans, Walnuts, even Wine. We saw a sign for the 'Southern Correctional Facility' – facility! – and a couple of 100-wagon trains, each pulled by four locomotives.

'The traffic's very light,' I remarked with pleasure, as I was driving.

'Everyone's in San Antonio being assailed by the Mariachi Bands,' Jeff riposted.

The road continued to climb. It became windy. Soon there wasn't much to see except dust. Lots! Eddies all over the place became mini whirlwinds stirring up the sandy desert until it became a blizzard of murky grey, at first obscuring the distant mountains then sweeping closer all around until visibility was greatly reduced.

A dust storm!

After lunch at a Denny's, a much-needed respite from the elements, Harvi carried us on the wind into Arizona, and warning signs: 'Caution High Winds – Dust Ahead' and 'For Next 30 Miles – Dust'.

'Too late! Not much use giving warnings now. I'm choked.'

'Me too.'

Shrouded in grey gauze, at last we found the small camping, in the middle of nowhere, for which we'd spent an age searching.

Chapter Sixteen

'This is Ricky,' the woman cooed affectionately.

Smiles at the ready, turning to look behind us to greet a treasured son, dropping our gaze to the floor, there stood Ricky. A roadrunner! How do you respond to an introduction like that? No paw to shake – both feet needed on the ground to balance. His twenty-four inches: *horizontal* from beak to tail, it's a long way down to pat a head, even a crested one. Sizing us up quizzically, he was enjoying being the centre of attention.

'He's quite tame; bin with us for years. They live 'til they're seven or eight, you know,' middle-aged Jackie, in reception, went on, while I filled in the registration slip.

'We've seen them in the desert as we've been driving,' I replied. 'It's amusing to see a tame one.'

Ricky wasn't hanging about to be sociable; scooting off on stiff, stout legs ending in bizarre feet, with that comical burst of speed typical of roadrunners – a ground cuckoo, they can run at an amazing seventeen miles per hour, fast enough to catch a rattlesnake – chasing after Jeff, who had returned to the RV. Ricky recognised where there might be food. Not that his usual feed-up of some insects, or gourmet fare: a lizard or snake, would be on board Harvi, but he liked human company and the offer of titbits.

For the campers, cooked dinners were available on site, as being isolated there were no restaurants for miles, just the day we'd been to Denny's and had a main meal at lunchtime. We ordered lasagne for later in the evening.

'It's *always* windy *everywhere* in Arizona in April,' Jackie responded to my comments about the dusty conditions. 'It can blow up quickly. When it's real bad you have to get off the highway and sit it out, 'cos you can't see to drive.'

'We've been lucky, then. It wasn't *that* bad. We have experienced blinding dust storms, in Canada, on the prairies, a bit like desert, so we know what they're like.'

'Never been to Canada,' Jackie replied, in a tone of voice suggesting that she wasn't anxious to remedy that omission any time soon. We'd got used to the fact that not many of the Americans we'd met on our extensive travels in *their* country, had ever been *north* of the international border. It was to be expected here, close to Mexico, where many people, including Jackie I would guess by her appearance, were Mexican or of mixed race.

It's not usually acceptable to wash down RVs or cars on sites not equipped for that, but seeing the condition of Harvi and with few others about, Jackie readily agreed that Jeff could use a hose to remove a couple of layers of grime. While *machines* did *my* work, I sat in the laundry room reading magazines and newspapers. An article on Mexico, though not specifically Mexico City, in a recent Arizona paper, concluded with the verdict that, 'Mexico is safer than the USA'. Should I send it to Norma, in the AAA office in El Paso, I mused, with apologies for having cast aspersions on her native city.

The wind dropped. The dust settled. Now it was possible to see and admire the mountainous surroundings; though not all of the mountains in the Southwest *look* high, as the desert floor from which they rise is itself at a minimum elevation of 3,500 feet. Another bitter night followed, but we were prepared for it. It was the awesome *silence* of the desert that kept us awake! Unfortunately, for me, there is never silence, because lack of external sound only accentuates the perpetual hiss of tinnitus, as any sufferer will confirm.

Although we were not far from Tucson, our intended destination, next morning, instead of going there directly, we headed south and took all day following a scenic, almost-circular route to Tucson. Tombstone, nicknamed 'The Town Too Tough to Die', one of Arizona's old mining camps, where in 1881 the infamous Earp-Clanton gunfight took place at the OK Corral, was our first stop. Situated in E. *Toughnut* Street, Tombstone

Courthouse State Historic Park had interesting displays relating to the 'lives of former citizens'. Is there anywhere else on the planet with a museum featuring a *rose bush*? Rose Tree Inn Museum has the world's largest rose bush, its size verified yearly by the Guinness Book of World Records. In another, the prized exhibit was a bullet from *that* gunfight. With little else showing any sign of life, the town had the dreary air of an out-of-season resort. In Tombstone, the town packed to capacity all weekend, nothing much happens until late afternoon during the week. That suited us fine!

A horse-drawn stage with a handful of sightseers clip-clopped along the deserted main street. Near The Bird Cage Theatre (of the song, 'Only a Bird in a Gilded Cage' fame) strutting about on very high heels, a woman, long past middle age, ample bosom spilling over the top of her blouse, tarted up to resemble, well, a tart of bygone days, was keen to sell us tickets for a show. Blinking in the blinding light of morning, looking incongruous in her attire, she gushed, 'This show won first prize in the US for its gunfights.' When she spoke, her lips, outlined in pencil, a darker shade than her thickly applied lipstick, displayed uneven, discoloured teeth.

'We won't be here this afternoon,' we explained, declining the proffered tickets.

'Now ain't that just bad luck,' she commiserated, her black eyebrows meeting in a frown, as she adjusted her feather boa.

'Anyway, I don't like guns and I wouldn't enjoy a *live* gunfight, even one that doesn't end in death,' I said, thinking of the noise and what it would do to my hearing.

'Oh, woe-na be live this afternoon – havta wait 'til Saturday for that. . .'

Away from the main drag, it was a different world: the well-cared-for houses had trim gardens, full of fragrant roses, yellow creepers, small cypresses and paloverde trees, ringing with bird song. We chatted with an older couple (about our age!) tending the grounds of a church. They had lived in the town all their lives and, though they hadn't travelled much in America, they had been to Ireland. They waxed lyrical about the 'softness of the moisture laden air and Gulf Stream warmth', accounting for the lush vegetation of West Cork, among the places they had visited and enjoyed.

Craving some *moist* air myself, I felt as if I was shrinking with dryness from the inside outwards, as well as my sore throat, sore breathing and sore, itchy skin. Both yawning with tiredness, the altitude (at Tombstone 4,539 feet) and the arid high-desert air of the past couple of weeks was sapping our energy.

We carried on along a sometimes-winding, scenic mountain road, with tumbleweed, flowering yuccas, scattered cattle grazing, and an occasional sign: 'Watch Out For Animals' and 'Entering Wine Country'. The Santa Cruz River, whenever glimpsed, almost devoid of water, not unlike the Rio Grande, and the customary vultures circling, lords of the cloudless, cobalt heavens. In Patagonia there were directions for Patagonia Lake State Park, a tempting side trip. Not to detour each time we felt inclined needed firm self-discipline, or we wouldn't get back to Canada – ever! Keeping to the planned route, it descended through a valley of trees, passing Arizona Vineyards, into Nogales, the largest of the Arizona/Mexico border towns, referred to as Ambos Nogales, both Nogales. It was exceedingly hot. It had been a gorgeous drive, but we were tired, thirsty and hungry. Taking refuge in an air-conditioned restaurant for an hour, fortified by an appetising meal, enabled us to continue north on I-19, still surrounded by beautiful mountainous scenery, to historic Tucson.

The Saguaro National Park's two sections, lying east and west of the city, contain thriving stands of saguaro cactus of awesome proportions – some are fifty feet tall, weighing as much as fifteen tons – with multi limbs that stretch out in strange configurations. No prizes for guessing that the saguaro is Arizona's state flower. We first encountered these weird giants on the vast, arid plain of San Xavier Indian Reservation. At the far end of a long straight road rise the white plastered walls and towers of the Spanish Baroque/Moorish church, dazzling in the desert sun against an ultramarine sky. Among other plants there were tall saguaro, maybe as old as the Mission itself. Sprouting stubby bunches of vivid yellow flowers at the tips, they seemed alive as small birds nest-building were disappearing into, then popping out of, the numerous holes, which punctured the tall trunks and contorted arms. Gila woodpeckers make the holes in the saguaro; then they and other small birds and elf owls all take up residence. A bird co-operative. Bird skyscrapers!

A painter, fiftyish, palette held in his left hand almost at eye level, attired in dark blue baseball cap and matching shorts, long sleeved shirt splotched with paint, even the back, was standing at an easel.

'Mind if we watch?' we asked.

'That's OK. Feel free.'

He was putting the finishing touches to an accomplished representation of the Mission buildings, except that, in the sky over the church, he had added some fluffy clouds and a large figure in white robes arms raised, ascending upwards, akin to a Raphael Ascension.

'Do you live on the Reservation?'

'No! No! I love this place. I love it like crazy, but only American Indians may live here. I have their permission, though, to come daily to paint, which is real neat,' he continued, never taking his eyes off the painting. (Indian Reservations, regarded as sovereign nations, make and enforce the laws regarding their own land.)

'There's Mass every morning. . . like this since Spanish/ Mexican times,' he asserted, as if he had lived that long and that's why he knew. 'There're four Masses on Sundays, all crowded. Lots of tourists come then. I like it on quiet days, like this.'

Mission San Xavier del Bac, dating from 1700, is the oldest Catholic church in the United States still serving the Indian community for whom it was built. Not surprisingly, the adjoining gift shop had similar beautiful artefacts to those we'd admired in Mexico City. Twenty per cent of the population of the southwest derive from Hispanic descent, which explains why we found the atmosphere in all the places we'd been in southern and western Texas and in Arizona from the Mexican border to Tucson, and the city itself, 'foreign' except, of course, on shopping malls! On a spanking-new, spacious one, boasting five department stores selling everything imaginable, all we bought were some socks. Later, each of us felt tidier, and lighter, for having a haircut. In a specialist store, I lashed out on some expensive cream, in the hope of quelling my once-again erupting skin before I went completely bonkers.

'It's not like Tucson you know. No way as nice. No way!' the chirpy man said, from the big RV, that had just set-up on the adjacent pitch, the aroma of freshly brewed coffee filling the air, as we chatted about our proposed visit to Phoenix, while rolling in our awning and disconnecting the water and electricity in readiness to depart. Situated in Central Arizona, Phoenix, 111 miles north of Tucson, is the state's capital and largest city – the two don't always coincide.

'Phoenix is one of our nation's fastest growing places,' he gabbled on, in between taking slurps of coffee from his mug. 'Folk retire there. Amazing, 'cos it's in the desert. Jes' *I* wouldn't want to live there,' he declared.

'We don't want to *live* there,' I mumbled to Jeff, after waving him goodbye, 'but we've seen so much of Arizona this year, together with the year we visited the canyons, that we might as well have a look at Phoenix, especially as we're so close.' And a *look* at the city, from Harvi's high seats, was all that we got.

The saguaro, paloverde, groups of palms, sand-coloured, flat fields, an ostrich farm with signs offering ostrich-feather dusters, eggs, meat. . . gave way – *miles* from the city – to extensive land clearing by great machines tearing up the desert flora. ('The place spreads on a *daily* basis,' the guy in Tucson said, contemptuously.) Billboards, so big they could be read from outer space, advertised the properties (more man-made places of ugliness) that would rise on these prairie-like destruction sites.

Interstates I-8, I-10 and I-17 hurtled traffic towards San Diego, Los Angeles and Flagstaff, and for a while we followed the four-lane asphalt towards 'Central Phoenix'. The city, famous for world-class resorts, golf courses, wealthy retirees, is reputed to have museums, theatres, a symphony hall. . . Not finding anywhere to park the RV, we didn't see any of those, only shopping plazas – by the hundred.

'Do you really want us to try to find the campground we've earmarked in the camping book?'

'No!' I answered swiftly. Being the navigator, *I'd* have to *locate* it! Anyway, any desire I had to become familiar with the place had long vanished. As soon as he could, Jeff doubled back. We took an exit road. Parking on a sprawling shopping mall (they do have their advantages!) to buy groceries and, while having a meal, we flicked through the pages of the site book to find an alternative campground.

Apache Junction surrounded by desert and lakes, with the Superstition Mountains nearby, had an RV park on the edge of town. Its big, individual pitches screened by flowering cacti, roses, hibiscus, had good amenities, a pool and spa, making it a pleasant base for a few days, despite not every day being entirely restful.

Next morning Jeff was bumping around early. I wasn't in the mood for breakfast before 7am on a rest day! He had a cup of tea and went for a walk. Unable to return to the land of nod – thanks a bunch Jeff! – I got up. Nobody was about. A flock of funny-looking, plump birds each with a semi-circular hooped feather on the front of its head, which looked as if it would roll away when bobbed up and down, were feeding on a patch of ground nearby. Later I discovered the correct term for my birds was 'a covey of Gombel quail'. After an hour Jeff arrived back, agitated. Flinging open the side door, he clambered in blurting, 'I can't find the RV keys.'

'What do you mean you can't find the keys?'

'I can't find the RV keys,' he bellowed each word slowly, as if saying it slowly and very loudly would explain all.

Why did he need keys to go for a walk? How did he *know* that he'd lost them – the door he'd just barged through was unlocked? On these occasions silence on my part causes the least trouble. He'd lost the ring with the full set of keys – for everything – which normally 'lives' safely in the RV; we just use individual keys as required. Why did he take the full set? I helped him turn the place upside down, but no keys.

I cooked breakfast. Afterwards he went looking again, retracing his walk, while I attacked the shambles the search on board Harvi had created. He returned. No keys. He set aside that problem. And confronted the next one. 'While we're here (meaning in Apache Junction) I'll see if I can find a repair shop to fit the switch I bought in El Paso.' The switch on the oil pressure gauge (the second *new* one, that had been fitted the previous year) was playing up again, giving false readings. Another faulty switch didn't seem possible. It was!

'I'll take the RV into town. Do *you* want to come, or what?'

'How long will it take?'

'Probably hours. First got to find someone to do the job.'

'No. Better not. There's masses of laundry. These seat covers need to be washed, too. Help me to cart everything over there, before you disappear leaving me homeless.'

In the laundry room, a girl and two guys – Krista, Brad and Craig – all about twenty years, had commandeered two of the four washers, and the four dryers. I divided my clothes between the two available washers, but with no Harvi to retreat to, I had to remain in the laundry, where their unbelievable amount of clothing in varying degrees of wetness was piled on every available surface. Giggling, Krista explained that, while driving, all their 'gear had fallen off the top'. The top of what? Something pretty big to hold the magnitude of stuff they had. It had taken them ages to retrieve most of it, but not all, bit by bit, back along the highway and surrounding countryside. 'We've been using the washing machines for *hours*,' they wailed; now, feeding coins into the hungry maws of the dryers was threatening to become a ruinous drain on their combined finances. On this occasion, I was thankful for the 'No Washing Lines Allowed on the Campground'. Imagine what it would have looked like! They were still there hours later, when my laundry was finished.

Jeff had tracked down a place that *could* do the job, only they refused to fit the switch he had already bought, even though they hadn't a similar one in stock. Can you believe? Eventually, after much wasted time and energy looking for another workshop, all was completed satisfactorily and his taut nerves could slacken off a bit.

'This is the third switch. Let's hope it's a case of third time lucky.' Considering the day he'd had, he was in reasonably good form. As always, I was deeply grateful for his ability to successfully deal with problems, especially those concerning Harvi, which allowed *me* each day to discover something new – if not exactly earth-shattering! – like 'funny-looking, plump birds' being desert creatures called quail. The bunch of keys was never found!

One afternoon we took a stroll, dog-legging along narrow, up-and-down, paved roads – a school bus disappearing into the dips to emerge hugely a minute later – and dirt side roads past homes and small holdings. It was fascinating to see desert gardens, not a blade of grass in sight, just areas of sand marked out by stones, containing cultivated, blooming cacti including ocotillo and organ pipe; stands of saguaro towering above the buildings, the ground around paloverde: yellow circles of fallen flowers, a few fruiting orange and lemon trees. Many of the houses had small notices at the entrance saying 'Private' or 'No Trespassing', which abundant rabbits, roadrunners and small birds with red fronts blissfully disregarded. Those with sufficient space had horses, or ostriches. One we saw had mules, another goats.

For two hours we were the only people walking. Obviously conspicuous by our rarity – or eccentricity – a passing cyclist greeted us; the few car drivers waved. Several dogs, including a pure white one resembling a wolf, all securely tied up within their gardens, thank goodness, noisily objected to our presence near their territories.

Back at the campground it was fully dark at 7.30pm.

'Because of the time difference it's too late to call Canada now,' Jeff said. 'We'll make sure to do it tomorrow, early, wherever we are.'

Arizona not observing daylight-saving time, but some American Indian reservations within the state doing so (and a quarter of Arizona's total land area is occupied by twenty reservations) meant that, sometimes, our timepieces were at odds with local time.

Three miles west of Apache Junction, the road there running through sandy hills of strange shapes and pinnacles, is Boyce Thompson Arboretum State Park, 420 acres of desert plants from around the world. There were boojum trees, a eucalyptus forest, a Sonoran desert trail, a forest of giant cacti in which there were yucca trees so tall their enormous, pendulous blooms drooped ten feet above us. A desert meadow – a contradiction in terms? – was a riot of colour with a variety of small cacti shrubs. Quiet, birds flitting about, warm sun, it was delightful, perfect tranquillity until. . . somebody, someday, decides that what the arboretum really needs is a fast food joint. Perish the thought!

We hit the road again, scenic US 60. A sign promised (or threatened), 'Coming Soon One-Eyed Jack's Tatoos'.

'Too bad we'll miss it,' Jeff laughed. 'I wouldn't trust Jack not even if he'd two eyes.'

As we drove east the sun disappeared and was gone for the rest of the day. It became heavily overcast and downright chilly. After Globe (a trading centre for the San Carlos Apache Reservation) there was a change in the vegetation too, with the mountains on both side of us clothed in pine trees, quite a surprise after weeks with little except cacti. Leaving the Tonto National Forest the

Sign for Moose near Conway, New Hampshire.

Quiet campground at Zanesville, Ohio.

Cape Foulweather, Oregon.

Nice to be welcome!

Gold Dredge, near Fairbanks, Alaska.

Fanny displaying a hand-crafted fur Parka and her
new trainers! Alaska.

Caldera Kilauea Volcano, Big Island of Hawaii.

Lei of Plumeria Flowers, Island of Oahu.

The Pearl Harbour Memorial, Honolulu, Island of Oahu.

The border between Tijuana, Mexico and California.

The Pyramid of the Sun, Mexico.

The Capitol:
Washington DC.

Barred from the
White House!
Washington DC.

Central Park
on a sunny
Sunday, New
York City.

Harvi; early morning New Jersey across the Hudson River from Manhattan.

Lighting-up time in Manhattan.

Watching the world go by on 5th Ave, New York City.

The Twin Towers,
New York City from boat to
Ellis Island.

The Statue of Liberty,
New York City.

Baltimore
Ravens'
Stadium.
Baltimore,
Maryland.

We began and
finished each
trip in Ontario,
Canada.

road continued north-east across the Reservation and The Salt River Canyon. There were lots of viewpoints giving sweeping vistas over the immense canyon – all would have looked marvellous in sunshine. Even without, it was impressive and we had several – shivery – stops along the canyon floor. From one overlook we could see the road that we had yet to travel on three levels, going from mountains down to the river and aloft again. As there were no campgrounds listed for the area, we booked into a motel in Show Low around 3.30pm. During the night, when the temperature dipped to 23°F, with snow showers, we were glad of the comfort. At an elevation of more than 6,000 feet, Show Low with a resident population of roughly 5,000, takes its name from a winning hand in a poker game. Most of the motels, restaurants and shops were situated on Deuce of Clubs Avenue. Many of them had a 'mean' winter because, 'We didn't have enough of the white stuff,' for winter sports enthusiasts, the waitress explained, when we ate dinner.

Leaving the motel, black clouds threatening, snow swirling and the temperature below freezing, Jeff gassed up both RV tanks and turned north, passing through a town called, appropriately in the conditions, Snowflake. It was May 1st. At Holbrook we changed on to I-40E, the highway passing through The Painted Desert, where we visited a few years before, at a different time of the year, in very different weather.

We crossed into New Mexico and put our watches forward an hour. Stressed by the dreadful driving weather making visibility difficult, badly in need of a break and some warming sustenance, Jeff pulled into a service area. There was a post office. I asked if they sold stamps, as the place was cleared in readiness for closing some ten minutes later.

'Sure thing.'

'Could I have four 50s, please?'

He looked puzzled by the request. 'Doyaknow I'm righ' outa 50s.'

Unblinking, he stared at me and repeated, *twice* more, 'I'm righ' outa 50s.'

'Well could I have 40s and 10s?' I ventured.

'Sure thing,' he answered, flicking the pages of the stamp book back and forth to confirm that he *did* have them. 'How many?'

'Four 40s and four 10s, please.'

k

'So you're wannin' four 40s and four 10s, OK?'

'Yes, please, and could I have airmail stickers.'

'Naw. Naw. Don't have no airmail stickers. They'll be OK jus' with stamps.'

Unless friends mention to us that they've received cards, I never check, so heaven alone knows how many of those dispatched with such effort ever arrive. The Family Restaurant, where we ate, had a sign outside it: 'Open 24 Hours'. Why? What family needed grub in the middle of the night, even in this land of non-stop eating? Thinking about it, maybe it would be a good way to spend the night with a wakeful, cranky child. I recall that friends of ours in England, desperate to get their two toddlers to sleep, used to put them, pyjama-clad, in their car and drive around and around until they nodded off, then gingerly transfer them to their beds, praying all the time that they wouldn't waken and start yelling again. For them a cosy restaurant to recoup their energy would have been great.

'Ain't this just awful?' the waitress groused. 'Never like this at this time of year. Not bin bad when it shoulda bin. Gettin' our win'er now.'

We've learned from experience that *anywhere* in the world can have unseasonable weather, it's not just peculiar to the British Isles. As we continued east the swirling snow gave way to heavy, soggy stuff, changing eventually to rain and then it too petered out, but it remained miserably cold.

Albuquerque – what an intriguing name – apart from knowing that it was a town – somewhere! – in the US, I knew nothing else about it until three years before, on a sunny Sunday morning, when we bought a piece of sculpture from an American Indian selling his wares from a table in the doorway of a shop in Ventura, California. In glowing terms he spoke about Albuquerque, his home city, and with a population of half a million, New Mexico's largest. That's where we were now headed. Passing the exits for several campgrounds, including one billed 'as the best in New Mexico' to reach one claiming to be 'the most central', we came off the interstate for *that* one – only it was no longer a campground! Fractious and frustrated, Jeff manoeuvred the RV back to the busy highway, soon to tag on to the tail end of a long hold-up. A truck had shed its load of cabbages, which skittered in all directions, hell bent on avoiding being shovelled up.

'All that's missing is beetroot, and then they've the makings of oceans of borsch,' Jeff quipped, good-humouredly, despite his exhaustion. Eventually we found a campground far on the other side of Albuquerque. We were past caring what it had to offer, just wanted to get off the road. Now! After we'd recovered a little, longing to catch up on news from all branches of our family, via our kids in Canada, we phoned there and had a one-way chat with an answering machine. It was definitely time for an early night. Tomorrow had to be a better day!

Well, it wasn't snowing. Or raining. In fact, it was quite pleasant and we had a relaxing time on the campground. One day, hitching a ride on a bus for several miles, we set off for Albuquerque's Old Town. 'Take a look at Central Avenue as you go along; that's a section of *magical* old Route 66,' the guy in the camp office said, proudly. The construction of Route 66, The Mother Road, began in the 1920s. The two-lane, paved highway starting in Chicago, travelling through three time zones and eight states, ended 2,448 miles later in Santa Monica, California. The Historical Route 66 Association, which has a devoted following, came into being, in the nick of time, to save some stretches of the famous road, before its entire length was lost by being built over. We had seen the *end* of it in California and driven on stretches of it in other places. (A couple of years later we'd stand at the *beginning* of it in Chicago.) Europe has sections of Roman Roads. The United States has Old Route 66. Miles-long Central Avenue, with its flashing neon, had many examples of 1940s architecture.

A bit older than that, the four-block Old Town, where we got off the bus, the site of the first non-native settlement, dates from 1706. Named after the Duke of Albuquerque, a real duke, there was a big statue of him. (Next door, in the state of Texas, their idea of a duke is John Wayne!) San Filipe de Neri church with its massive adobe walls, and other adobe buildings now serving as shops, restaurants and galleries surround the tree-lined Old Town Plaza. Rio Grande Blvd. was the original Camino Real. The New Mexico Museum of Natural History, exploring the geological history of the Southwest, offered unusual experiences such as a walk-through volcano, a replica of an ice age cave, full-scale dinosaur models, as well as a salt water aquarium (a long way from any ocean), all in a striking modern building. Turquoise from around the world, together with that mined locally, was on display in the Turquoise Museum. I always thought that the colour of turquoise was, well, turquoise, but it can be any colour between white and deep blue or deep green. The more copper in it the deeper the shade of blue; the more iron: the more intense green. The quality of the stones can be from crumbly to No. 7 (a diamond is No.10).

'Hey, Melvin take a look at this,' a plump, middle-aged woman called. Melvin joined her beside a showcase displaying The George Washington Turquoise. 'It's massive. Weighs 2,620 carats,' she squeaked.

The Mayans and Aztecs of Mexico traded with the Indians of the Southwest for their turquoise. Bet in those days all of it was genuine. Nowadays, according to a notice, 'less than fifteen per cent of Turquoise Jewellery is natural', and another warned that 'Authentic Indian Handmade is the only term defined by law regarding turquoise jewellery'.

For me, the best thing about Albuquerque was that in a Walgreen Pharmacy I was recommended some cream for my itch which, after applying it diligently for a week, cleared the persistent irritation that had plagued me for what seemed an age.

The sixty-one-mile Turquoise Trail links Albuquerque with Santa Fe. Not taking the turning for the 10,678-foot Sandia Crest with its observation deck, which that day, to our huge disappointment, would have given us only a view of extensive mist and not the usual 'panorama of 15,000 square miles', with sparse traffic, the road climbing imperceptibly, we drove on past areas of thick pine and aspen forests and a few ghost towns with old turquoise or gold mines and always mountains rising not very far away.

Perched on a plateau at 7,000 feet, ringed by the snow-capped Sangre de Cristo Mountains, we thought that Santa Fe might be cold. We weren't wrong! The small RV site on Cerrillos Road was well-placed for buses into the city, or to malls on the periphery. Our first purchase was an extra sleeping bag. I slept in it in the fully made-up bed, which helped to combat the below-freezing night-time temperature. Not that sunny daytime was balmy. 'Wasn't the usual win'er snowfall in ski areas,' we were told repeatedly. 'Now, in May with these bitter winds we're having March weather.' (In contrast, 2,000 miles *north* in Canada, at 7.30pm, their time, our son was playing golf, the temperature:

25°C, [upper 70sF] we were told when we phoned.)

With not a wisp of cloud marring the deep blue sky, the first thing that's striking about Santa Fe is the remarkable clarity of the air. (Though the downside was – there's always a downside! – that the thin mountain air made both of us headachy and a little nauseous.) Spanish influence is everywhere, but it's unlike any city in Spain, or any place else – anywhere. Anglo, American Indian, together with Mexican and Spanish cultures intermingle giving New Mexico's capital city a special charm. There are no high-rise buildings. The warm-brown adobe structures, private and public, not all of them as old as they look, with their rounded outlines have the timelessness and innocence of children's sandcastles.

The area of New Mexico is the same as that of the British Isles, but the population of Santa Fe is tiny compared with London's; however, both cities have in common many museums, art galleries and above all bags of history. Dating from 1610, The Governor's Palace, on The Plaza, the oldest continuous seat of government in the United States (it moved elsewhere early in the 20th century) houses a history museum. On display in a prominent position is the pen used by President Taft, 'on 6th January 1912', to sign the proclamation admitting New Mexico, as the 47th state, to the Union. Most of the exhibits were much older, giving the chequered history of Sante Fe and New Mexico from the Pueblo Revolt of 1680 and Native rule from the Palace, to Statehood and the Second World War. I was surprised to see a copy of a Velasquez painting, *Water Carriers of Seville* circa 1620 (the original is in London) though, on reflection, it wasn't really remarkable as The Governor's Palace was built about the time of The El Escorial Palace, near Madrid, and Velasquez was a court painter. For homesick Spaniards, from Seville, maybe? Gazing at it must have given them solace in lonely, inhospitable circumstances, much as we, always, carry photographs of our kids and grandkids, though we are on *chosen*, greatly enjoyable expeditions.

There was a very different style of painting from Velasquez's in The Georgia O'Keeffe's gallery. Though born in Wisconsin of Irish ancestry, her vivid palette depicts the landscape and desert flora of New Mexico. Her intention was, she said, 'To make people *see* flowers, whether they want to or not.' She succeeded:

flowers filled entire large canvases – there was no escaping them!

The modern State Capitol Building is unique. Kiva-like, resembling the Zia sun symbol, the official emblem of New Mexico, it has a large statue of an American Indian woman in front. Along the Old Santa Fe Trail, the Loretto Chapel has a 'Miraculous Staircase' in that, the double spiral to the choir loft has no visible means of support, nor does it have any nails in its construction, and the wood used was/is not found throughout New Mexico. Crossing the trickle of The Rio Grande we visited the Old Mission of San Miguel with its centuries-old, sturdy, adobe walls. Among many priceless artefacts is the San Jose bell cast in Spain in about 1356, having been used in churches in Spain and Mexico, before being transported to the Mission.

'Imagine the journeying it's done, and we don't like carting holiday souvenirs through airports with their tardy carousels and stoney-faced custom officials!' Jeff commented.

One afternoon, Jeff, not wishing 'to visit any more museums,' (ever again! – judging by the tone of voice) went shopping (he loves shopping, often buying lovely food, and on that occasion I got a pair of beautiful earrings) while I took a bus which chugging up a steep, winding road, gave a magnificent panorama over Sante Fe and extensive mountainous countryside. 'You missed a great view, Jeff,' I would tell him, but on second thoughts maybe I wouldn't, because then I'd have to admit that there were *three* museums up there!

I was the only fare on the bus up and back. Changing buses in town to return to the campground, a man fixed his bike, free of charge, to the rack on the front of the bus, before boarding, followed by half a dozen other people. Of those, one youngish man nursing a large bottle, with no money to pay his fare, walked to the back and slumped down, taking the odd swig from time to time. A woman had only a dollar bill and bus drivers don't give change; so she, too, had a free ride. One other man and I were seniors, paying the princely sum of 25 cents each (for quite a long ride); therefore I wasn't surprised to read a notice stating that a Public Meeting was to be held the following week because, 'Either the Bus Schedule will have to be Reduced or Fares will have to Go Up'.

One morning, listening to the radio as usual while eating breakfast, our whingeing about how the sunny weather was spoiled by the cool wind was put into perspective – in an instant. A ferocious tornado had ripped through the state of Oklahoma.

'There is widespread destruction and great loss of life, particularly in the area of Oklahoma City.'

We listened, chastened. We'd been grousing about a bit of cold wind! Looking at one another in silence, I cleared away the dishes. Oklahoma was on our itinerary for a few days later. . .

We'd travelled 4,000 miles since leaving Canada and to get back there we'd have to cover another 2,000. A family celebration was scheduled for one of our grandsons in two weeks' time. There were places we'd planned to see along the route, including Oklahoma, a state not visited previously. However, we wouldn't be able to spend more than a couple of days at any particular place. Sante Fe was marvellous, but it would be our last long stop-over.

'When we get nearer, we'll have to see what the situation is like in Oklahoma City and go a different way if necessary.' Jeff got busy with his maps again.

Chapter Seventeen

Harvi seemed as delighted as we were to be on the move again, happily bowling along the single-lane road, almost devoid of traffic, through semi-arid, rolling ranch country. The sun already warm, with hardly a whisper of a breeze, a dome of blue overhead, it was going to be a great day.

Not for long! An almighty bang from the rear of the RV had us scurrying out to investigate – my heart thumping ready to explode, what about Jeff's? – after a mere twenty miles of the 300 that we hoped to cover that day. We often saw strips of burst tyre in ditches. Well, it was our turn to make a contribution. A wide strip of thread had shorn off the canvas of the nearside back tyre and the bang was it slapping the underside of the RV. Now what? Up to this, in all our travels, we hadn't even had a *slow* puncture. Why did it have to be a big one? Something major. Without warning. A superb mechanic, Jeff had checked everything meticulously the night before, as always. The RV was too heavy, the spare wheel likewise, for him to do the replacement as with a car, or as he would have done with something this big prior to his illnesses. Should we use our CB radio to contact road services?

'We're in the middle of nowhere,' Jeff said. There was no denying that. 'We could sit here baking for hours.' That was true, too. 'Even if I give directions, it will take the breakdown people ages to reach us.' The road had no shoulders; we couldn't pull over; not a scrap of shade in any direction, and no habitations. 'Much better to carry on till we reach a landmark before contacting them,' he reasoned, calmly. He decided to drive on slowly.

Chunks of thread nosily departed at frequent intervals. Each time Jeff would stop, scramble out to assess the situation, before creeping along again. Each time we rounded a twist in the road to be confronted by more miles of nothingness and worse: sometimes an incline, there were suppressed groans from both of us, but we didn't speak at all. I marvelled at Jeff's uncharacteristic patience and *silence*. His bluster had deserted him. In forty-three years of marriage I'd never seen anything like this cool control. Totally unexpected! Could it be replicated next time he started bellyaching about something *unimportant*, I wondered?

After a 30-mile crawl, now bumping along on bare canvas, we reached Clines Corner. Clines Corner is just that: a *corner* where roads cross. A travel stop, it had a shop, a cafe, a gas station, but nowhere for repairs and not much else within sight on the flat landscape. We telephoned the Triple A. And waited. And waited.

'Better get the spare wheel ready.' Jeff then found that the spare wheel nuts were rusted to the holding bracket. *That* discovery was not made in silence! And who could blame him? After a sweaty hour with a hacksaw, in the desert heat, the nuts, as if to say, 'Sod you!' were still firmly in place. An angel of mercy with a blow torch – not a commonplace combination, I admit – alias the hefty handyman from the gas station, released the wheel, with the usual American opening and closing phrases: 'No problem,' and 'You're Welcome,' admirable, because they're always genuinely intended.

Three hours after the telephone call, the Triple A man arrived – with a low-loader. He had come from Albuquerque to the west. We liked Albuquerque. Sure, we liked it lots, but heck we didn't want to go back there, not now – maybe another time. But not now, *please*. We didn't have to. All was resolved. The job was completed on site. The empty low-loader returned to its home. No time for a much-needed repast, but immediately on to the highway east in search of a replacement tyre. It was late afternoon Friday, not the best time for that kind of shopping. A tyre proved elusive. Stopping many times in fruitless search, travelling more than fifty miles we at last got one. And had it fitted.

Jeff told me, quite some time afterwards, that he had known that there was a serious problem in the US with new cars involved in crashes, proved to have been caused by their faulty tyres; because of the age of our RV, he hadn't suspected that we would have similar trouble. The way in which the thread had parted company with the canvas indicated the same problem. How lucky we were to have been on that traffic-free road. Someone was looking out for us. Thanks!

After ten hours, with not much to eat, we'd covered only one hundred miles. Hot, hungry, tired, to find an overnight campground was a priority. When we climbed back on board Harvi, happy with his new tyre, our stomachs rumbling, he refused to budge. We weren't going anywhere. The starter had packed in.

Another wait. Another Triple A man arrived. He got us mobile, then led the way to a repair shop to have a new starter fitted. Hand on heart, in 35,000 miles driving in North America we had never before called the emergency services.

New Mexico's motto is: Land of Enchantment.

Really?

After a comfortable night, we set off at 7.30am from the campground, in brilliant, warm sun, hoping to make up lost time, blissfully unaware that we had a *faulty* new starter fitted. Changing to Central Time two hours later, when crossing into Texas, we put our watches forward, thereby 'losing' an hour.

Amarillo is Spanish for yellow and it was the colour of the earth and the water in a stream that the road passed over. It's the main city in the Texas Panhandle and the home of one of the United States' largest cattle auctions. We certainly saw – and suffocatingly smelled! – lots of cows on the flat, featureless countryside as we drove. Later, back in England, tracing our route on an atlas with one of our daughters, she exclaimed, 'Amarillo is an *actual* place! A *real* town?' She thought it was just the name of a famous song. We stopped to fill up with gas, delighted with Texas' prices: only $1 a gallon. Jeff kept on and on east, signs at intervals proudly declaring: *Old Route 66*. Driving through Shamrock we passed the blackened jagged shell of a burnt-out motorhome on the central reservation, a sobering sight, and a long tailback of traffic going west. A roadside marker for our 46th state: Oklahoma, was shaped like the state itself. Oklahoma, Choctaw for 'Red Man' – I'm sure the name was not given by *white* settlers! – is home to numerous Native Americans divided

226

between thirty-nine tribes.

During the evening Jeff was vomiting again. Extremely worrying for me, I always feared these bouts of choking, or vomiting, would bring on a heart attack. He recovered each time fairly quickly, always to say, 'I'm OK. Stop fussing!' In England some months later, following exhaustive hospital tests, the discovery was made that he had a 'twisting stomach' as well as the hiatus hernia dating from many years before, inoperable because of the extent of his heart surgery. I think that *I* had every reason to worry, but when Jeff said, 'Stop fussing' that's what he meant!

On our overnight campground, west of Oklahoma City, everyone was talking about the killer tornado. At the time, they had escaped its full fury, though strong winds were still whirling around the campground. A weekender, who lived on the outskirts of the city, described how she watched the sky grow dark until it was fully black. 'I knew then it was going to be a big one,' she said. 'All evening I watched TV, repeating over and over, Oh my God, help them. Oh my God, help them.'

Not having a TV on board the motorhome we'd been spared the visual horror.

Folk in the Southern States, or here in the Central Plains, live with the threat of hurricanes and tornadoes as a fact of life. They happen frequently, not noted much outside the area in which they occur, unless it is a Big One that makes the National News for a day or two until another 'event' replaces it, leaving the locals to cope on their own. This time, The American Red Cross and Salvation Army were both federally mandated to take care of the immediate response. More than forty had been killed. With 50,000 homes destroyed, one in eight people was directly affected by the tragedy. In one district, only one building was left intact: a Baptist church.

'You guys English?' a fellow camper asked. 'Do you know there's an English couple, travelling in a RV, missing in the City? Nobody's seen them since the tornado struck.' (A couple of days later they were found, safe.)

We hadn't known, so lost no time in phoning Canada and 'Yes' there were calls from all our kids who knew that Oklahoma was on our itinerary.

In Arizona and New Mexico we'd been told, 'It's always

windy in *April*.' Well, in Oklahoma it's *always* windy!

'The grass is never still. Ever! Just like now,' a pretty, young woman said to us outside the local church, gesturing to an extensive green field of wheat swishing back and forth. And so it was all the way along our route. Quite unnerving! It was also very humid, with thunderstorms forecast, strange after weeks of dry conditions. In the gusty wind Jeff found steering difficult across the billiard-board flatness, the sparse trees all leaning northwards evidence of the prevailing wind. We heard on the RV radio that in Oklahoma City 65,000 people were gathering for an open air religious service.

The main devastation was in the southern city; avoiding that area by joining the I-44 north we then got on to busy 23rd Street, its entire surface stripped in readiness for repairs (nothing to do with the tornado), all vehicles bumping about endeavouring to dodge the raised manhole covers. Well-shaken about, three miles later, we were delivered to 2,300 Lincoln Blvd., the State Capitol Building, flags everywhere at half mast. Unlike the Kiva-style of New Mexico's Capitol, Oklahoma's is the more usual, white classical. In front it had an expressive statue of a Native American woman, carved by the Apache sculptor Allan Houser. Believe it or not, the Capitol sits on top of one of the State's largest oil fields, which explains the oil derrick in the grounds and accompanying information board for *Oklahoma City Oil Field,* and a picture of a 'Structural Cross Section' drawn in rainbow colours.

Nothing open on a Sunday, there were only five cars on the reserved parking for 'Government Officials and Governor's Staff Only', where escaping the unpleasant wind, we ate lunch on board Harvi; afterwards taking a toll road heading north-east. A pawnshop had a big notice outside: 'Disaster Relief – Interest Free Loans'.

Though whole areas to the south were devastated, the Capitol and centre of the city were unscathed, then, many miles further north there was evidence of the rampaging wind and the freakish path the tornado had taken. To the west of the road, an entire Outlet Mall had been obliterated, and a newly-erected road sign warned: 'No stopping on the Highway – Keep Driving – Don't Slow Down'. Further on, east of us, tractors and heavy farm machinery were strewn in fields like abandoned children's toys;

fences buckled; trees ripped apart; road signs scattered. One battered one still standing read, 'Don't Trash Route 66'. 'A pity tornadoes ignore signs,' Jeff said. There was evidence, too, of structures having been lifted from one place and then, only partially damaged, coming to rest somewhere else. A report told of a dog being borne skywards to land, unhurt, many miles away.

In the late afternoon, we pulled on to a campground in the hilly, northern outskirts of Tulsa, Oklahoma's second city. Jeff was hot and dishevelled with a mood to match the rotten drive. Not that I was sweetness and light. I hate windy weather at the best of times. And recent days were not the best of times, by any reckoning. Also, sitting for long stretches I found very uncomfortable and emerged bodily crumpled. Trying to straighten up, I could have made good use of a big oil can, like that of the Tin Man in *The Wizard of Oz*, to lubricate my joints.

While booking in the woman warden asked us what the conditions were like to the south.

'Here we got away clean, but for them it's all gone. All gone!' she lamented, gazing into space, blinking away tears for several moments, before running our credit card across the machine.

The male warden with her explained that the destroyed Outlet Mall we'd seen was the only one in the state and was an economic centre for Oklahoma City and Tulsa. 'A hospital, shopping malls and other businesses are also badly affected,' he went on, a catch in his voice.

The local Wal-Mart was a collection point for donated stuff, *anything*, no matter how mundane, for the thousands who had lost *everything*. We had already donated cash in several places.

The campground was situated Easy Off Easy On, as they say. After a restorative breather for a couple of days it was Easy On again to a toll turnpike, later becoming Route 66/I-44. There are 400 miles of Route 66 in Oklahoma. We drove through wooded, rolling farmland, passing little towns each with a small, simple church: Assembly of God or House of Prayer, with single-storey, clapboard houses stretched thinly along the edges of the road. Claremore, the first town we passed, had the tomb of Will Rogers, a well-loved character, being both a Cherokee *and* a famous Cowboy. The area has Artesian mineral wells reputed to be good for arthritis and skin complaints. Too bad there wasn't time to stop to sample them!

We crossed into Missouri. Then detoured a bit to have a look at the George Washington Carver National Monument. He was an African-American scientist, who developed more than 300 by-products of – wait for it – the peanut. And more than 100 of the sweet potato, also finding new uses for cotton, soybeans and other crops. A super Jeff, I thought! But Jeff's an engineer not a scientist. *He* can find a use for any *discarded* object and can repair all manner of things that submit to his healing hands. (There was bound to be a collection of breakages waiting for him in the basement, in Canada.) None of that costs money in research and, anyway, we don't like peanuts or sweet potatoes. We did concede, however, that George Washington Carver must have been some swell guy.

Historic 66 carried on past trees, trees, trees, farmland with earth a different colour from Oklahoma's, no more red water, red wild flowers, red earth. There were horses and cows at a waterhole, a winery. . . We stopped, not for wine, but for gas. Still $1 a gallon. Cleaned the windscreen encrusted with splattered insects and carried on to a rest area. Before setting out this year, we had talked over whether or not this would be our last, *long* trip with Harvi, both time-wise and in distance. As on previous trips, we'd had a great holiday experiencing all that was on our itinerary and much more besides. While having lunch we discussed the possibility of *selling* him – only briefly – because that seemed too much like treachery, anyway if he overheard he might refuse to get us home!

Back in the land of Billboards, I sat behind Jeff, the better to read them, and conjured up a fantasy life. There were ads for a barrel museum, numerous motels, walnut bowls, Russell Stover candies, pre-owned mobile homes, boats, cars, foodstuff, clothing; outlet malls for every conceivable item. . . Take my advice, when you feel like a change, go on a trip. Stay in a motel; visit the local attractions in your chosen area, all from the advertisements on billboards. No wonder publishers are concerned about falling book sales. (Somewhere, but I can't remember where, we'd been in a shop so desperate for sales that it sold books by the *weight* – honestly – '$3.28 per kilo'.) A house on a low-loader passed by with the slogan 'Dream Home Being Delivered' – an unfinished dream. The other half-house was a long way behind. One thing for sure – the time whizzed by while

230

reading through the window.

The next day we drove to St. Louis, which is always pronounced, despite Judy Garland's singing otherwise, St. *Lewis*. Three years before, we'd driven through the city with no time to stop. Well, we were back! We crossed a bridge to the RV park, in East St. Louis, on the Illinois bank of the Mississippi, an extensive hard-topped park adjacent to a casino riverboat, giving a great view of the wide river and the unique skyline of downtown St. Louis with its 630 foot parabola, The Gateway Arch, which commemorates the city's role in westward exploration, the centrepiece of the Jefferson National Expansion Memorial. All especially thrilling when lit up at night.

'Are you goin' to the game?', the ticket clerk asked us at the Metrolink station. (Why? Was that fare different?) We weren't, but the train throbbed in tune with the throng heading for the St. Louis Cardinals' Baseball game, at Busch Stadium.

The *outside* of the stainless steel Arch is mightily impressive, standing taller than the Presidents' Heads on Mount Rushmore, South Dakota, about sixty-three storeys, with the span from leg to leg being the same as the height. Surprisingly, it also has an *inside*.

The forty minutes spent in a line-up gave plenty of time for an exchange of pleasantries.

'You've come all the way from England to visit *our* city!' gushed one woman. 'Know somethin',' she continued, indicating the woman with bright red hair beside her, 'We only live *ten* miles away and this will be *our* very first time to go to the top.'

That we'd been in forty-six states drew much admiring comment from those around us. In truth, after many years travelling on our own throughout Europe, relying heavily on sign language and phrase books for communication, we found the openness of friendly Americans, everywhere, a delight.

It became our turn to crouch into a claustrophobic, barrel-shaped capsule, seating five passengers. Eight capsules joined together form a 'train' of which there were two, one riding each span. Equipped with a levelling device, every capsule repeatedly changed position as it travelled, to keep us upright on the four-minute, jerky ascent to the top, for which, never having a stomach for upside-down, fairground rides, I was thankful. From the glass observation deck there was a view over a sea of red enjoying the game at Busch Stadium; the Old Courthouse where the slave, Dred Scott's historic case was tried and, though he didn't win his freedom, it paved the way for a better life for others; (I visited the Courthouse and found that it has a magnificent iron staircase rising through four tiers to the dome, housing old photographs recording the development of the city and the settling of The West); riverboats lining the levee; paddle-wheelers on the mud-coloured river – had my Yorkshire grandfather been here, when he worked on the boats? – and, across the Mississippi, way on the other side of the RV park, a minute dot was Harvi.

Located beneath the Arch there's the Museum of Gateway Expansion. Lewis and Clarke, whose exploits we encountered some years before in Montana, set out in 1804, at the request of Thomas Jefferson, the 3rd President, to search for the source of the Missouri, and much of America west of here dates after that time. There was a great deal in the museum relating to the explorations of Lewis and Clarke often supported by quotations from their diaries. The museum also commemorates, together with the Gateway Arch, the thousands of 19th century pioneers, who stopped for provisions in St. Louis before travelling west.

There were other places of interest. The Old Basilica of St. Louis has the distinction of standing on the *only* piece of land in the entire city which has never changed hands; while the New Cathedral/Basilica, built in the Byzantine tradition, has set its own records by having in its mosaics more than 41,500,000 pieces of tesserae in 8,000 shades of colour. From churches to breweries – the place has the world's largest, Annheuser-Busch. Not recorded anywhere, but never-to-be-forgotten by us, a first for this year's trip, we got soaked to the skin in a thunderstorm deluge returning from the station to the RV. Drumming deafeningly on the roof, it rained without let up for five hours – no visit to the casino that evening.

Leaving St. Louis, driving all day, we crossed Illinois, into Indiana to Indianapolis and the campground east of the city. We'd been in this place two years previously. Here, obviously, overnighters don't get the prime pitches. I swear that we got the same humpy-bumpy, weedy-grassy spot as before. Wilting, I found that the swimming pool hadn't yet opened. The season, apart from in the South, runs from Memorial Day, at the end of May, to Labour Day, the first Monday in September. Regardless of temperatures, often hot enough to fry eggs on the concrete, in our experience these dates are adhered to, not only by campgrounds but by public outdoor pools generally.

Next morning, crossing under a roadway arch declaring *Ohio Welcomes You* we continued along a flat, straight, uninteresting highway busy with traffic. On the truck in front was painted in giant letters: 'Integrity Driven Comments Welcome'.

'What kind of comments would they like?' Jeff asked.

'Explaining what *integrity* driven means would help.'

Soon after 3pm we arrived at a campground in Zanesville. Quickly becoming aware of the idyllic lakeside setting, with extensive meadows and woodland, we decided to stay for the weekend. The uniformity of layout in hotels and motels – worldwide – often contributing to the soulless, impersonal ambience, doesn't apply to campgrounds. In thirty-five years, we have never come across two campgrounds which are the same. For good or bad, each has its own individual character.

A guidebook for the surrounding area listed fifty-eight 'things', in date order, from 1797, when Colonel Ebenezer Zane was given land grants to settle what is now Zanesville, under the heading: *Did You Know?* Well, of course, we didn't know any of it. Put politely, I don't think our not knowing was any great loss! In all our travels we have not visited many places beginning with the letter zed, in American English: 'zee', and we were glad to have stopped off.

In the 1840s, a group of potters came from England to manufacture Rockingham Ware, using clay mined in the area; several potteries are still thriving. We bought a bowl. I don't find it attractive, but many others obviously do, because the makers claim to be 'The World's Largest Manufacturer of Stoneware Crocks'. Astronaut John Glenn, the first American to orbit the earth, in 1962, and later a Senator, was educated at school and college in the vicinity. Maybe his appreciation of the beauty of the earth as seen from outer space, and described in his poetry, developed during his early life in the lovely environment of this part of Ohio. (Incidentally, Ohio has the world's largest Amish population, but they are not a tourist attraction as they are in Pennsylvania.)

The Y-Bridge (the fifth construction at the same location), in downtown Zanesville, spanning the confluence of two rivers, claims to be the only bridge in the world which you can cross and still be on the same side of the river. Another attractive curved span, that we saw in the area, is the S-Bridge.

Jeff, unfortunately, had another couple of stomach upsets. Giving him the opportunity to rest we spent a tranquil day on site, not even going out to eat. From my lounger I watched the antics of gorgeous blue birds, and others, flitting about the lacy trees shading our pitch, while relaxing after a morning walk around the lake and through woods when we saw lots of wild life.

Reluctant to leave the sunlit campground, driving east through pleasant up and down countryside, after a couple of hours we crossed into West Virginia.

'Our 47th state!' I said.

'Only Oregon, of the 48 lower states, has not been graced by our presence,' Jeff mocked.

Squeezed between advertisement jingles on the radio news, there was an item about a tornado in Iowa which had caused several deaths. Later in the day the jingles were repeated – often, the radio station dependent for its existence on the revenue from advertisers, but the account of the tornado was no more. We drove on to Wheeling and stopped at the Wheeling Convention and Visitor Bureau on Main Street.

'We don't know much about West Virginia except that it is very rural (more accurately I should have substituted 'anything' for 'much') I responded to the plump, middle-aged woman's offer, 'How can I help you?'

'You from Canada?'

'Sort of. But we live in England.'

'Not been to West Virginia before?'

'No. That's why we don't know a lot about. . .'

'Many *Americans* don't know a lot about us,' she interrupted ruefully. 'Some don't even know that there is a West Virginia. Think we're western Virginia.'

The Union-supporting West Virginia broke away from Virginia during the Civil War. Rather a long time ago, maybe her comment about some Americans not knowing that it was a separate state was made tongue-in-cheek? She explained that eighty-five per cent of the mountainous state is forested and that, compared with other states, tourism was not developed very much. She listened with interest when we told her about our travels by RV

234

around America.

'This is our 47th state,' we went on.

'Forty-seven!' she blurted, her eyes growing wide. Indicating the visitors' book on the counter, she asked us to, 'Put that in please! Forty-seven!' she repeated. 'That's more than we've had visitors!'

We made a quick tour of the city. Had a look at the world's oldest major long-span suspension bridge, The Wheeling Suspension Bridge, built in 1849, the first bridge across the almost-1,000-mile long Ohio River, an extant feat of civil engineering from before the Civil War; then got a bird's-eye view of everything from Point Overlook Museum.

Back into Pennsylvania, we stopped at the Welcome Center. Having got the information we needed for campgrounds we didn't delay, as five buses disgorged chattering, gesticulating teenagers, who seemed to grow in size and number as they noisily dispersed in all directions. In late afternoon, we missed coming off at the required exit for our intended RV stop, but that was fortuitous, because a few miles further on, in lovely countryside, adjacent to Lake Arthur, was another. All the buildings on the well-kept campground were rustic, festooned with floral greenery. We were the only overnighters.

Our pitch a bit humpy-bumpy; a sweaty, fractious time followed getting Harvi level, but there was plenty of shade under scented, pink blossoming trees and there was no traffic noise.

Jeff wasn't well after our evening meal, complaining of bad pain. He went inside to lie down. As always, *my* stomach started churning. Will it lead to a bout of vomiting, or choking, or angina, or a heart attack? I have had so many frights over the years with all of these things. After twenty minutes he came bounding outside. 'Fully recovered,' he claimed, eager for a walk! 'What about viewing the sunset over Lake Arthur?'

Sparkling in the evening sun, equally captivating early the following warm, misty morning, deserted apart from an abundance of feathered creatures of different species on the long fringe of sand. There were two Canada geese with two tiny goslings. Unhurried, they waddled to the lake as we approached. In the water they moved more quickly. The female repeatedly extended her neck to its limit, then contracted it again. Each time she did this the ball-of-fluff babies put on a spurt of speed for a few moments, then slackened until urged to greater effort again. Inaudible to us, 'Get a move on you two!' must have been the stern command. Other geese were having noisy squabbles, and, some distance from the squawking, both parents, not just one as is usual, stood guard, while their well-grown offspring pecked along the water's edge.

Not needing to vacate the campground until four in the afternoon, we resisted the temptation of staying until then. It would get hotter and thunderstorms were expected. It's not just in the British Isles that people make frequent reference to weather forecasts for later in the day, or further on in the week. Living in the great outdoors as we have always loved to do – in any country! – it makes good sense to be alert to the fickleness of the elements.

Despite lumbering machinery at roadworks, one stretch was ten miles long, driving north we reached Lake Erie in a couple of hours. Otherwise landlocked, Pennsylvania has a forty-mile stretch on the lake. We continued along scenic Route 5, hugging the shoreline, into New York State and booked on to a camp-ground for two nights. Like elsewhere, the swimming pool was not ready for use, but more surprisingly, this far north, not all of the trees were yet in leaf, reminding us of the continental scale of the United States and just how far we had travelled. Was it on *this* trip that we had visited Mexico City, more then 3,000 miles south from here?

After a substantial late lunch we each fell asleep! An almighty clap of thunder and torrential rain, lasting for about half-an-hour, roused us.

'Glad we left the last place when we did and didn't linger,' Jeff said, closing the roof vent against the downpour. 'Otherwise we'd be driving in this.'

Both nights on the campground were chilly, following lovely sunsets viewed across a bay on Lake Erie, and at breakfast with heavy dew on the grass twinkling like frost, we needed the warmth of the fire; the same fire that Jeff had bought second-hand in northern California on our first long journey in Harvi, and here, in New York, we were wrestling with the notion of selling him, would this be one of our last outings?

On our non-driving day we walked the four-mile round trip to the nearest small town. It had three churches, two grocery stores,

236

a McDonald's and several 'Antique' shops – well, in truth, not that kind of antique. Jeff calls these emporiums 'Rummage and Rubbish Shops'. And he adores them. Too bad, like the churches, they were closed. One had a big, battered sign: *Open 1–6pm. Some Days – or – By Chance.* Well, Jeff was in luck (unfortunately!). After we had a snack in McDonald's, the door of that 'Aladdin's Cave' was ajar on our way back. He bought a box of tools for $10. I have learned not to question his prized purchases; like, this time, why does he need any more tools? He has all he requires on board the RV (which maybe we're not going to use much longer). Our son will gently decline them, 'No, Dad, really, thanks all the same.' They'll be too heavy to transport home, where anyway, he has so much 'stuff' in the garage there's never any space for the car, which we have to leave with relatives whenever we are absent from home for long periods. Like now!

Next day we crossed back to Canada at Niagara, making time, as always, to marvel at The Falls. We had tailored this year's trip to take in a big family celebration. As anticipated, it was hugely enjoyable.

In serious vein, Jeff agreed that on our return to England he would insist on having his stomach problems more rigorously investigated than previously. Alas, also the *possibility* of parting with Harvi was becoming a *probability*. To ease our upset at the prospect, we decided to take him to New York City. We'd heard on the grapevine that the RV park in New Jersey, where we'd stayed the previous year, was due to close permanently at the end of the season. Might as well go while it was open and we still had Harvi. How many people arrive for a visit to The Big Apple by motorhome?

Forty-two years to the day since we set out into the unknown, on a journey of 3,500 miles, from Toronto to Vancouver through Canada, much of it on unmade road, in a nine-year-old car piled with all our possessions, and I pregnant – the first and most daring of all our treks? – we headed off for New York City, through the familiar, well-loved Empire State. We had chosen this date for the start of our yearly trip on three occasions. It was a fitting date, we thought, for a fourth one, which might also be our last excursion in Harvi.

Crossing from Canada into the United States at Buffalo, on through New York State (roughly the area of England) that we know so well, on good road, apart from the odd burst tyre, or unfortunate, flattened, dead animal, even a small fawn, staying for a third time in Tunkhannock; then duly arrived, for a second visit, at the New Yorker RV Park. Yes, it *was* going to close permanently, later in the year. Yes, the gorgeous red roses *were* blooming near our pitch, as before.

We had a great week. I indulged my penchant for museums and galleries, meeting up with Jeff, in between visits, to explore other places together. A long, sunny Sunday spent in Central Park was an entertaining experience, including watching an alfresco Jewish wedding conducted by a female Rabbi, while several post-wedding groups vied for the best sylvan backdrop for photographs. World-famous Central Park in mid-Manhattan was designed by Frederick Law Olmsted. How many people are aware that he modelled it on Birkenhead Park, designed by Sir Joseph Paxton, situated across the River Mersey from Liverpool? We knew! The memorial, *Strawberry Fields*, for Liverpool's John Lennon is situated within Central Park – there isn't one in Birkenhead.

Late one evening, the temperature still in the 80sF, we watched enthralled from across the river, the setting sun turn Manhattan ablaze. As the crimson light faded, the scene resembled a painting, when a full moon rose from behind the famous skyline throwing its silver beam on the Art Deco Chrysler building and transforming the Empire State to a slender, blue finger pointing skywards.

'Oh no! Not again! I don't believe this. . .' Jeff groaned. 'Why? Why now?'

On our return journey, nearing Canada, the new starter, fitted a few weeks before in New Mexico, jammed. A fraught time followed. There were little affectionate discussions, which usually finished with, 'It's not *my* fault!' 'Well it *certainly* isn't *mine*!' It didn't seem possible – it was another defective starter. It was Jeff's birthday. Not one of our best celebrations, though it's etched in our memories.

Extensive travelling has to have some low points. Overall, on our trips in the US, there were few, and at no time did Jeff end up in hospital, or need medical care as had happened in Europe, each time with a different – unforeseen – health problem.

(A few years later, while in Australia, travelling on our own,

Jeff contracted meningococcal meningitis *and* septicaemia. Desperately ill, unconscious for several hours, the ambulance on a long journey to hospital got a puncture. . . Against all expectations, he survived – just! 'Thought only young people got that,' folk commented, when, at last, we arrived back in England. 'I am young!' Jeff asserted. 'More like indestructible. . .' people mumbled.)

'You've journeyed through 47 states, only missing out Oregon,' our son said, with considerable pride, we thought! 'Bet there're not many Americans who can equal that.'

'So far we've not met any.'

Our daughter-in-law butted in, giggling, 'All because, in a letter to England, I suggested that maybe – sometime – you should consider booking a vacation to Arizona and The Grand Canyon, as we'd enjoyed it so much.'

'We didn't expect you to buy Harvi and go there *from Canada*!' they laughed.

'When we bought the RV to do that trip in celebration of our Ruby Wedding, we didn't intend to keep it,' we reminded them.

'Or to go on using it year after year,' they replied.

The starter was replaced under guarantee. We gave Harvi our usual loving brush-up and polish, before taking him to storage for the winter, postponing any definite decision to part with him – just yet!

After a few precious weeks with our Canadians, there was, as always, the painful exchange of good-byes and tearful hugs for another long year. Our overnight air flight took us from gloomy 'Au Revoirs' with one section of the family, to a joyous 'Welcome Home' from the rest of the gang, eager to hear our news and pour over maps tracing our route, requesting: 'Let's see the photographs!'

Chapter Eighteen

Visits to Oregon, and Alaska at midsummer, were on the agenda for this year. Four road treks across North America had shown us enough prairies to last a lifetime. No way were we going to *drive* west. Sorry Harvi! Our son arranged the tour. Anticipation tinged with apprehension – after forty years independent travel, our accommodation always with us, would we feel constrained by schedules and pre-arrangements? Would Jeff have enough to occupy him? Confinement with a *bored* Jeff was not my idea of fun.

Departure day, en route to the airport at 6.00am, a mere *twelve* hours since making an emergency visit to a doctor. Having beaten a track from bedroom to bathroom all night, Jeff spent the day on the sofa, ashen faced, dozing, while upstairs I packed, not really believing that we would be travelling. Every half-hour I peeked at him, still prone, still pale.

Solicitous suggestions got negative replies: 'I don't *want* a drink. . . I can't sit up. . . I don't want to go to bed. . . just leave me here.' To expire?

Describing his symptoms on the telephone locally, and to our doctor-daughter-in-law in England, all advised a visit to a medical centre. (Doctors do not make home-visits in Canada.)

'I can't get up. . . go to a clinic. . . let me be.' What particularly disturbed me was the *dog's* behaviour. This friendly, never-quiet, never-still dog (a bit like the usual Jeff, really!) lay facing the sofa, his head on his paws, one ear cocked, hour after hour stretched out motionless. The arrival of the post, a ring at the doorbell, the telephone, my ins and outs provoked no response, but always a half-open eye trained on Jeff. Accounts of dogs being prescient came to mind. What did *he* know?

Our son returned home and before Jeff had time to object we were in the clinic.

'There's no way you'll be able to travel tomorrow,' my son said to me.

I agreed, relieved that I wouldn't have to tell Jeff that, then listen to his protest: 'Of course we can go!'

'Cancel the hire-car in Oregon. If Dad recovers maybe you'll be able to do the land-cruise in Alaska.'

Totally exhausted from lack of sleep and unnerved by past experiences in foreign parts, 'I favour cancelling the entire holiday,' I said, 'not just the first week.'

'We'll see what the doctor says,' my son soothed.

Twenty minutes later Jeff emerged, wan and wobbly, dark circled eyes, face as white as the paper he was clutching.

'It's only a virus. . . not my stomach. . . or heart,' he whispered. 'I can expect to feel unwell for several more days. Here's a prescription. . . got to be careful what I eat. . . and no alcohol.' More words than he had spoken all day!

Like cats, if we have nine lives, I once calculated that Jeff was on life six.

'What about flying?' my son queried.

'That's no problem,' Jeff replied weakly, with just a hint of his usual optimism.

'That's good! How soon can you travel?'

'Tomorrow morning.'

Silence! Inwardly I was furious with Jeff for being un-cooperative all day only to flutter to life the minute he saw a doctor. What about the dog's behaviour? He'd let me down, too! Just as well I'd done the packing – there wouldn't be time now; anyway I felt drained. I had no enthusiasm left. Always, when Jeff has been taken ill, I've been alone with him. Though on the same landmass as the family, we would be 3,000 miles away at our nearest point. Not encouraging!

We'd been treated to the air journeys, in Business Class – a novelty! 'No thanks, none,' Jeff replied to the proffered wine and brandy, as he picked at his food. (And I don't drink alcohol!)

The captain said, 'We'll fly over Lake Michigan, North Dakota, Spokane in Washington.' Though hundreds of miles apart, we'd been in each of those places with Harvi. Five hours after leaving Toronto Pearson Airport, we descended from 39,000 feet – my ears popping painfully, as usual – to a cloud-shrouded Vancouver, the temperature only 57°F.

Much later than scheduled, because our connection was delayed, in pouring rain, we joined heavy traffic straight from the exit ramp at Seattle Seatac Airport in a brand new hire-car, same model as ours in England. Jeff applied the windscreen wipers the *windows* opened. Locating the wipers' switch to tackle the coursing water, we were soaked before he discovered the buttons to close the windows.

'The car's not identical!' we said in unison.

110 miles in torrential rain and spray on busy Interstate 5, some of it wedged behind a smoke-belching van, driving again the road travelled at the beginning of our first trip in the United States, to our overnight motel. Jeff had planned the route carefully because unlike previous trips, this one was not open-ended; there would be no meandering, not as much time to explore. Jaded, when we collapsed into bed dawn was breaking in Toronto. Was it really only this morning that we'd been there?

The Columbia River forms the state line between Washington and Oregon with The Lewis Clarke Road: The Oregon Trail, running alongside. Grey, billowy clouds smoothed the outlines of distant mountains, wooded hill nearer with vultures circling, men fishing, here and there water lilies breaking into flower, and cascading broom flinging great splashes of yellow against green lushness.

'A car ferry crosses the river somewhere here,' Jeff said.

There was a sign: 'End 409', then another: 'To The Ferry'. Down an incline, past a scruffy board giving an hourly schedule, crossing the ramp, only four cars in the space for ten, we paid the princely sum of $3 to a jovial guy in a peaked cap. 'Well timed! That was lucky!' Jeff grinned, as we chugged across at swimming speed.

'Our 48th state! To Oregon by boat!' I exclaimed, when we docked.

The intrepid explorers, Lewis and Clarke, beginning their trek in Missouri in May 1804, finished in Astoria, at the mouth of the

Columbia River, in November 1805, and set up a camp. We'd encountered the famous pair in many places; our contact with the Columbia River, however, goes back more than forty years, when we travelled the hairpin that was The Big Bend Highway in British Columbia, 200 miles of gravel road with *no habitation* between the three equidistant small, service stations. In the early 1800s, at the top of this hairpin, two paths crossed, one of which led to The Oregon Trail. The building of dams flooding the area made the mighty Columbia a series of lakes and reservoirs – alas! – relegating The Big Bend Highway to history.

Dominating Astoria, atop Coxcomb Hill, is the 125-foot Astor Column, patterned, surprisingly, on Trajan's Column in Rome. Having scaled many, including the Leaning Tower of Pisa, whose high platform was then unrailed, we decided to forgo the 'breathless panoramic view' from the top. With its grand Victorian houses, churches, mostly Lutheran, small single-storey shops, sparse traffic, the place had a caught-in-a-time-warp air. Posters plastered abundantly announced their annual Scandinavian Summer Fair, promising Nordic dishes to be sampled, 'music, parades, folk dancing and much more'. Even with *mucho* 'much more' it wasn't going to be a rave-up. That's for sure!

Scenic US 101 skirts the edge of the continent all the way to Mexico. Travelling it in British Columbia, Washington and the whole of the Californian section, in the past, we set off to drive the wild 400-mile, surf-swept, sea-stack studded Oregon Coast.

Haystack Rock, a 235-foot basalt monolith, was reminiscent of the French painter Claude Monet's famous series of hayricks (which I'd seen in exhibitions), a trick of light turning rock into Monet's tangled red and purple hay.

Every bend of the ocean-hugging, two-lane road afforded panoramas of empty beaches fringed with surf. On outcrops of rocks sea-lions basked, the dark-pelted adults contrasting with their golden-brown pups. From an overlook on a high headland, the muffled roar of the Pacific sounding like a jet plane warming up as the mile-long breakers tumbled in a froth of creamy lace on a vast expanse of sand was a stupendous sight! Oregon, *our* 48th state, is surely one of the most spectacular.

The highway descended. 'This place might have a motel by the ocean,' Jeff said, turning down a side road.

An upstairs room gave us a grandstand view. With only brief, bright spells all day, the sun was struggling to penetrate cloud again; quickly dumping our gear, jackets buttoned up against the breeze, we strode along the deserted, driftwood-strewn beach, reminding us of other similar places we loved: Tofino, on the west of Vancouver Island, or northern California. After a long walk, clambering over a pile of ocean-battered debris, up the soft sand bank we took a meandering path through an assortment of unoccupied holiday dwellings of weather-beaten clapboard.

From previous experience knowing that the coffee machines in motel rooms don't produce *boiling* water, the sachets of coffee, whitener, and plastic cups provided, not needing it at that temperature, we brought tea bags, cups, cutlery, two small emersion heaters, bowls. . . A hamlet had a couple of shops and a pizza takeaway. Using the microwave oven we soon had an appetising meal, sitting at the table by the window, overlooking the endless beach. Before the black clouds, mustering along the horizon, joined forces with others hovering menacingly ready to release a deluge, the huge sun dropping seawards sent ribbons of crimson dancing across the waves.

It was a bitter night, squalls rattling the windows and roof keeping us awake. It had never been this uncomfortable in the RV! Numerous cups of tea thawed us; then we slept for a few hours. Having brought sachets of quick-cooking oats because, since his heart bypass operation, Jeff likes to have porridge for breakfast, we devoured bowls of steaming cereal.

Dashing through the drizzle to return the key, the blonde, middle-aged woman in the office chirped, 'It's goin' to be a gorgeous day. By ten or eleven all this is gonna-be-gone.'

Gone? At ten and eleven, and for hours afterwards, beyond the furiously flicking windscreen wipers, there was horizon to horizon rain falling in bucket-loads. With water sloshing everywhere, God's Lighthouse was an aptly named church. We stopped at rain-lashed Depot Bay, reputed to be the smallest port in the world, and then carried on to Cape Foulweather. Yes, that's its name! So called by Captain Cook in 1778 when, heading north from Hawaii, he sought shelter here in a ferocious storm.

'The locals must agree with the appellation or they would surely have changed it,' I said, tightening the hood of my rain jacket.

'Maybe it has rained ever since!' Jeff grunted.

There was a shop crammed with beautiful objects made from distinctive myrtlewood, a rare hard wood native to south west Oregon, extremely difficult to carve. Considering workmanship and quality, the articles were not overpriced. Further south, a basalt headland, Cape Perpetua, was also named by Captain Cook. Nobody knew why it was named after a 3rd century Christian martyr from Carthage.

Confined in a car, we found travelling much more wearisome than it had been in Harvi, with his high-off-the-road seats and big windows. OK, today all was swamped in gloom, but in the spacious comfort of the RV we would have felt less enveloped by the elements.

'How many inches of rain do you reckon we had?' I groused.

'About 100,' Jeff replied.

A disappointing day! There's a Cape Disappointment in Washington, named by an English guy who ended up there instead of finding the Northwest Passage, where he expected to be.

The next morning it was not raining! Time to head north, driving through the famed Oregon Dunes National Recreational Area, forty miles of undulating sand, in places reaching three miles inland, with some dunes as high as 500 feet, and beaches, forests and wetlands. Maritime pines, golden broom and a riot of wild flowers on sandy banks flanked the road. We stopped here and there to view – in sunny weather!

In Florence the Dunes Overlook had viewing docks on three levels. The lowest one gave access down through lush vegetation to powdery sand beaches; from the others there were sweeping panoramas. The dunes region is used by campers, hikers, mountain bikers, buggy enthusiasts and, believe it or not, dog-sledders. Amusing to read that the ocean off the Pacific north-west is actually warmer during winter than in summer, when prevailing currents carry cold water from Alaska southwards, whereas south-west winds push warmer currents northwards in winter, forcing colder currents further from shore.

Heading inland on the 126 through leafy, river-laced countryside, we had lunch in Eugene. Vacating the place in one-way traffic, the University of Oregon area was lovely first time around, trapped on a run-amok-carousel, admiration waned on subsequent circuits. By the time we escaped, the sky was emptying again.

'Probably raining in Portland, too, glad we didn't try to get back there today.'

Portland, Oregon's largest city, was having its biggest spectator event of the year: The Grand Floral Parade of the city's Rose Festival, something I'd planned on seeing, but decided against as the weather channel warned of 'a massive rain storm sweeping in from the ocean.' Instead, in the comfort of a snug motel room, we watched a TV recording of the rain-soaked Rose Festival and Grand Parade. Twenty-five floats each had occupants togged out in rain-gear with enormous umbrellas to match the colour scheme of their flowers.

The Oregonian had a float celebrating its 150th birthday. The newspaper existed before Portland was a city, or Oregon a state. We were very impressed!

The 1190-Kex-One-More-Time-Around-Again-Marching-Band not only has surely the longest title, but is one of the world's largest. It was memorable for the baton twirler, throwing her silver stick twenty feet into the air, doing a couple of turns and two-steps, with a broad smile to the onlookers, before catching her stick – all without missing a beat. She, like the troupes of dancers; smartly dressed high-school bands; mounted posses with well-behaved horses, riding four abreast; had no protection from the elements.

'Heck we've spent all year preparin'; we're not gonna let rain stop us,' participants smiled to the TV cameras.

Drenched, bedraggled onlookers explained: 'Well, reckon'd it would rain this time. It was dry for the past two years.'

Sunday was a washout! Catching through a rain curtain glimpses of attractive buildings along Portland's wide, deserted streets, a deluge-induced disappointment: we didn't visit the renowned rose gardens. Instead, we stopped off at the Servite Monastery, set in lush, landscaped grounds, on various levels, everything dripping, not just the many water features. An elevator ride gave access to a hilltop plateau, with an amazing garden, famous for its *1,100* varieties of trees and shrubs. A floor-to-ceiling curved glass enclosure, promising a 190-degree view over Portland, was *in* dense cloud, swirling white.

Next morning, travelling another scenic route running east,

rain dancing on the road and augmenting the numerous waterfalls, sending them crashing in billowing foam down cloud-obscured mountains, the whine of the wipers competed with the drumming on the car roof. Everywhere: wet! Wet! Wet!

In The Dalles we traipsed to the post office, a smart new building. After twenty minutes in a line-up we gave up. We were about to give up on Oregon, too. We crossed the Columbia River back to Washington. The weather station promised 'No Rain on Wednesday'. By then we'd be flying to Alaska. This had been our only chance to see Oregon. The really frustrating thing about poor weather is that there's no one to blame! A Jewish friend, having saved for many years, was thrilled to visit Israel. Her vacation included one day in the holy city of Jerusalem. Relentlessly it rained all that day, but not on any other.

'Welcome to Washington the Evergreen State – Mile 1' the sign greeted us at the end of the Yakima Bridge.

'Evergreen because ever-raining,' I grumbled.

'No gas for 50 miles' warned a notice. The single-lane road with 'No Stopping Places' across the Yakima Indian Reservation was 'A 24-hour Headlight Area'. The Yakima, also called Cayuse, were famous horse dealers. Oregonians called horses: cayuses. Leaving the Reservation, we stopped at Arco for gas. A notice boasted: 'am/pm Selfserve Gasoline'. 'Glad to be back, eh?' the girl asked Jeff, when he paid. In Oregon it is *illegal* to pump your own gas, but not in Washington.

At a pullout a man entreated: 'Take a look, that's the top of The Mount'n pokin' thro' mist on the lower slopes.' It wasn't till later that we appreciated how lucky we were to see it. Mount Rainier, an active volcano, affectionately called The Mountain, is Washington's tallest peak. That mountain *tops* were visible, when for days we hadn't seen the *bottom* of anything, made us empathise with Noah's frisson of excitement when that dove bearing its olive twiglet swept into view.

Nearing the end of our 1,000-mile trip, in Mount Rainier National Park we headed for somewhere called Paradise. Promptly the sun disappeared. Stopping at a viewpoint for Laughingwater Creek, the rain tumbled from on high once more.

'Laughingwater Creek, Paradise, maybe these places were named to encourage well-being,' I whinged, beginning to identify with the message I'd read on several big billboards: 'Depression

247

is the #1 Cause of Suicide'. Was Gene Kelly the only person ever to *sing* in the rain? By the way, did you know that the heavy 'rain' in the film was a mixture of milk and water? *And* he caught a cold while prancing about in the wet; bet he wasn't singing then.

Driving up and up, green gave way to startling white banks of snow and white trees, then white *fog*. After all, this place has been described as 'an Arctic island in a temperate zone'. The Mountain was laughing its head off at the cold, sodden folk here from far flung places all over the continent, judging by the car registration plates, and two from England for whom, like my friend in Jerusalem, this visit would be their only one. The weather had won again!

The view of dazzling, white-capped Mount Rainier, in a cloudless blue heaven, an expanse of flower-fringed reflective water at its base, was reproduced ad nauseam. A man in the shop admitted that he hadn't often seen The Mountain, though living there, seasonally, for years. There was a post office (on a mountain peak!) with stamps for the cards that I'd been carrying around.

An observation deck gave a 360-degree view, not of 'twenty-five glaciers' just fog. A cheery notice instructed: 'In case of earthquake (or a prolonged rumbling noise) GO TO HIGHER GROUND', accompanied by a drawing of two tiny figures walking uphill, 'Get to 160 feet or more above River Level'. There was nothing to say what you did *then*. A warning about bears went on: 'Black bears may be Brown, Tan or Blond'. Apparently, too, we were in Mountain Lion Country, 'also known as Cougars or Pumas'; the chilling accompanying advice: 'If attacked, fight back aggressively' and nearby a request: 'Please Report All Sightings asap'. Sightings? Whether from survivors, who fought back aggressively, or those recovering *their* grisly remains wasn't clear.

Descending from Paradise we covered the seventy miles to Seattle and booked into a motel near the airport. In an airy restaurant Jeff declaring his health a little improved, in celebration, ordered a T-bone steak, chomping away appreciatively before groaning, 'Oh! No!' as he removed a tooth imbedded in his steak. He now had a hole in the centre of his top teeth. A similar incident occurred years before, also near the *beginning* of a holiday. I had to listen to him whistling through a gap. Now the same would happen on our first luxury cruise. He hasn't lost any other teeth – ever!

'No way am I going to try to find a dentist here. No way!'

No way does he ever go to a dentist apart from that one visit.

In the morning, returning the car, we boarded the plane for Alaska. Before gaining height there was a great view of Seattle with its Space Needle then, from 31,000 feet, vessels diminished to miniatures: ships negotiating the Inside Passage.

Alaska, a corruption of the Aleut word, Alyeska, meaning 'the great land', officially became the 49th state on 3rd January, 1959, though an American flag had flown there since 1867 (the same year that the Dominion of Canada was established), when the huge landmass was bought from Russia for two and a half cents per acre. If superimposed on a map of the US, Alaska is almost a quarter of its size, but sparsely populated. Straddling the International Date Line, it's on a time zone of its own, four hours behind New York, nine hours behind GMT. Flying in over the treacherous mud flats of Cook Inlet (how that fellow got around!), against a backdrop of the ice-capped Chugach Mountains, lay Anchorage surrounded by a vast wilderness.

In a display case in the Hilton Hotel's lobby, standing seven feet tall on its hind legs, mouth open showing enormous teeth, nails long as fingers, stood a stuffed brown bear and in equally ferocious stance, nine feet tall, a polar bear, its paws with hairy soles for gripping the ice, both animals reminders, if rather incongruous here, that Alaska is their territory. The hotel promised: 'spectacular views' from its windows; our bedroom overlooked a tiny triangle of concrete, the size of the bathroom, formed by three towering walls, necessitating artificial light always in this city of *twenty-hour days*.

Outdoors, we weren't sure what to expect. The first thing that struck us was the clarity of the light; the second: the feeling of space; the third: that it was a pleasant 70°F, but not humid. It was going to be great! There were few tall buildings along the wide, straight streets of the usual North American grid. The Visitors' Center, a rustic cabin, had a *sod roof* of luscious grass and standing outside a 5,144-pound jade boulder, mined inside the Arctic Circle. There were hanging baskets, tubs, containers of all sizes bursting with blooms, large and vivid, thanks to the long hours of summer sunshine.

Hit by an earthquake in 1964, the ground beneath some buildings in Anchorage, situated as it is on glacial silt deposits, slid into the sea; however many original structures survived including the Art Deco 4th Avenue Theater. Holy Family Cathedral was transported, in the early 1920s, to 5th Avenue from the distant town of Knik by – would you believe? – horse and sleigh.

Later that year, an article of mine, about our visit to the Shrine of Our Lady of Guadalupe, in Mexico City, was published in a magazine in *England*. Published, subsequently, there was a reply in appreciation of it from a lady in *Anchorage*. I wrote saying that we'd visited *her* cathedral – a small world, eh?

Feeling unwell from airplane sickness, tiredness, Jeff's virus, or whatever, I bucked up on seeing the double-decker, dark-blue and silver train, *The McKinley Explorer*, its locomotive a cheery yellow with blue trim, for the journey into The Interior. Tracy, a student on vacation from university, was our guide on railcar Chena. As the train slid gently out of the station, she told us about The Iditarod Trail Dog Sled Race; a marathon, 1,100 miles, from Anchorage to Nome, taking about twelve days, held every March. A 'musher' is the person in charge of a dog team. A 'husky' is any dog that pulls a sled (once, a team of poodles competed). An unexpected thaw in Anchorage one year meant that snow was brought in by dump trucks before the race could begin. In recent times Susan Butcher won on three consecutive years. 'The male dominated sport was not amused,' laughed Tracy, turning around. On the back of her T-shirt was the slogan: 'In Alaska where men are men, And women win the Iditorad.' .

Giving us points of the clock, she said, 'Right now at 9 o'clock the jets are ready for their mornin' run.'

Sounding a bit like *Alice in Wonderland* crossed with *West Side Story*, it referred to the Elmedorf Airbase with its jet planes and 6,500 airmen. The roar of aircraft, silver streaks in the bright sun, was not easily associated with the wilderness on Anchorage's doorstep. From dog sleds to jet planes Alaska has it all.

On the 3 o'clock side a marker indicated every mile for 470 miles. Raising her voice above the train's clackety-clack Tracy called, 'Watch for milepost 141; we'll go over a bridge and soon after is Exluta, one of the largest Native villages in this area. Look out for the onion dome of a church.' Peeping up among foliage was St. Nicholas' Russian Orthodox Church, which is listed on the National Register of Historic Places. This mingling of eastern European religious culture with Native Indian we encountered in various parts of the state, a reminder that Alaska was Russian long before being American.

We crossed creeks, blocks of ice tumbling in green waters, snow tucked in pockets, in an area where many trees were lost in an earthquake. Tracy recounted how silt and fish from Alaska were found in caves in Arkansas, 3,000 miles south, carried there by tsunami generated by the eruption. In the 3-month-season of long, sunny days, given fertile soil, crops of lettuce, potatoes, carrots and peas are grown. If moose don't get there first, giant pumpkins and cabbages are commonplace, for instance a 190-pound pumpkin, an 80-pound cabbage. What would you do with an 80-pound cabbage? A bit heavy for basketball! It's not surprising that coleslaw accompanies so many meals. During the frigid, dark months of winter trees make no growth. In the vast, austere landscape we passed through, they were dwarfed to insignificance.

Every thirty miles or so, there was a cluster of wooden houses. At some distance from any dwelling, perched on four sturdy poles, ten feet off the ground, is the cache (food store), as important today as it's ever been. Bear proof! Access is by portable ladder, removed after each use.

To the west, a range of towering, white-topped, black mountains, their slopes widely striped with glacial streamers, looked for all the world like an endless procession of zebras: the 600-mile-long Alaska Range with twenty-three peaks over 10,000 feet, with more glaciers and ice fields than in all the rest of the inhabited world.

From time to time there were shrieks, 'Look! A bear! A bear!'

An excited scramble to the side of the train.

'Where?'

'There!'

'Ooooh!'

Jeff and I, though seeing bears in the wild in Canada, were equally delighted.

I hadn't eaten for twenty-four hours. Sitting with Ginny and Frank, in the restaurant, *I* asked the question that *we* were always being asked, 'Where are you from?' Our fellow travellers came from all over the US, with a few from Canada and Europe.

'From Vermont,' (on the far side of the continent) Ginny answered.

'Which part?'

'Near Burlington on Lake Champlain. Doya know where that is?'

'Yes, it's a beautiful area and a lovely city. We stayed in Ferrisburg to the south.'

Astonishment crossing their faces, 'Wotcha know, Ferrisburg's where we live!' they chortled.

They were greatly impressed by our jaunts through all 48 lower states, especially when they learned that we lived in England, not Canada.

On relating my meeting with Ginny and Frank, Jeff spluttered with laughter, 'While filming outside, I was talking to a fellow from home. About half a mile from our house. We've come 7,000 miles to meet here!'

The train slowed for a while, not that it had been rollicking; after all it was a sightseeing trip; Tracy called out, 'On the 9 o'clock side, folks, a 100 miles away, Mount McKinley, North America's highest mountain, can be seen on a clear day. Not visible now. Sorry!'

At Talkeetna, 'meaning river of plenty', the train stopped. Originally an Indian village, today it's geared for the flight-seeing and climbing expeditions for Mount McKinley. Earlier in the week a successful rescue had been mounted. 'Last year,' Tracy recalled, 'a man with two false legs, injured years before on Mount McKinley, succeeded in reaching the top,' – a heady 20,320 feet. Susan Butcher, of Iditarod fame, *mushed* to the summit. Tough people these Alaskans!

For sixty miles north of Talkeetna, with no trails, the local twice-weekly train is the only lifeline for those living in the bush. I joined Jeff on an open section of the lower deck. Beyond a frieze of dark, stunted spruce were the never-ending 'zebra' mountains, with no opportunity today of seeing Mount McKinley (like not seeing Mount Rainier, in Washington); though other high peaks were awesome with stunning scenery on both sides of the *single* track. Slowly we thumpied, thumpied, thumpied across the Hurricane Gulch Trestle, the creek 296 feet below. At times we could see the locomotive ahead rounding a curve and then looking behind the end carriages completing the turn, but mostly it was straight ahead for mile after mile. Crossing a beautiful, broad taiga valley, the train climbed to Summit, the watershed divide: south of here rivers flow into Cook Inlet, while to the north, waters eventually reach the Bering Sea. This enormous world, the breeze on my face, was exhilarating!

The train pulled on to a siding. The southbound train's three large headlights in a triangle were visible in the distance, then the yellow and blue engine with its trail of dome cars smoothly drew to a stop. Personnel transferred between trains. It's a long way down, or up, when there's no platform; a box-like step was placed by an open door of each train and the departing, or boarding, staff got hauled the rest of the way by helping hands. An exchange of greetings, a few waves and the *Spirit of Alaska* was southbound.

Continuing northwards, in the late afternoon, our train arrived at Danali Village. Denali – a Tanana Indian word, meaning 'The Great One', Mount McKinley, of course! – is surrounded by snow-capped mountains. It was thrilling strolling around taking photographs, at 11pm *in sunshine*! Sleep was patchy, then at 8am we set off for a Natural History tour into Denali National Park, greater in size than the state of Massachusetts, in a shuttle bus – not built for comfort! – along a gravel road giving vistas of the taiga and tundra landscape, with low, green hills nearby, jagged, glacial peaks in the distance. 'Mount McKinley's not visible,' Mike our driver-guide said. Like elusive Mount Rainier, so with Mount McKinley. A guy working in the village told us that he'd only seen it *once*, and he'd lived there for *six* years!

Several moose, some with young, a bull six feet high at the shoulder, with a fantastic spread of antlers, ambled morosely, ignoring the bus, in an out of scrappy bushes; a vixen with an animal in her mouth, like a pet dog with a newspaper, kept pace with us for some distance, before disappearing into the undergrowth; later we saw her litter by an icy stream, frisky bundles of golden fur. We all spilled off the bus to focus binoculars on green hills speckled white with grazing Dall sheep, shy creatures with the sense to keep well away from camera-toting tourists; caribou were also spotted, while sailing nonchalantly in great sweeps in the wide sky were golden and bald eagles. The park is the habitat for thirty-six species of mammals and more than 150 species of birds. We watched a big grizzly snuffling around on the far side of a partly-thawed stretch of water in the moss-clad tundra valley, his lumbering gate and black nose enabling us to see him, despite his camouflage fawn coat merging with the ground cover of sedge and dried grasses. From the safety of the bus we saw another, up close – huge and ferocious.

Rejoining *The McKinley Explorer* we travelled north through coal fields, flat lowlands, then swamps. Permafrost close to the surface inhibiting water drainage causes swamps and bogs: a perfect breeding ground for millions of mosquitoes called, because of their size, Alaska's State Bird. Summer temperatures can reach 90°F to 100°F dipping to minus 70°F in winter. It was sobering to visualise working conditions in that range of temperature when we travelled through places associated with the Gold Rush.

Fairbanks Station is the terminus of the Alaska Railroad. There are no rail tracks, nor roads of any kind north of here, only airways, or sled trails! Situated on a river plain, Fairbanks charmed us from the moment we arrived and were driven to the hotel along quiet, wide streets full of light. 'At mid-summer, it never gets darker than twilight, though the sun dips below the horizon for a couple of hours,' the driver explained.

We weren't aware of the 'dip'. At midnight golden light flickered across our room each time the gauze window drapes billowed inwards on the gentle breeze and before 5am we were awakened by the startling brilliance of the sun. Five hours' sleep was good, we realised, when Heidi, with the longest hair I've ever seen, our driver-guide, a Mormon, on vacation from university in Utah, said, 'I love this place, but with almost constant sunshine I don't switch off; my body refuses to wind down; I hardly sleep – no matter how tired I am.'

Fairbanks, Alaska's second city, founded during the Gold Rush, retains the air of a frontier town, and the first building Heidi pointed out was a shotgun cabin. Built as a one-room dwelling (shack, really!) it could be added to if the owner was successful, if not, the poor guy used his shotgun to put himself out of his misery.

We stopped off to see Alaska's prestigious 800-mile-long oil pipeline, 'One of the largest such systems in the world,' Heidi explained proudly, adjusting the hairband that kept her mane away from her face. 'Built to withstand earthquakes, crossing three mountain ranges and more than 800 rivers, it delivers twenty per cent of the nation's domestic oil.' Half the length of pipeline is elevated five feet overground to allow the uninhibited migration of caribou; the buried half, ironically, has to be insulated to prevent heat generated by flowing oil from melting the permafrost. What a scarring incongruity it looks in this beautiful wild place!

A cruise aboard a sternwheeler gave us a taste of the 'real' Alaska. In Fairbanks, two of the three hotels are boarded up outside the brief summer, from break-up to freeze-up being only about 120 days; but our trip took us past year-round detached homes, each had walls with twenty to thirty inches of insulation and windows with quadruple glazing. Skis replace the floats on planes, now moored on the river, when the ice reaches a depth of five feet.

'In winter it can be a comfortable minus 40°F up the hillsides here,' Jon, our commentator said. (*Comfortable!* – I loathe, absolutely loathe, any *minus* temperature, but *minus* 40°F. . .) Fairbanks has the widest temperature spread of any city on earth, 'from minus 66°F to plus 99°F.'

The sternwheeler tied up at a summer village. Alaskan Natives from the four main Native groups demonstrated ancient skills. There were remedies, extracted from plants, for everything from constipation to serious diseases; beautiful baskets; bead embroidery; babiche: rawhide strips – from moose – could be used for snowshoes, fishing nets, or if really desperate boiled for soup.

'In the lower 48, some folk don'wanna wear animal skins, up here, though, furs are worn for *survival*,' Gina, dressed in jeans and T-shirt, batting away mosquitoes, stated in a no-nonsense-take-that tone of voice. Then, maybe catching sight of disapproving faces, she went on, 'My family live in Huslia, in the Arctic. Gets mighty cold in win'er, remember there's very little light,' she paused – as if to aerate her point – 'and *no sun* for months!' Having anticipated any possible resistance, she proceeded to show a vast array of pelts. Among them were ones of a moose and a grizzly – so enormous that even those vehemently opposed to the fur-trade, must surely salute the bravery of the persons who got *this* close to those beasts; timber wolf; lynx (bobcat); wolverine, 'the warmest fur of all'; marten, mink, 'not warm enough for clothing only trimming'; and two fox furs: one brown (red) the other, silver. 'Both colours can be in the same litter,' Gina explained.

Fanny, about twelve years old, an Eskimo from Kotzebue, within the Arctic Circle, in its early life a reindeer station, went walkabout, proudly modelling a magnificent parka-style fur coat with two hoods, one fitting her head snugly, her thick, jet-black fringe, jutting out underneath, the bigger one trimmed with a great hoop of fluffy white fur like a halo around her stunningly pretty face, her dark eyes a-twinkle. She readily agreed, posing with a beaming smile, for a photograph. *My* suppressed smile was at her footwear. From under this sumptuous, authentic Native parka of incredible workmanship protruded feet encased in new, startlingly white *trainers*! – proof that younger people of the Native culture are not much different from other young folk, while remaining proud of their traditional skills.

The big 24-hour Supermarket in Fairbanks was deserted. 'See, this weekend we've The Summer Solstice Celebrations. This evenin', at ten, the 10K Midnight Sun Run begins. . . with thousands of runners. Everyone's out along the route,' the checkout girl said, 'except me,' she added ruefully, joining us at a table in the cafe.

'I'm fascinated with all this marvellous light and sunshine, but I shudder to imagine what it must be like in winter,' I said.

'Most of the year is win'er!' the girl laughed. 'That's why so much fuss is made of the week's *mid-summer* celebrations. From now on, each day there's less light. . . it happens quickly. . . until we've just a few hours of twilight daily. Still we're not as bad as Barrow, on the north slope; they've two whole months when they've no light at all!'

'How awful! I'd die! I find our temperate, gloomy winters bad enough. D'you get used to the lack of light?'

'Some do. . . some just go nuts! Take my mother, she's not nuts mind you,' the girl quickly assured us, 'but she can't take it anymore. She's lived here all her life. Now, she can't tolerate the perpetual twilight. . . The family's bought her a special daylight lamp; she sits under that for hours everyday to beat her darkness depression. Keeps her sane.' Before taking up her position again at the checkout, she brightened, declaring, 'The good side is in win'er we have the Aurora Borealis – often as many as 200 times in a season.'

'200!' I exclaimed. Years before, living in Vancouver, we'd seen the Northern Lights a few times. To behold that dazzling display of dancing coloured light 200 times must be some compensation for the lack of daylight – for those who live there, not for me, though, not even with a special daylight lamp, more likely I'd resort to a shotgun, like the poor blokes in the shotgun cabins.

From the aircraft we looked down on Fairbanks, each house, on a quiet Sunday morning, had a car on the driveway and a 2, 4 or 6-seater plane on a landing strip nearby. None of us saw Mount McKinley, despite the Captain's saying that it was 'visible today'. Now we were never going to see it!

On arrival in Anchorage, with no time for a meal, we'd been promised a 'packed lunch on the motor-coaches' taking us from Anchorage to Seward, to join the cruise ship. For the three-hour ride, Jeff and I, with another couple across the narrow passageway, were on the last seats of the trailer section of a bendy-bus. I'm not a good bus traveller at the best of times. . . Our garrulous driver could talk without drawing breath; with overhead speakers along the bus there was no escaping the torrent of information – a captive audience, but not a captivated one.

It used to be a dog sled track; now the single-lane road twisting through the Kenai Mountains is regarded as one of the ten best scenic drives in the entire US. It was a gloomy day with low cloud, small trees, stretches of water shivering in the stiff breeze, bald eagles perched disconsolately in twos or threes, snow lying in places, glacial streamers striping rugged mountains, the surroundings were striking, if we had not already surfeited on spectacular scenery, in *sunshine*; anyway, hungry, bundled in bulky jackets, eager to attack lunch, there was much ripping open of paper bags, swiftly followed by gasps of disbelief at the frugal contents, accompanied only by (very cold!) bottled water. The driver's statistics rattled on. So did the bus. Each time we hit a bump, which was frequently, all the passengers in the trailer section leapt upwards from their seats.

'Everyone OK at the back?' our cheery chappy called.

For those of us at the end of the trailer, our jumping upwards alternated with hanging on for dear life each time we rounded a bend, which was frequently.

'Everyone OK at the back?'

Directly behind Jeff and me was the toilet cubicle. With a broken lock, there was no way of jamming the door shut. It swung open outwards, then clattered closed again with monotonous rhythm. On one occasion a startled gentleman hurtled out of the cubicle trousers at half-mast, and was deposited in the lap of an equally startled woman across from us.

'Everyone OK at the back?'

After another hour or so, turning off the highway, The Voice called, 'Here we are folks at the Wildlife Refuge I was telling you about.' We bumped along a dirt road past enclosures with, 'Caribou, reindeer, moose, there's one with calves, that bald eagle has only one wing. . ' to a picture-postcard, red-roofed, log cabin against a dramatic background of towering, snow-covered mountains. It truly was lovely.

'We'll stop here for thirty minutes.'

Silence. No one moved.

'Doya wanna get off. . . stretch your legs. . . have a hot drink?'

A hot drink would have been great; I longed for one, some food, too, but – no one moved.

'Nobody wanna get off?' More than a hint of desperation in The Voice, 'Sure?'

'Nope.' 'No thanks.' 'Just get us to the ship.' 'To Seward.' voices chorused.

Nonplussed, the poor guy turned tail and we bounced back to the highway. From then on he was silent! Next time we weren't given any option. He pulled into a parking lot saying only, 'Well I need a break,' turned off the engine and departed.

Served us right! Here all we could do was watch the long line-up for each door of a row of 'Rent-a-Cans': none-too-salubrious portable lavatories.

There was rain on the blustery wind, on arrival at Seward, about 4pm. It was a relief to get aboard the cruise ship where, 'all shook up' after the bus ride, we made straight for our cabin, the stench of stale tobacco smoke halting us in the doorway. While the powers-that-be readily accepted that the cabin was 'disgusting', with no alternative accommodation available, the bedding, window drapes and room-dividing hangings were all replaced, but it was the *shampooing* of the carpet, which took hours to get

258

nearly-dry, that delayed us until *midnight* before we opened our bags, had showers and fell exhausted into bed. Not a great beginning to our luxury cruise!

That evening, with just one sitting for dinner – apart from the meagre snack, it was eleven hours since breakfast – there were no latecomers. We trouped into the dining room to hear an announcement that several hundred passengers had been stranded owing to aeroplane problems – the ship would sail four hours behind schedule. Great news! Being 'homeless' owing to the problem with our cabin meant that we hadn't freshened up. Sitting at table with a couple from Canada, who, like everyone else, had *dressed* for dinner, discussing the advantages of being retired, Robert said, 'Right now I'm too busy, but I'm considering. . .' his voice trailed off. In slow motion, an elderly lady at the next table slid from her chair to the floor beside us. Calmly rising to his feet, then kneeling beside the prone figure, 'I'm a doctor,' Robert said. Medical staff arrived with a wheelchair. . .

'So much for saying that you were considering retirement; *that* happened as if on cue,' Jeff said, when we resumed our seats.

Later on (still homeless), we learned that the lady had fainted from *hunger*. Honestly!

Next morning, the fog with rain was not the only reason for the cancellation of sightseeing around College Fjord. The ship sailed closer to land to enable a helicopter to airlift a sick passenger, his wife and a nurse to hospital. In place of the helicopter pad on ferries that we'd travelled on in Europe, this 55,500-ton liner had a huge swimming pool (fat lot of use in this weather). From a lower deck I watched the helicopter making wide circles before hovering, about fifteen times, a brave soul at its open door lowering a stretcher only to have to raise it again each time the wind blew it sideways, before the three were winched, individually, aboard.

The ship then sailed across open stormy water. Not expecting that a cruise ship would roll and toss as it did, I hadn't anticipated being sea-sick, but I was. Very! The Captain's public apology for not stabilising the ballast quickly enough was no compensation for my missed Captain's Gala! Things could only get better.

By the following afternoon the storm had abated. We even had sun for the magical four hours spent on the top deck, in Glacier Bay, viewing up close the crystal blue ice of sixteen awesome glaciers, tidewater ones calving with tremendous crashes sending up great walls of stiff spray. Here, ships of all sizes being regulated, ours was the only cruise liner, with a few small boats and kayaks. The ocean strewn with ice floes, seals and birds drifted nonchalantly on moving ones. Leaving the bay, accompanied by a couple of acrobatic humpback whales, we watched their antics from our cabin. For the next five days, sailing against a backcloth of stupendous scenery, we relished our wide window on the world.

The Tlingit (pronounced Clinkit) is the dominant Native tribe of Southeast Alaska, numbering about 11,000. Sitka, a Tlingit name, the capital of Alaska until the beginning of the 20th century, in the shadow of Mount Edgecombe, an extinct volcano, was our first port of call. Going ashore by tender, I joined a tour; Jeff preferred to wander on his own. 'Alaska is known for its "liquid sunshine" take one of these,' Judy, our driver-guide said, indicating a heap of large umbrellas.

Situated on Baranof Island, with rustic rain forests and an ocean-swept, pebble beach, in Russian times the place was called New Archangel. At St. Michael's Cathedral with its malachite onion dome and gold Russian cross and bell tower, following the Julian rather than the Gregorian calendar, some people celebrate two Easters and two Christmases. Its famous library was lost in a fire in 1966, when fortunately its many other religious treasures and icons were saved.

Escaping a downpour, the group sought shelter at the Alaska Raptor Center, and dripped dry while hearing about efforts to rehabilitate injured bald eagles. With a wing span of six to eight feet, they can spot a fish from a mile high and dive at an amazing 100 miles per hour. Their 7,000 feathers weigh more than their bones.

'Eight Stars of Gold on a Field of Blue, The Bear and the Great North Star', the distinctive Alaskan flag was much in evidence here as throughout the state. Several classy shops had displays of fur coats and other quality non-fur things. Also lots of stuff, in this unique frontier, marked 'Made in China'.

Looking out our big window (I know it's called a porthole), early the next morning, we were amazed to be 'parked' at the base of a towering, ice-striped mountain in Alaska's capital city, Juneau. No need for a tender, just walk across the gangplank into town. Situated along a narrow, saltwater channel, founded by a down-and-out gold prospector, Joe Juneau, it is the only state capital inaccessible by road. Eighty-five per cent of visitors arrive by sea, the rest by air. There were only modest Alaska Marine Ferries plying these waters before the flourishing cruise ship industry barged in. 'If Tourism thrives, the Wild won't survive' – there's mounting concern that the previously small fishing towns along this coast are losing their original character. *Cruise Control*, a lobbying group, wishes to limit the number and size of ships. A liner, docked at the same time as ours, was taller than the tallest buildings in town. (Another which visits was *three* times the size of the ship in which we sailed the Atlantic to Canada in the late 1950s; the 75,000-ton monster has a golf course on board, for heaven's sake!) Often four ships a day call. *The Peace and Quiet Coalition* want to limit the number of roaring *helicopters* and 'These flight planes flipping overhead like demented moths,' complained a disgruntled man.

It was not somewhere that we could have visited by RV; and though in full agreement with the need to protect this marvellous environment, *we* were *here* now and never would be again; however, we found plenty to enjoy without taking a helicopter or plane ride. A notice displayed prominently in several places read: 'Caution – you are travelling in Bear Country' with advice on what to do and not to do because 'Bears don't like surprises. . .' Not half as much as those meeting one, I'd say. In a pharmacy, next to the famous Red Dog Saloon, we got linctus for our coughs, probably brought on by the not-yet-dry carpet, which had kept our cabin much too chilly for comfort.

Picturesque Ketchikan, our last port of call, is Alaska's most southern outpost with floatplanes lined up like taxis along the waterfront. Its attractions are myriad from flight-seeing trips to the Misty Fjords National Monument, four times the size of Rhode Island, to Saxman Village and Totem Bight Park, possessing the largest collection of Totem Poles in the world. There's Creek Street, built on pilings over Ketchikan Creek, the former red-light district of Gold Rush days with its museum, Dolly's House, in the former home of Dolly, a successful madam, and lots of 'quaint' shops – no indication that Ketchikan wished to restrict tourism! Feeling better than we had done all holiday, during a long, interesting day, we escaped with just brief showers.

Ketichikan, with 170 inches of rain annually, is the wettest city in the United States.

No more trips ashore. During the sunlit evening, changing to Pacific Time at Dixon Entrance, the international boundary between Alaska and Canada, the American pilots disembarked and the Canadian pilots came on board for the remainder of the cruise, through the coastal waters of British Columbia.

While the pilots coped with navigational challenges, we spent most of the last day on deck in glorious weather, as the ship threaded its way between evergreen islands within touching distance and timbered hillsides all around. Watching small fishing vessels, bald eagles, a couple of killer whales, some porpoises, busy in their home territory, I really *did* feel guiltily that *big* ships were intruders here. The names of places of forty years ago floated back into memory, as we sailed the calm, sunlit waters of the British Columbian section of the Inside Passage through some of the world's most stunning scenery.

We well remember from our time in Vancouver the excitement and relief expressed when the top of Ripple Rock, the two-headed pinnacle hazard, in Seymour Narrows, causing the sinking of more than 100 vessels, was blown off by the, then, world's largest non-atomic explosion. Without the Rock, but with currents that can reach sixteen miles per hour, Seymour Narrows is still a challenge for ships. Today, though, all was tranquil for the conclusion of our trip.

Vancouver was a mere seventy years old, the first *white* woman born there still alive, when we lived in the city! The place has grown up and out and sea transport proliferated since then. Big ships in our day were bound, not for Alaska, but New Zealand and Australia. Vancouver's celebrated Heritage Buildings, now dwarfed by others, were the *only* large ones then.

'*We* are *History*,' Jeff chortled at the idea.

'Well, now we've made more History. Maybe, even, created a Record,' I laughed. 'Bet not many have covered as much ground throughout the North American Continent as we have.'

'Especially as we don't even *live* here,' Jeff agreed. 'Apart from the Yukon and Northern Territories in Canada, and the state of Hawaii in the United States we've been everywhere else. Amazing!'

Skipping breakfast, early the next morning we were among the few on deck. I wasn't prepared for the overwhelming nostalgia that swamped me as I gazed misty-eyed across the misty waters of English Bay towards Point Grey, where we had lived with our first child – now, he'd booked this trip for us! (Our other three children were born in England.) How lovely were the memories as we drifted under The Lions' Gate Bridge past Stanley Park in the soft morning light, towards the majestic white sails of Canada Place Cruise Ship Terminal.

Our married life was coming full circle. If our son had not been Canadian by birth would he have returned as an adult and settled in Canada? Would we visit him and his family every year? Would we regard Canada as our second home? Would we now be returning from Alaska, our *49th* American state? If. . .

Chapter Nineteen

With much heart-tugging, on our return to our family in Ontario from Alaska, we parted with Harvi, posing beside him for a last photograph, before wishing his new owners as much thrilling travel on board as we'd had. Anyway, we couldn't take him to the Hawaiian Islands, the only state not yet graced by our presence!

In Vancouver, when we lived there, some friends arrived back from a vacation in the Hawaiian Islands, not yet an American state. (The Islands received statehood in the same year as Alaska, 1959.) 'The islands are just so gorgeous!' they enthused. 'You must go,' they urged. 'Go see for yourselves!'

Taking their advice – forty years later! – we did.

Our 50th American state, ironically, despite those well-meaning friends of long, long ago, the only one not visited from Canada, but from England on an escorted tour. The temperature, a mere 55°F in San Francisco where we changed planes, five hours later and 2,500 miles from the Californian coast, landing at Honolulu, on the most geographically isolated archipelago in the world, it was 84°F. Scented breezes, swaying palms, exotic flowers. . . Paradise awaited us!

Watching the spectacle of our first tropical sunset at Waikiki Beach alleviated our travel weariness. Then, totally dark at 7pm, too early for bed, despite the thirty hours since having any sleep, we turned our attention to the show on the open-air stage, where lissom girls, their skirts oscillating rhythmically to chants and music demonstrated *Hula*, while a good-looking, overweight,

264

Hawaiian woman, dressed in a gown called a *Muumuu*, a cloud of yellow silk, explained the complexity of their dance.

The familiar *skurd* is all important, 'using about 100 leaves. If the rib bone at the back is not removed it bends and snaps, so first the *gurl* debones each Ti-leaf to make it flexible. . . like *paber*. . . pliable. . . softer.'

'Wish her voice was softer,' Jeff groaned. The louder swelled the music the more she screeched into the mike above it.

After deboning, painstaking hand-sewing is done, overlapping all the leaves individually on to a waistband. Following every performance, the *skurd* requires maintenance: 'each leaf is laid *flad*, then sprinkle' with *wader*, rolled up and put in a refrigerator. That way the *skurd* might last for two months, but in the sun,' she shrugged, 'no such luck. . . *aboud* one month only.'

'What a lot of fuss – for *that*!' groused Jeff.

'You've no appreciation of the finer things in life,' I teased.

'Hours stitching 100 blasted leaves – for pity sake!'

It was time we got some shut-eye!

Hula, often just regarded as entertainment for tourists, is more important than that – its origins and place in the life of the Islands is woven into Hawaiian history. Before their written word existed, *mele oli* chants and *mele hula* chants with movements were used for passing on information from one generation to the next. *Hula* schools, following rigorous guidelines, taught sacred music and dance forms for performance on ceremonial occasions, and to record historical happenings, legends and customs. Hawaiians believed that physical events could be controlled by responding to them through words and gestures. All a far cry from the 'performance', much as it was enjoyable, at Waikiki Beach.

Waikiki, Hawaii, Honolula, *hula*, *aloha*. . . familiar words, Wiki Wiki (quick, quick) was the name of the shuttle bus taking us from Arrivals to Baggage Claim. *Aloha* meaning 'love' or 'peace' is both a greeting and a farewell, and *mahalo*: thank you, and other Hawaiian words, were in use on the aircraft. Missionaries were the first to *write* Hawaiian, giving the alphabet five vowels, like ours, but only *seven* consonants: h,k,l,m,n,p,w. A consonant is *always* followed by a vowel, so that, consonants never come in pairs, but vowels often do, sometimes even in threes or more. *Oo*: is a Hawaiian honeyeater, *Heiau*: a temple or place of worship. Their alphabet with only twelve letters doesn't

m

mean that all words are short – heavens, no! A fish: humuhu-munukunukuapuaa, a word of twenty-one letters, requires just seven letters of their alphabet, leaving unused two consonants and three vowels!

Such is jet lag that, after five hours sleep, we were awake again and making tea with miserable tea bags and not-quite-boiling-water from the coffee percolator in our airy room heavily scented by our leis, received at the airport, draped on the back of a chair.

'Wish we'd brought our water heaters with us.'

'Yeah, and some decent tea bags. . .'

After an early breakfast, we assembled for a tour of Honolulu.

'Aren't you guys big!' Gary, the tour manager, from California, exclaimed to the driver of the Polynesian Adventure bus, attired in gaudy shirt of tent-like proportions, more than filling the entire doorway, when we took our seats. Both sexes were dark haired with smooth skin, usually attractive; the women lithe, sylph-like when young, older ones plumper, most Hawaiian men were tall and broad.

Ours made no reply to this personal comment, maybe accepting it as a compliment. Anyway, there was no disputing so blatant a fact, though 'big' was an understatement, really. Built like a wrestler, with an intake of breath to reduce his girth he angled his shoulders through sideways, then heaved in the rest of his bulk. When he flopped into his seat, the front of the bus sank a foot or two jerking the heads of those sitting nearby backward then forward.

'I'm Curly,' the jovial giant introduced himself. 'My Hawaiian name is. . .' to us, something completely unintelligible. 'I'll call you Cousins 'cos here we're all family.' With the suspension only partly recovered, we were off. Curly, too, was off with a litany of facts and figures.

About a quarter of the population is white. Less than three per cent of Hawaiians lay claim to being pure blood descendants of the first Polynesian settlers, though about thirty-five per cent, having some Hawaiian blood, are proud to call themselves Hawaiians. 'I'm quarter Hawaiian,' Curly crowed, not elaborating on the other three-quarters. The rest of the population is a mix of many races with a predominance of Japanese, Chinese and other Asians. After travelling more than 40,000 miles with Harvi and many thousand more miles by other transport, Jeff and I found this place American yet un-American. *Native American Indian* influence has been absorbed into the fabric of life in all states so as to be unnoticeable, until here, where it was starkly absent.

'Cousins, we're headin' for the Pearl Harbour Memorial,' Curly informed us, 'which all our visitors wanna see.'

From early in the 20th century the US Military began arriving on Oahu Island, when it became an American Territory. Pearl Harbour, near Honolulu, was dredged and equipped to service the Pacific Fleet, while the army occupied barracks further inland. The Japanese attack on Pearl Harbour on 7 December, 1941, with catastrophic losses, brought the United States into World War Two.

Curly continued his patter. The cost of living on these exotic islands is prohibitive. 'Men with guns guard their mango groves,' he chuckled. 'Wotcha call the place in England when your grandmother lives with ye?' he asked.

Puzzled silence for a few minutes. Then someone volunteered, 'Granny flat?'

'Yeah that's it! Well here it's young married folk who've to build on to their parents' place and live with them, for years sometimes, 'cos real estate's so dear.'

Amazingly we were travelling on an *interstate* – and the next state, California, was nearly 2,500 miles away across an ocean. Curly explained, laughing, 'To get funding it had to be called an interstate.'

Parking the coach, Curly said, 'Cousins, see you all back *here* at eleven. The full programme takes seventy-five minutes,' he boomed, waving a waist-size arm indicating the entire area of the USS Arizona Memorial, as we trooped with him and Gary towards the ticket office, at the Visitor and Information Center.

In the Interpretative Area, the catalogue of military gaffes, which left America unprepared for the onslaught, was downplayed. 'It was not a failure of technology as much as it was a failure of organisation.' While radar *did* detect the incoming planes there was no way to *assess* the information and communicate this knowledge to those in command. No reference was made in documentary film, or on the numerous display boards, to the ineptitude which allowed two waves of Japanese fighter-bombers to pulverise the American War Machine. 'Ordinary men in extraordinary circumstances, they performed their duty as expected.' Hardly!

Shuttle boats take visitors to the Memorial Building spanning the mid-section of the sunken USS Arizona, the resting place of its 1,177 crewmen lost when the ship sank within *nine minutes* of being attacked. An iridescent circle like a radiating halo on the water's surface is a poignant indication that, even after a lapse of sixty years, oil was seeping from the shattered structure.

Though only becoming a State in 1959, the Hawaiian Islands have been a US Territory since 1900. Now it is the most militarised of all the states. Along with tourism the military plays an important role in their economy. A ploy appealing to modern tourists – especially Americans! – is the exploitation of their royal family: 'We are the only state in America to have had our own king!' boasted Curly.

The last Hawaiian royal was Queen Liliuokalani, a passionate nationalist, whose determination to preserve 'Hawaii for the Hawaiians' was no match for a group of thirty United States businessmen, who, without consulting Washington, forced the queen to abdicate, in January 1893, to be replaced by a provisional government headed by an American plantation owner. The monarchy, existing for little more than a century, came into being through bloody combat between the rulers of each independent island, until the warrior, Kamehameha the Great, dispatching all opponents, declared himself King Kamehameha 1st of the entire Hawaiian Chain of Islands.

There was no wafting of fronds or fluttering of flags, (their state flag has a small UK Union flag in a corner) everything limp in the steamy, afternoon heat when Curly took us on a walking tour of what he termed 'Historic Honolulu'. A huge black, naked statue of Kamehameha stands near the Iolani Palace, draped in a resplendent heavy, gold brocade cloak, a wide band of cloth falling from his left shoulder covering his masculinity. 'His garments can be removed for dry-cleaning,' Curly informed us. Nobody asked if they then used a real fig leaf to maintain his modesty. In contrast to that statue's opulence, outside The State Capitol Building there is a statue of Fr. Damien de Veuster, a Belgium priest. 'The Martyr of Molokai,' Curly said, respectfully. He devoted his life to the plight of victims of Hansen's disease (leprosy), on the island of Molokai, dying there himself in 1899 from the disease. 'The Damien Museum in Waikiki runs a soup kitchen,' Curly went on. A soup kitchen was needed in Waikiki?

Much of the population of the entire islands lives in Honolulu, the tenth largest city in the United States, but, away from there and nearby Waikiki, Oahu, fringed by soft-sand beaches, has many tranquil places. *Heenalu*: sliding on a wave, is the Hawaiian word for surfing. Petroglyphs show that Hawaiians have been doing this for 1,000 years. Different coasts are best at different times of the year. Some places were busy with surfers, others quiet.

Our tour left us plenty of free time. One morning, exploring on our own, en route to the Foster Botanical Garden, a notice on the number 4 bus encouraged: 'Learn to read FREE'; nearby, a man who had obviously mastered the art, sitting in the lotus position, soles of his feet together, hat on his head, was deeply engrossed in a book. The Garden is home to a plant collection from the world's tropical regions and possesses among its vast collection twenty-five trees designated, for various reasons, 'exceptional'. Among these was a Bo tree, Ficus Religiosa; a sacred tree for Buddhists, as it was beneath a tree of this species that Gautama Buddha received enlightenment. The Foster Garden specimen was propagated from a famous tree in Sri Lanka, regarded as being possibly 'the oldest historical tree in the world', dating back to 288BC. Termites are arch-enemy number one. The woman in Reception related that during the past week two trees were 'removed' (felled and destroyed) despite previous valiant efforts to 'save' them. Another 'exceptional' tree had a large Beware notice alongside; a member of the Brazil nut family its large, heavy spherical fruit (fruit!) gives it its common name: Cannonball tree. I reckon a speedy exit from this world would ensue if a 'fruit' fell on an unprotected head.

Apart from trees and startlingly vivid plants there was a Chilkat Indian Totem Pole, a gift to the people of the Hawaiian Islands from Alaska (nice link for us with last year's trip) and, surrounded by lush lawn, a large statue of Buddha. Oahu, meaning *The Gathering Place* has a gathering of cultures and religions. Just outside the garden there was a Buddhist study, next door to a Lutheran school with nearby, an Episcopalian church of the Scottish Rite, and a Catholic church. (There was similar juxtaposition, too, on other islands.) Friendly strangers introduced themselves by giving their name, followed by their ethnic mix: Chinese/Japanese/Norwegian; Samoan/Portuguese/ Filipino and, if they could lay *any* claim to it, their Hawaiian name. Several were Mormons, a fast-growing religion on Oahu. Amazingly, on this small island, The Mormon temple in one town was the most visited one after that in Salt Lake City, Utah.

Other islands, referred to as the 'neighbour islands', are reached by hopping on a plane, as we would a bus or train. We arranged for a 4am alarm call for a long day trip to Kauai, known as the *Garden Isle*, not on our scheduled tour. As we waited in the lobby for our airport cab, three young women emerged from the lift, bid goodbye to the night porter, then whispering and giggling to each other, clicked away on high-heels up the cool, pre-dawn, shadowy street.

Promptly at 8am the 12-seater bus, picking us up at Lihue airport, set off along the coastal road on the eastern side of Kauai, the *Coconut Coast*, the sparsely populated part of this mostly rural island. Alicia, a Mexican from California, at the wheel, and marvellous seascapes and white-sand beaches on one side, luxuriant greenery and fields of taro in the valleys below verdant mountains on the other. Mount Waialeale (5,148-foot), in the centre of the island, with approximately 486 inches of rain yearly is called 'the wettest place on earth,' Alicia said. 'Folks, no problem today, the weather round the coast is going to be gorgeous.' She went on, 'I'm still regarded as a *Malihini*, a newcomer, even though we've been here for sixteen years, our two boys born on the island,' she giggled, light-heartedly.

Someone commented on the non-touristy appearance of the hamlets we passed through. 'There are strict sign ordinances in operation here. Each hotel, or business, is permitted just one sign, no more. And no neon lights at all,' Alicia explained. 'Yet, now, tourism accounts for ninety per cent of the economy on Kauai.' The once thriving sugar industry has almost ceased, it being cheaper to import from Indonesia. 'Seventy-five per cent of everything we eat is imported, would you believe?' she said. 'Even fruit and vegetables, even *pineapples*, for heaven's sake, for which we were famous. That's why our cost of livin's so high. Crazy!'

As with Native Americans in the other 49 states, here native Hawaiians had grievances regarding land ownership. 'On Kauai most of Hawaiian Home Lands (land set aside by US Congress in

1920 for homesteads) is leased to Big Business. Less than five per cent of Home Lands is available to native Hawaiians,' continued Alicia. On Oahu, thousands of native Hawaiians had been waiting for a homestead for up to thirty years! The United States recognises over 500 American Indian tribes as sovereign nations and political entities; now, *Kanaka Maoli* (Native Hawaiians) are seeking the same recognition for their indigenous people. Wonder how long they will wait?

A farm tractor lumbering in a field was followed pied-piper style by about fifty egrets; then at Kilauea lighthouse there were boobies, albatrosses and tropicbirds along the precipitous cliffs. 'There are no gulls on any of the Hawaiian Islands,' Alicia informed; strange surrounded by sea, not to hear their squawking.

We visited a guava plantation, the trees about the height of peach trees. This is something not imported: the plantation produces about fourteen million pounds of fruit annually. I didn't think that the pink-fleshed fruit tasted of much, but the fresh juice was wonderfully thirst-quenching. Big-leaved banana trees and a riot of flowers: arthuriums, birds of paradise, red ginger and orchids, flourished there too.

The north shore of Kauai is stunning! The vistas truly breathtaking! Superb views across small farmsteads with fields of taro and rice, 'No sugar now;' and gorgeous empty beaches with not a cloud in sight on this often rainy island. Alicia, negotiating a one-way bridge into a sharp-angled right turn, explained, 'This is why we're restricted to mini-buses: to keep the place unspoilt; even film crews have to make do with small vehicles when they come here.' Lumahi is referred to as 'South Pacific Beach' and the rock on which Mitzi Gaynor sat while washing 'that man right out of my hair' is recognisable from the film. Soon the road was brought to an abrupt end by the impassable Na Pali Cliffs. With no roads into the mountainous interior, Alicia retraced the coastal route south.

After lunch we headed north along the western side of the island.

'Oh shit!' Alicia exploded, when, despite her skilful manoeuvring up the narrow, twisting track, which had climbed 1,000 feet in the first mile, her wing mirror, caught by spindly scrub, shattered.

Gasps too, this time of wonderment, when we reached the

lookout over deep Waimea Canyon, ten miles long and a mile across, *The Grand Canyon of the Pacific* with its massive red, purple and green cliffs. 'Oh not now. . .' wailed Judy, from Minnesota, as she ran out of film. I took some photographs for her and sent them from England.

Hawaii: *The Big Island*, having more than half the landmass of the entire chain of islands, is described as a world in miniature, as it has eleven of the thirteen types of climatic region found on earth, with everything from rainforest to desert. It has lush tropical gardens; two massive active volcanoes; one of the largest cattle ranches in the United States; and is ringed by beaches, some with white sand, others black.

The tour beginning on the 'wet' windward coast, though it didn't rain while we were there, wound around the island to finish days later on the 'sunny' leeward side. After travelling extensively on our own, Jeff and I found it strange to be in our 50th state with an all-English group. In hotels and other places we did get chatting to vacationing Americans and, more often than not, we knew their home ground: Oklahoma, Texas, New England. . . Always they were truly amazed at our knowledge of their country.

Our co-travellers were good company and not having to plan driving routes left us free to enjoy the myriad pleasures and marvellous scenery. Because of Jeff's ongoing stomach trouble, we had to forgo the traditional *luau* (feast). It has been said that Hawaiians don't stop eating when full, only when tired! And that applies to other nationalities also; most of our group were not hungry for days afterwards!

Hawaii Volcanoes National Park covers some of the state's two active volcanoes: Kilauea and massive Mauna Loa. From the aptly named Devastation Trail, outside the Kilauea Crater, part of the eleven-mile Crater Rim Drive, we viewed the awesome destructive powers of lava, succumbing over time to the regenerative powers of nature. Forty years before, an eruption had buried an ohia forest under ten feet of pumice and cinders, yet, after just one year, regeneration had begun. Now, new black-barked ohia trees had blossoms, bristles bursting out of greyish buds to become red pom-poms. In places we had to keep to a boardwalk for fear of carrying alien seeds on our feet. From lookouts there were views across the caldera, a convex shield, like an enormous dried mud pool, oozing hissing steam. A sulphurous pong filled the air. The overcast sky did nothing to alleviate the greyness, in marked contrast to blue skies and exploding colour that we'd seen elsewhere.

A fine drizzle began to blow about when Tony, our driver-guide, stopped briefly at Punalu'u. The black-sand beach was closed to humans. Sea turtles were in occupation. They and their eggs are protected by state and federal laws. On a deserted stretch of beach further along the coast, one of my most enduring memories of these magical islands is of a native woman sitting at the water's edge, crooning softly to her baby cradled protectively in encircling arms. A scene as old as time.

Taking a detour, Tony said, 'I'm headin' for Ka Lae, which means South Point.' Ka Lae is not only the most *southerly* point of the Hawaiian chain of islands but of the entire North American continent. Less than a year before we'd been north in Alaska. Jeff and I *quietly* congratulated ourselves! *Wordlessly*, we were thrilled with our achievement. Our trips had taken us all the way around the coast of the continent. We'd journeyed from the Arctic Circle to the Tropics, and from the most westerly to the most easterly part of the United States, and everywhere – well, almost everywhere! – in between. However, we thought it inappropriate with an all-English group, or with Tony – who'd never even been to the mainland! – to rejoice in our independent travels. Here we had no one with whom to celebrate our adventures in North America, our amazing accomplishment. So we phoned our kids in Canada who shared our delight! Apart from this trip, all others had begun and ended with them. This time those living in England would be the first to celebrate with us.

At Kealakekua Bay, on the Kona Coast, a monument commemorates the death of Captain Cook, but being inaccessible to coach traffic, Tony did not take us there. In January 1779, Cook put ashore, his ship *Resolution* needing repairs, and in a skirmish between some of his crew and Hawaiian natives Cook was killed. A sad end to the intrepid explorer who had journeyed tirelessly around the world.

Kona coffee farms flourish in elevations between 800 and 2,000 feet. Tony, making the obligatory-tourist-coach-stop, disgorged us at one of these numerous farms, where not only the highly valued coffee could be purchased but macadamia nuts (the Islands produce ninety per cent of the world crop) dressed up in various fattening guises (one *unadorned* nut is a delectable, twenty-eight calories), chocolate made from criollo cocoa, and all manner of gift items, everything luxurious with a price tag to match.

Our hotel balcony overlooked a bay with a cruise liner at anchor, a sister ship of the one we'd sailed on from Alaska to Vancouver, the previous year. In town we noticed that the drove of passengers spent their time ashore not sight-seeing, or revelling in all that the Big Island had to offer, but shopping. Americans love to shop! Wealthy Americans love to shop for anything *expensive*. There were abundant displays of jewellery, especially items created using Taitian Pearls. In celebration, we splashed out on a pendant: a gorgeous black pearl nestling in a whorl of gold, which I seldom wear as it's ostentatious for our lifestyle! By the way 'black' pearls are not black but deep blue/green.

A twenty minute flight delivered us to Maui, The Valley Isle, after Oahu the most visited, and geared to up-market tourism. This was one occasion when we were quite happy to trade the freedom that camping afforded for the sophistication of a Kaanapali hotel and its orchid-filled open lobby with ocean views. Every afternoon clouds gathered over the mountain backdrop, releasing showers through great arching rainbows, but never advancing to the sun-bathed coast. I made good use of the resort's three swimming pools, though not of its eleven tennis courts, but in truth, above all, Jeff and I enjoyed walking the water's edge of the endless soft-sand beach.

Throughout the Islands more than 150 environmental groups are involved in various issues, from saving rain forests to protecting beaches from over-development. Feeling smug, as we don't play golf, we were aware that much agricultural land has been swallowed up for golf courses. On Maui, an oft-repeated slogan scolded: NO CAN EAT GOLF BALLS. 'We should be growing our own fruit and vegetables, instead of paying so much to import them,' they said.

The old whaling port of Lahaina (of *Moby Dick*'s time) today buzzes with sailing yachts and charter boats. Jeff did a dive in a submarine, getting a certificate to prove that they had submerged to a depth of 100 feet. Too threateningly claustrophobic for me, I found the glass-bottomed boat trip out to a coral reef just about fascinating enough to overcome my nervousness. Banyan Tree

Square in the centre of Lahaina has the largest Banyan tree in the United States. Planted in 1873, it had sixteen major trunks, covering almost an acre, filling the entire square. A seat in its shade, away from the bustle of Front Street, was a prime spot for people watching. Young boys swinging Tarzan-style in branches overhead competed with one another to cover as much distance as possible before dropping to the dusty ground. A village of stalls, splashes of colour, selling everything from T-shirts to snacks did a roaring business underneath the great, leafy canopy.

Returning to Honolulu airport, we collected our baggage and left it, as directed by the Tour Manager, with that of the rest of the group, for transfer to the aeroplane to San Francisco. That was the last occasion that we saw our *big* case – ever! Is there anything quite so disconcerting as watching the baggage carousel make its tortuous revolution over and over again, the multitude pieces of luggage gradually diminishing until it slows to a halt: empty?

Noted in California for its lower-than-other-places-temperature, San Francisco was cool compared with Hawaii; Jeff had just the shirt and shorts he was wearing! We did some shopping, then set out to re-acquaint ourselves with lovely San Francisco.

Apart from clothes, in the lost case there was a commercial video of an active volcano; illustrated books on flowers, trees and birds (ninety per cent of the Hawaiian Islands's bountiful fauna and flora are found nowhere else on earth); a quantity of cream made from kukui oil (from candlenut trees) for Jeff's psoriasis; many unusual gifts. . .

'It's easy enough to replace clothes, but what about all the other things?'

'Isn't that a great excuse to visit the Hawaiian Islands again?'

'Yes! Soon!'

Nothing could dent our sense of achievement! We were elated!

In retirement, after Jeff's major open heart surgery, we, whose home is in England, had toured on our own in a small motorhome, the *entire United States of America* from north to south, east to west, the endless coastline, all of the sections in eight states of Route 66, and hundreds of towns and cities. . .

Can any non-American Senior Citizens equal that?

Epilogue

In August, a few months after our Hawaiian holiday, we visited our family in Canada, always one of the highlights of our year. Exchanging news, enjoying their company, making good use in gorgeous weather of the swimming pool, all too soon it was back to school time. . .

We regard Canada as our second home, but their 'Neighbour to the 'South' was beckoning once again! We felt a pang of guilt – well, many pangs really! – that we'd sold Harvi, but hoped that his new owners were giving him the loving care that he deserved. We decided to hire a car. Crossing into the United States, we headed for Washington DC. After time in the capital, we planned to have a look around Baltimore (Maryland) and Philadelphia (Pennsylvania), neither city had we previously visited.

As we were driving through Baltimore, a female announcer interrupted the programme on the car radio: 'An aircraft has collided with the north tower of the World Trade Center in New York City. There has been an explosion. A huge fire is raging.'

'What an appalling accident! It's such a tall structure. . .' I exclaimed, remembering that, two years before, on our last trip in Harvi, I had spent a couple of hours on the 107th-floor observation deck of the trade building, revelling in the extensive views, picking out landmarks, looking down to the Statue of Liberty, that welcoming gateway for millions to a better life in America.

'It must have been a private, or maybe a sightseeing, plane. . . Commercial aircraft don't fly low over Manhattan. . .' Jeff said.

'The observation deck won't be open at this time, but the workforce will be there,' I replied. 'How terrible!'

For some minutes the woman's voice continued, repeating the details, speculating on the cause of the collision, retelling eyewitness accounts. . . Then her voice rose in disbelief, 'Another aircraft has slammed the south tower!'

It was no accident.

'There's a trade building in Baltimore,' I stuttered, breaking our silence.

'Quite near here,' Jeff agreed.

Swept along with the traffic, the radio was our only contact. There were several commentators now, endeavouring to keep up with events. Both towers were ablaze. Fire crews, at the scene within minutes, immediately entered the buildings. Skyward leaping flames and a huge pall of dense black smoke made any rescue by helicopter impossible. Thousands were trapped.

(We felt trapped – in our car.)

'The President has been flown to an undisclosed destination. . .'

'The two aircraft were hijacked. Two others have also been hijacked.'

Where were *they*? I panicked.

'A plane has smashed into the Pentagon in Washington.' (The world's biggest building.) A few days ago we'd been in the Galleria Shopping Complex near there.

'The White House is considered to be a target. The whole of Washington DC has been closed off.'

'Only planes already airborne will be permitted to land. All aircraft are grounded throughout the nation, as all airports are closed.'

The fourth hijacked plane was still aloft, somewhere? Where might it attack?

'What should we *do*?' I asked.

'What can we do, except drive?' Jeff answered, as, by then, we were on an interstate. 'I'll stop at the first rest area,' he said.

'Oh my God, the South Tower is crumbling. It has *collapsed*!' a radio voice gasped.

'Annapolis has been sealed off to protect The Naval Academy.' (We'd had a delightful time in the town just the previous day.)

'New York, and Philadelphia (where we were heading) and the surrounding areas are closed to all but emergency traffic.'

Half an hour after the collapse of the South Tower, the North Tower took a mere *twelve seconds* to buckle and fall, taking with it hundreds of fire-fighters among the thousands of victims.

Encased in the car, listening to all of this was terrifying, and there was still no news of the fourth plane. . .

Flashing signs, along the interstate, warned that all approaches to New York City and Philadelphia were closed, but we had to continue driving until we reached a rest area, where we could consult a map and decide where to go instead of Philadelphia.

'A plane has crashed in western Pennsylvania, creating a huge crater.'

Was *that* the fourth plane? Who could have done this? Why? Why? Why?

It was a relief to reach the turn off for a rest area. Finding space to park was difficult. All the cars and trucks, small and huge, destined for anywhere in the east took up every scrap of parking, even the grassed areas, their drivers talking on CB radio, cell (mobile) phones, or joining the snaking queues for the three public telephones.

Where were all these people going to go? I wondered.

'*We* mustn't stay long. I don't want to get boxed in,' Jeff said, opening the big *AAA Road Atlas*, on the bonnet of the car, 'otherwise, we'll never get away. We're here,' he pointed to the map. 'One of the places we intend to visit, after Philadelphia, is Allentown (Pennsylvania). We'll try to get there now.' He found Allentown on the map and quickly noted where we could divert from the interstate.

Arriving vehicles jostled to park. Queues for the telephones grew ever longer.

'Let's go!' Jeff urged.

The voices on the radio gave grim details. . . New York City's firemen and ambulance service were overwhelmed. An urgent appeal went out for volunteers, for doctors, for nurses.

Passing cars had hand-scrawled notices: 'God Bless our Firemen' and 'God Bless America'; small flags hung from car windows. We reached Allentown. There were few pedestrians about; many shops were closed, flags at half-mast and, in windows and on lamp-posts, numerous hand-written notices of support for the emergency services and 'our neighbours in NYC, DC and. . .'

We found the church we wished to visit; it has a copy of the Image we'd seen in Mexico City; apparently such a good copy that, it is said: 'Go to Allentown, if you can't go to Mexico' and it is the national shrine for the United States. The church, with a steeple 185-feet high and considered to have some of the finest examples of German stained glass windows in the country, was firmly locked. A *locked* church in daytime America?

In late afternoon we located a hotel. The broad-shouldered man in Reception was weeping quietly. Across the lobby from him the TV screen gave us *views* of the atrocities we'd been *hearing* about. For hours these scenes had been flashed around the world, yet we, who had been so close in distance, were *seeing* them for the first time.

We needed to contact our family in Canada. They would be frantic with worry. The telephone system had collapsed. Not even cell phones were working. 'Try during the evening. . .' a supervisor advised. 'They're struggling to re-connect. *Everyone* in the entire United States needs to telephone *someone. . .*'

It was the eve of my birthday. Not having eaten all day, in a near-deserted restaurant in town, we ordered a meal from necessity, not in celebration. Instead of the usual chirpy greeting: 'I'm' – Debbie, or Mandy, or Tracy – 'your server for tonight,' our young waitress was red-eyed and subdued. Background music played quietly and the TV had been switched off. Jeff usually gives me jewellery as presents, this time a pair of ruby and diamond earrings. I call them 'My September 11th earrings'. I wear them frequently, with sadness, yes, but also huge admiration for the American people.

At last, about 7.30pm we got through on the telephone to Canada. They had taken repeated calls *all day* from England. Now, nearing 1.00am on the 12th, English time, they could tell everyone that, thank God, we were safe.

'Are you going to try to get back here? The international border has been closed. Don't know when it'll reopen. Long line-ups are forming,' they said.

We decided against returning to Canada just yet.

'Please call frequently!'

We promised.

After a night tossing and turning, reliving the on-going horror, we set off early (my birthday!) crossing into New York state; then

279

Jeff drove and drove, all the way to Lake Placid, in the northern Adirondacks.

Everywhere was quiet while we travelled, no jet trails in the dome of blue in this country where skies are often as busy as the roads. Two days before the attack on the World Trade Center, the season's opening game of American Football was played at the Baltimore Ravens' Stadium close to our hotel. Throughout the city the carnival atmosphere was palpable, as families and friends gathered for the event, from far and wide, to share picnics in the car parks – a sea of purple and white for the super champions. The work ethic is strong in the US, as it is also in Canada: weekdays are busy, weekends are for enjoyment, outdoors if possible. North Americans have great enthusiasm for life, which is commendable. I wondered what all those folk who'd been in Baltimore were doing now. . .

Friday, September 14th, was to be a day of prayer, or quiet recollection, throughout the nation. From great city cathedrals to the myriad churches everywhere, of all denominations, services were planned. Tens of millions in this vast country were united in grief and in love for their homeland.

A Catholic church was across the street from our motel. Just before 9am about sixty children, aged three to twelve years, trouped down the aisle to sit in the front rows. Speaking directly to them the priest explained why Mass was in church instead of school, as was usual on Fridays: 'To give lots of people in Lake Placid the opportunity to pray for all the sad families in New York City, Washington and Pennsylvania.' In the crowded, silent church, this tall, middle-aged man spoke gently to the children as he continued, '*Everyone* loves you. Your Moms and Dads love you. All your relatives and friends love you. Your teachers love you. I love you. Jesus loves you. *Love* is so important! Remember that always!'

Adults in the congregation struggled to forgive in their hearts those who had caused such unimaginable destruction and loss of life. Sitting beside me was the woman who'd tearfully asked, 'Why would anyone *hate* us like this? Why?' The 20-year-old son of another, a fireman in New York City, was still on duty, though he had lost several colleagues. An older woman's husband, a retiree from the fire service, had just left this unbustling resort town in upstate New York to drive more than 350 miles south to offer assistance. Medical personnel had also volunteered. A brother and sister-in-law of the Catholic bishop of Burlington, Vermont, (of that makeshift-temporary cathedral we'd seen, three years before) directly across lake Champlain from Lake Placid, had been in one of the hijacked planes. I recalled how, over thirty years before, Martin Luther King had preached 'Darkness cannot drive out darkness; only light can do that. Hate cannot drive out hate; only love can do that.'

Six children, their clear, young voices ringing poignantly around the church, each read his or her own prayer. All of them dwelt on the heartbreak. Perhaps the greatest evil perpetrated was that it was impossible to shield these children from the graphic images of horror in their state's largest city. Waking or sleeping, the scenes on television ran relentlessly on and on through our minds: the sights, the sounds, the searching for the thousands missing, the individual stories, the heroism, the faces of the grief-stricken. . .

The Adirondacks Park in New York state (six million acres) is the largest wilderness area remaining in the lower 48 states, with mountains, lakes, and 30,000 miles of rivers and streams; almost half, being state owned, is protected by the 'forever wild' provision of the state constitution. After a few days the international border to Canada reopened, but queuing to cross was taking up to thirty hours. As our hired car didn't have to be returned yet, we remained in the Adirondacks, finding solace in the natural beauty of the area decked in glorious autumn colour.

Even in remote places there were flags, small and large, flying at half-mast. We understood the significance for Americans of their national flag, with often even the humblest front yard having a flag pole, but it wasn't until recent events that we appreciated how, for many, it had a *religious* significance: some notices said: 'God Bless America, our President and our Flag'.

Several times, people enquired if we were stranded, as thousands were throughout the continent, because of the grounding of aircraft and the difficulty of making alternative travel arrangements. Even in time of adversity, Americans take time to be polite, kind and considerate.

In beautiful late September weather, driving the US side of Lake Ontario, we could see that people were achieving a semblance of normality, with hand-made signs at house or farm gateways for 'Fresh Veggies and Pumpkins', 'Tomatoes', 'Peaches', 'Corn',

'Apples, Squash and Cukes' (cucumbers). One small town held its annual 'Salmon Fest'. Jeff was delighted to visit a small store with a sign for 'New and Used Antiques'! One day we saw an RV resembling ours – but it wasn't Harvi! It took about an hour and a half to queue, answer questions, and allow a sniffer dog into the car and boot, when we crossed back to Canada and our family.

In the early 19th century, along the Niagara Frontier, many battles were fought between Canada and the United States. During the 20th century, the 5,000-mile border dividing the two countries was described as being 'the longest peaceful border in the world', referred to with pride by both nations as 'a Border of Friendship'. At the dawn of the 21st century, because some terrorists entered the US by way of Canada, the political relationship between the two countries has soured somewhat, with one of the consequences being that security along the international border is now more stringent.

It is no exaggeration to claim that the events of Tuesday, 11th September, 2001, or 9/11 as it is commonly called, changed life for ever, not only in North America, but throughout the world.

But has the imposition of new regulations and the tedious hanging around airports curtailed international travel? Of course not! Why let terrorists be vicious victors?

We continue to visit Canada and the US yearly, where life goes on in both countries as before. We haven't yet met anyone who has travelled, in a small motorhome, as extensively as we did in Harvi. The most frequently asked question is: 'Which is your favourite state?' Our answer: '*Every* state has something special and we would be thrilled to visit all 50 again!' The problem is there isn't sufficient time – we were already *retired* before we began! Our advice: start young!

I have heard from people who decided to visit Canada after reading my book about it. One enthusiastic woman took a book with her, when visiting the Rockies and Vancouver, and exclaimed aloud to the entire coach, 'It's here in the book,' each time they came to a place mentioned in the text!

When you spread maps on your dining-room table, realise that a few inches on paper might be several hundred miles on tarmac. Apart from that, travelling in the US is easy and enjoyable. If you hire a motorhome, on collection give it a name, any name, but *please* don't call it Harvi!

THE UNITED S

WASHINGTON

OREGON

IDAHO

MONTANA

NORTH DAKO

SOUTH DAKO

WYOMING

NEBRASK

NEVADA

UTAH

COLORADO

KAN

CALIFORNIA

ARIZONA

NEW MEXICO

TEXA

ALASKA

HAWAII